D0323455

Mary Fielding Smith

Mary Fielding Smith.

Mary Fielding Smith

Daughter of Britain

Portrait of Courage

DON CECIL CORBETT

Published by Deseret Book Company
Salt Lake City, Utah

Dedicated to my dear wife Marion,
a descendant of pioneers
and a faithful supporter
in the preparation of this story.

First printing in the Classics in Mormon Literature Series, May 1995

Library of Congress Catalog Card Number 66–29293

ISBN 0–87579–990–6

Printed in the United States of America

10 9 8 7 6 5 4 3 2 1

Publisher's Preface

As The Church of Jesus Christ of Latter-day Saints approaches the one-hundred fiftieth anniversary of the arrival of the pioneers into the Salt Lake Valley, it is appropriate that attention is once again focused on one of the heroines of that courageous and faith-filled body of Saints. Mary Fielding Smith exemplified the character traits that made those pioneers so magnificent. She, like many others, was a woman of faith, determination, and courage who endured hardships unimaginable when judged by the comforts of today's standard of living.

But Mary's difficulties and trials did not commence with her pioneer experiences. From the day she was baptized into the restored church, she faced constant challenges; yet her faith never wavered. Perhaps the resoluteness of her determination to endure might be summarized in words extracted from one of her letters: "Blessed be the God and Rock of my salvation, here I am, and am perfectly satisfied and happy, *having not the smallest desire to go one step backward.*" Her faith and commitment to follow the counsel of the Lord and his servants stand in sharp contrast to another significant woman of history who, contrary to divine admonition, "looked back" and lost her life. (See Genesis 19:17–26.)

Yet combined with Mary's desire to be obedient and her ability to follow counsel was a fierce independence. This was aptly demonstrated during her confrontation with Peter Lott, the cantankerous captain charged with leading her and others from their camp in Winter Quarters, Nebraska, to the Rocky Mountains. Told by the insensitive man that she, a widow with scarce resources, would be "a burden" upon the little company of pioneers "the whole way," Mary resolutely replied, "I will beat you to the valley and will ask no help from you either!"

Such was the faith and determination of Mary Fielding Smith that she kept her word, beating not only the captain but also the entire company into the valley by many hours. However, her promise was not easily kept. There were many challenges during the long trek across the plains that might have stopped one of lesser spiritual strength.

One such challenging experience was the occasion when one of her oxen, evidently spent of its strength, simply lay down in the dirt and appeared to die. Ignoring the caustic comments of her nemesis—the company's captain—Mary returned to her wagon to retrieve a healing remedy: a bottle of consecrated oil. She asked her brother Joseph Fielding and another worthy priesthood bearer to anoint and administer to the fallen beast. The Lord responded to Mary's silent prayers and the pleading of two humble bearers of his priesthood. To the amazement of those who watched this strange but sacred event, the animal rose to its feet and the journey continued.

Later, yet another ox of Mary's similarly dropped in the dust devoid of life, and the divine drama was repeated as a priesthood blessing restored its life.

What were the origins of the strength of this special woman, Mary Fielding Smith? As the title of this book declares, she was a daughter of Britain. Mary was raised in a religious family in England, and her parents cultivated in her a faith in and love of God. She was raised in the countryside on a small farm where she loved the animals and knew the meaning of hard work. Mary also learned the graces for which the English are noted and developed a finely tuned sense of dignity and culture.

Her dignified charm did not go unnoticed by men. One such was a gentleman whose interest in Mary was not reciprocated. Not feeling good about his pursuit of her, Mary decided to emigrate to Canada. The spurned suitor was a lay preacher in a Protestant faith, and Mary's departure was looked upon by some as providential for him, leaving him more time to devote to his ministry. How little did the well-meaning detractors realize how providential such a decision really was—but on Mary's part; for God had other plans for this daughter of Britain. Surely she stood among the great and noble women in premortal councils who received special appointments in this life.

This marvelous woman was to become the wife of Hyrum Smith, the patriarch-prophet, and the mother and grandmother of yet other prophets of God. Her impact upon the history and destiny of the Lord's latter-day work is well expressed by Susa Young Gates in a tribute written in 1915: "When the roll of the greatest women of modern times is called, we make no doubt that the name of Lucy Mack Smith will head that roll. The second name on that list will be that of Mary Fielding Smith. . . . Her greatness, her power, her beauty and her charm have lain hidden in the modest silence and reserve with which she covered all her own acts. But the pages of history will yet record what she was, what she did and why she is entitled to this exalted rank." ("Mothers in Israel," *Relief Society Magazine,* 3 [March 1916]:123.)

As a relatively new convert to the Church, Mary was immediately exposed to turmoil that tried the faith of many. Shortly after her baptism in Canada, she traveled to Kirtland, Ohio, headquarters of her newfound faith. At this time, apostates were speaking against the Prophet Joseph Smith, seeking to wrest control of the Church. Mary was undaunted. In a letter to her sister, she said, "I do thank my Heavenly Father for the comfort and peace of mind I now enjoy in the midst of all the confusion and perplexity and raging of the devil against the work of God in this place."

During the seventeen years she lived from the time of her baptism until the time of her death, Mary Fielding Smith would experience much of the devil's raging against the work of God in many places. She was driven from the comforts of her home on numerous occasions. She watched her saintly husband ill-treated and finally martyred by rabble.

Perhaps as she viewed the mutilated and lifeless body of her beloved husband, Hyrum, words she had earlier written gave her some degree of comfort: "I feel more and more convinced that it is through suffering that we are to be made perfect, and I have already found it to have the effect of driving me nearer to the Lord."

Such was the character of Mary Fielding Smith, whose earthly life is portrayed in this engaging volume written by one of her faithful descendants, Don C. Corbett. This gifted writer has added a human dimension to historical fact. He paints word pictures, adding color to black and white pages. As noted on the cover jacket, "Here is a biography that will stimulate and interest her countless descendants and all who seek inspiration from the lives of great individuals."

The life of Mary Fielding Smith has inspired speakers, teachers, painters, and historians. Famed Latter-day Saint artist Minerva Kohlhepp Teichert painted a masterpiece depicting Mary's faith and struggles. A building on the campus of Brigham Young University was dedicated to Mary Fielding Smith's memory in 1954. Yet no painting, building, or monument will ever sufficiently honor her. More lasting than these is the model of faith, courage, and determination engraved on the hearts and in the minds of those who have come to know of her good works.

This volume on her life affords all the opportunity to know the good works of this saintly woman whose gravestone reads, "She Died as She Had Lived . . . Firm in the Faith of the Gospel."

Hoyt W. Brewster, Jr.
Great-great-grandson of Mary Fielding Smith

Introduction

The pages of history are graced with the names of exceptional women who live on in the annals of time—women of great faith and courage. They are found in ecclesiastical and secular history. They are known because their lives were outstanding. They made history and someone took note of their accomplishments to make them more than just legend.

Dipping back into antiquity, there were, for example, Ruth, the faithful Moabite girl who left her people to become an Israelite and the great-grandmother of David, King of Israel; Hannah who was so grateful to God for taking away her reproach and blessing her with motherhood that she gave Samuel to the service of the temple; Esther, the Jewish girl, who became queen and was able to help her captive people; and, more modernly, Joan of Arc, the French peasant girl who led an army into battle and saved her country; Florence Nightingale, the great English nurse of Crimean War fame; Sacajawea, the Indian maiden who courageously led Lewis and Clark on their famous exploratory trip to the Northwest Territory.

And now these pages tell of another courageous woman, Mary Fielding Smith, an indomitable English lady, the daughter of a Bedfordshire farmer-preacher, who left her native land and became a heroine in her own right. We tell of her not that she led armies nor became the great-grandmother of a king, etc.—for these she did not do—but because of her overall courage, ability to rise above the crises in her life, and the will to overcome adversity and accomplish the extraordinary for a woman.

She joined her life with the Mormon cause and went

through the persecution in the early days of that Church when its members were buffeted and driven. After a mob had killed her husband, she outfitted herself with six covered wagons, took along a large number who lived under her roof, and eventually reached the heart of the Rocky Mountains. She went prepared with food, powder, and bullets. She braved the dangers of primitive Western America, such as savage Indians and wild beasts, and placed herself beyond civilization where she would be safe to build a home and rear her children free from the terror of mobs. She was subjected to hunger, drought, hordes of crickets which devoured precious crops, long, brooding winters locked in a mountain fastness, the uncertainty of survival, and all this for conscience sake and the faith that she had espoused. Moreover, she represented a rare breed of her kind who had the courage to stand fast for their beliefs.

After her conversion in Canada, she came to the United States. She witnessed the onslaught of intolerance against the Mormon minority in Ohio, Missouri, and Illinois. In a country whose constitution guaranteed religious freedom for all, she became a victim of relentless harassment from depraved mobs supported by elected officials. Incredible hostility, which today seems unbelievable, built up against the newly established Christian community. In the bitter conflict between the Mormon group and their merciless foes, the Saints were allowed no quarter. The persecution against them was persistent as was the case with other religious groups down through the ages.

Mary Fielding Smith's life was one of conflict. In a way, this was to prove compensatory. It sharpened her determination, made her a fighter, and drove her to great heights. Without conflict, she would not have attained the eminence that she did. Under the goading of her adversaries, she matched her ingenuity with the obstacles which arose. Under the burden she carried as a widow, she found extra-spiritual support which enlarged her capabilities. Faced with the problems of daily survival, she developed the power for making the right decisions. The vicissitudes of life humbled her and caused her to be grateful for all favors. Conflict was ever present and ruthless. It pounded her until it hurt; spurred her relentlessly to do her level best; energized her to achieve the impossible; wrung her to the breaking point; grieved her to tears; challenged her to the mountain tops; and rewarded her with fame and distinction.

She had the supreme experience of seeing the West opened up by a stream of pioneers and of being one of the hardy souls to settle far beyond the centers of commerce and established social complex of the nation. As the last entry, she joined a long emigrant train of 110 wagons and stayed in the gruelling march until she achieved her goal. She was a part of the huge assault on the far-out, unsettled continent, a member of the grand cavalcade that conquered vast buffalo country, western rivers, and alpine-tall mountains. She lived the excitement of the great outdoors—the wild frontier—resounding to the shouts of bull-whackers, the lowing of cattle, and the stampede of buffaloes. She felt the twinge of concern that goes with getting beyond the known and deep into the unknown, as was the case with the men who sailed with Columbus. She grew apprehensive upon leaving the grasslands of the plains and entering the rocky plateau country where feed for animals became progressively scarce. The encounters with traveling Indian bands or an encampment of the redmen caused her nerves to tingle. Verily, hers was a momentous experience that brought her special enrichment and the appellation of, true pioneer.

Mormon history is replete with instances of individual courage in a wide variety of circumstances. For a certainty, countless pioneer happenings shine with the deeds of both men and women during times of great affliction and stress. Many of them have been told and retold through the years and passed on to each new generation to become a part of western lore. However, few are quite as emphatic and of such duration as those of the heroine of our story. She scored in a dramatic fashion to leave her name high for all to see. Her accomplishments do not dim but endure to perpetuate her memory and give her luster. They point up her background and reflect the fold from which she came.

Foreword

I have always regretted that Grandmother Mary Fielding Smith died before I had the privilege of knowing her, and all that I do know is of course what I have read and have been taught. That she was one of the noblest of women evidently is perfectly true. The hardships she had to face from and including the days of Nauvoo, until her death, have been impressed upon my mind. I am sure she holds a place among the noblest women who ever embraced the divine truth of the Gospel of Jesus Christ. She was always true to the Prophet Joseph Smith and to her husband and his family. One day—as time passes—I am sure I will have the privilege of meeting her along with the other members of the family who have gone on before.

Joseph Fielding Smith

Preface

Mary Fielding Smith came by her qualities of character through a genteel English family. Her people, the Fieldings, were a devout group of Methodists possessed of physical and mental vigor and high ideals. What follows, however, is neither a lay-treatment in filial eugenics nor a delineation of genealogical background. Rather, it is to take Mary by the hand, as it were, and lead her forward in a new setting so that others may become acquainted with her and know her story. It is to reveal the singleness of mind that carried her past many obstacles. It is to focus the spotlight upon the exceptional faith and courage that brought her through many extremities and made her a credit to her sex and country that produced her.

In putting the accent upon Mary Fielding Smith, we are not unmindful of her husband, Hyrum Smith. His place in the history of the founding of The Church of Jesus Christ of Latter-day Saints is well established. Through his deeds, faithfulness, and character, he brought honor to the cause he represented. His forebears were of sturdy stock. His fourth-greatgrandfather was Robert Smith, a venturesome Englishman, who emigrated to America in 1638. Through Hyrum's mother, Lucy Mack Smith, his progenitors can be traced back to Edward Fuller, a Mayflower passenger.[1] The marriage of Mary Fielding and Hyrum Smith united two devout, old English family lines.

The story of Mary Fielding Smith is narrated against a background of religious excitement and contending doctrine

[1]Descent from Edward Fuller, Mayflower passenger, to Lucy Mack Smith: Edward Fuller, Samuel Fuller, John Fuller, Shubael Fuller, Lydia Fuller, Lydia Gates, Lucy Mack.—Courtesy of Carl J. Harris, Charter Member of Utah Society of the Mayflower.

embroiling family and friends. The Fieldings in America stepped from an obscure English hamlet onto a world stage and left their impact on the affairs of the Church. Various members of this respected, middle-class family played prominent roles. From the ranks of the family emerged forceful personalities, some who aided and some who hindered the cause of the restored Church. The net effect was a lasting gain for the Mormon cause in membership and spirituality.

The Fieldings, Joseph, Mary, and Mercy, were among the early families who came into the Church and put their stamp on its history. These three people at first tried to avoid the message of Mormonism. However, their spirits were ripe for its reception. They were devout farm folk who lived close to the soil. This was the situation when the "new covenant" came to them. As any rural project in the new world, Joseph Fielding's farm required hard work. He and his sisters refined the virgin terrain, planted their crops, and prayed with anxious appeal for the rain to descend and the soil to give forth that there might be "seed to the sower and bread to the eater." Their spirits were humble and their gratitude great for their many blessings.

Thus, on the Canadian frontier their hearts were conditioned and put in tune with the promptings of the Holy Spirit. They were prepared to receive the witness of a humble missionary to the restoration of an old covenant. The message brought by him distilled upon their souls. Most assuredly, this was for a purpose. There was a work for them to do at a time when the power of evil was unleashed against the work of the ministry in Kirtland, Ohio. Furthermore, there needed to be impressed upon the Saints a full realization of the universality of the new Kingdom and a redirection of thought to the greater concept of world-wide spiritual hegemony. This needed to be brought home to the Saints and fully realized. For the restored Church was to be more than a temporary, quick-birth-and-die sect of the type common on the frontier of America. It was larger than town, state, or national boundaries. It was to leave its natal chrysalis and go forth to many nations and people to tap the great repositories of the blood of Israel in those places and be given to all who would receive it.

The American Fieldings became a part of this unfoldment. Joseph Fielding helped spearhead the first mission of the Church abroad. It resulted in a marvelous work and a wonder, that of bringing into the Church thousands of faithful people who leavened the loaf and brought as an offering their means, skills, and mental resources and laid them upon the altar for the upbuilding of the new Zion. His sisters bore witness to the divinity of the work.

In the development of the operation, the three Fieldings in America played their parts well. Once enlisted, they never faltered, vacillated, nor murmured. They were special vessels in accomplishing the spreading of the new Word to the land of their forebears. The Fielding name thus became dramatically linked with the Church. It lives in dignity associated with the names of other worthy stalwarts of the new dispensation of the truth upon the earth.

Acknowledgments

The creation of any book is a story in itself. Between the covers is woven information from many sources, sought out in innumerable places, and from a large number of people whose willingness to assist and lend a hand is quite generous. Such was the case in fashioning this story. Into its making have gone contributions of many individuals, both living and departed. Appreciating the importance of the historical and a place of a book such as this, many gave material, pictures, references, etc., while others gave encouragement. The task of creating was made easier by the very nature of the subject—a human interest story—a pioneer saga— which had the virtue of evoking understanding and a willingness to help. To each who assisted in any way in furnishing suggestions, information, material, or services, goes the author's deep thanks.

Special thanks is extended to Joseph Fielding Smith, Church Historian, his assistants, A. William Lund and Earl E. Olson; also, Lauritz G. Petersen and Joseph H. Peterson, members of the staff. In addition, special thanks to the Utah State Historical Society for access to source material in that office—for photostats, pictures, and references.

Grateful appreciation to Josephine Burton Bagley, Eva Burton Franz, Howard and Rae Barker for their contributions; Mary Porter, Clarence F. Peirce, Edith S. Heaps (deceased), Leah Porter Griffin, and the Utah Genealogical Society for relevant material and genealogical data. Also thanks to Mary Jane Groberg, *Deseret News*, and Patricia Bell, Assistant Archivist, County Records Office, Bedford, England, for their kind help; and P. W. Bailey, Huntingdon, England for details of the old Fielding farm in Honidon.

My deep appreciation to my wife Marion, Mrs. Joseph Fielding Smith, Edith Smith Patrick, Martha Smith Jenson, and Harold H. Jenson for their reading of all or portions of the manuscript, their comments, and helpful suggestions.

Contents

Pictures

Chapter 1

Daughter of Britain

She had made it. The English woman had crossed the final mountain barrier, culminating a perilous journey of 1,350 miles through Western America, a country infested with Indians and wild animals. Her party moved triumphantly out of Emigration Canyon and headed for the frontier fort in the Valley.

Whether anyone knew it, the person in charge, the directing mind, was Mary Fielding Smith. She rode high on the spring seat of her lead wagon. Her slatted sunbonnet was pushed back on her head. Her supple figure swayed gracefully with the jostling of the wagon. She sat composed, shoulders erect, her face to the setting sun. Her blue denim dress was faded and snagged. Her high-laced "boots" were scuffed and precariously worn. They showed traces of mud picked up on the pass after the cloudburst. Her hands and face were ruddy from months of exposure to sun and wind. A faint smile of satisfaction played on her lips.

She was vital and alert—her eyes clear and keen despite her weariness. She had "savvy" and ability to back it up. She was now a veteran wagon-mistress who could hold her own in most any situation. She was familiar with every aspect of pioneer travel, including the use of her late husband's rifle which she kept close at hand. She was a forceful woman operating in the world of men.

The strength of her spirit loomed in her tired face to give it character. A lock of dark-brown hair, stirred by a light movement of mountain air, graced her with womanly charm. Intense anticipation showed in her eyes, as she looked toward the fort. There, she would find her sister Mercy who had arrived earlier with another wagon-train.

Her lean oxen moved wearily forward with sure steps, heads low, exerting steady pressure to keep the wagons rolling. The heavy yokes on their necks were scarred and weatherbeaten like the serrated felloes of the wagon wheels. The iron rims were rounded and brightened by the daily scouring of rough roads. The wagon boxes looked old and travelworn—the paint faded. Wagon covers were torn and tattered from wind and storm but newly washed clean of overland dust by the morning rain. Yet, her train of five wagons was an interesting sight. As a single family unit, it stood out and monopolized the road. It was a typical wagon-train heavy with equipment and supplies, including enough corn and wheat to see her through the coming winter and to plant in the spring. Lashed to the outside and rear of the wagon were many odds and ends that could not be carried inside—the water barrels, a plow and harrow, a cage of poultry, sacks of jerked buffalo meat, and the like.

Coming down the winding road to the Valley, she had noticed the colorful display of autumn leaves on the scrub oak and sumac that lined the canyon slopes. The splashing creek, swollen by the morning rain, caught her eye. The road went through a thick growth of trees and willows on the canyon floor along the creek bed. Progress was slow, as the road was tortuous—with many bends and turns, brush and log fill-ins of lateral water seeps and soft places, bad creek crossings, and detours to avoid boulders. Traversing this stretch was agonizingly slow consuming precious daylight hours.

Her pulse quickened with each sustained advance. This was a grand moment in her life, banishing her great fatigue. The day before, she had stood on Big Mountain and caught a glimpse of the Valley. That moment was one of exhilaration and joy. The many hardships through which she had passed flashed in review, as she contemplated the scene. The present moment, as she entered the Valley, was one of fulfillment.

Her journey had its beginning two years earlier when an armed mob camped on what had been her farm and then advanced and forced her from her home in Nauvoo. She heroically moved her household, consisting of eighteen people, away from the danger to avoid the wretches the like of which had widowed her at Carthage.

She had pitted her mind, skill, and resources against many obstacles which had blocked her way, including a doughty captain of a wagon company on the long haul to the Valley. He was now nowhere in sight. In fact, he was unexpectedly detained on Little Mountain where a sudden storm had upset his plans.

The contest with the Captain had its inception in some sharply spoken words on his part which galvanized the determination of Widow Smith in a do-or-die effort. She had not been fully equipped to travel with an emigrant train. She lacked the necessary team strength for such a major undertaking. The Captain curtly advised her to remain at Winter Quarters, that she would be a burden on the company. She answered that she would beat him to the Valley and ask no help from him. This set the stage for a unique race, undoubtedly the longest of its kind in history.

It represented a rare competitive situation within a wagon-train of Mormon refugee emigrants. In consequence of it, Mary and the Captain engaged in a running contest the ending of which was in doubt until the last moment before entering the Valley. It became a war of nerves, a test of self-control and sportsmanship. The race went along unpublicized, without fanfare, wagering, or cheering. When it had ended, there was no notice of it by the community, no newspaper accounts, no gloating, no laurels for the victor—simply the satisfaction of achievement for the Widow and something for her children to remember.

It had been an emotionally packed morning for Mary. This last day enroute had started disastrously when she couldn't find some of her oxen. They were recovered. She caught up with the Captain who hadn't waited for her. It was his turn to be stranded. She gave the order, and her wagons went out around him on a clear road.

Her caravan finally pulled up before the fort at 10 p.m. She descended, bone-tired, into the arms of her sister. Many of the leading men came to greet and congratulate her for a job well done. The teams were unhitched and turned out to graze. The next morning, being Sunday, she put on a change of dress and went to the services in the bowery. She offered up her oblations to her Heavenly Father.

Mary, by birth and rearing, was well qualified to accomplish the things that she had done. She had her beginning in England, as a member of a large family. The Fieldings of Bedfordshire were a rural family engaged in farming and the spread of Methodism. The locale of their activities was Honidon,[1] the hamlet near where they lived, and the surrounding towns and villages within walking distance of each other, such as, St. Neots across the river in Huntingdonshire where the family worshipped.

Bedfordshire, a south midland geographical area, was the fourth smallest shire in England. It had always been a prominent agricultural center. Nearly nine-tenths of the total acreage was under cultivation. The chief crop was wheat for which the valley of Bedford was specially suited. Bedford, located fifty miles northeast of London, lay principally in the middle of the basin of the river Ouse which entered from the northwest and traversed the rich and beautiful valley to the northeastern corner of St. Neots. It was a parliamentary borough and the county town of Bedfordshire. Bedford boasted of a grammar school founded by Edward VI in 1552. It is, today, an important school for boys. This and private schools for girls put educational facilities within reach of the Fielding children.

The market places of Bedford and St. Neots afforded

[1]Honidon (modern spelling Honeydon) is a hamlet in the large parish of Eaton Socon in the east of the county of Bedfordshire.

farmers the opportunity to sell many of their farm products. Early on market day, they arrived and set up their stands around the square. A vegetable counter might be flanked by a cheese counter or a poultry booth, and so on around the perimeter of the open area. Market day was looked forward to by farm children, as it allowed them the opportunity to accompany their fathers and mothers on the high cart carrying the produce. It was excitement for them to watch the heavy traffic of people milling about from vendor to vendor looking for the best bargains. Occasionally, a hawker would call out his specialty, his voice being little heard above the general din. By noon the activity commenced to taper off as supplies diminished or the demand was satisfied. Those who had sold everything brought around their conveyances, loaded their empty containers, and departed. Undoubtedly, Father Fielding and members of his family came often on market day to St. Neots or Bedford where they were known to many.

Market day was not only for trade and commerce, but, also, a time to exchange the latest news with neighbors and catch up on political matters. It also afforded an opportunity to do some shopping. If business had been good, a visit was made to buy a bit of sweets or a pretty print for a new dress.

Religion and contending doctrines were ever ready subjects which left their impact on the visitors. The shire was made up of a large percent who were nonconformists—people who had left the Church of the English Crown and affiliated themselves with various sects, such as the Methodists and Calvinists. By so aligning themselves, they forfeited certain perquisites permitted by the State church to the faithful. The Nonconformists were people of independent spirit, freethinkers, and freedom-lovers. They were willing to risk the sanctions applied against them by the Crown. They were the material which would form the fabric of the support that would be given to Mormon missionaries upon their arrival.

The Fieldings belonged to this class of rugged individuals who chose to worship according to the dictates of their own conscience. This trait of character was blended with a deep-rooted fear of God, a characteristic exhibited by the entire Fielding family.

Mary Fielding was born into such a Nonconformist-family on July 21, 1801, in Honidon, Bedfordshire, ". . . into the home of a pious, refined, intellectual, and educated family."[2] Her parents were John and Rachel Ibbotson Fielding, both of Halifax, Yorkshire, England. John's father was Marmaduke (Duke) Fielding and his mother, Elizabeth Dyson.

Earlier, John Fielding had married Sarah Kitson. This marriage was marked by a succession of misfortunes. Before her death, Sarah bore seven children, five of whom died soon after birth. One of the surviving children, Marmaduke Fielding, died at the age of eleven. The oldest, Sarah Fielding who never married, died in her forty-sixth year. She was the beloved elder sister of the Fielding domicile. While she lived, she was a faithful member of the Methodist Church in St. Neots.

In 1790, John Fielding married again, taking to wife Rachel Ibbotson, who was twenty-three years of age. He was eight years her senior. She came from an affluent and refined home and had received a good education. She bore John a large family. Mary Fielding, the heroine of our story, was the sixth child of a family of ten children born in the following order: John, James, Thomas, Joseph, Ann, Mary, Martha, Benjamin, Mercy Rachel, and Josiah (stillborn). Benjamin lived not quite two years.

More is learned about the Fielding family from a memoir of Rachel Fielding written by her daughter Ann Fielding

---

[2]Susy Y. Gates, "Mothers in Israel," *Relief Society Magazine,* III (Mar. 1916), 123.

Note: Letter from Sarah M. (Lillie) Wright, daughter of Rev. James Fielding, under date of Feb. 8, 1915, to Pearl Vilate Burton, Ogden, Utah, bears the suggestion that the Fielding family crest and coat of arms were removed from the "linen and plate" of the Fieldings when they became Methodists under the preaching of one George Whitfield. "They became Puritans and discarded worldly things and became extreme in their simple ways of living."

Matthews.[3] This memoir eulogizes the life of Mother Fielding and helps us to see where the children got their Christian graces. Moreover, it prefaces Mary Fielding who was a reflection, in religious feeling, of her mother.

In the year, 1781, when Rachel Ibbotson was fourteen, her mother died. Not much is known of her mother, except that she had been a devout member of the Calvinistic faith. Shortly after her mother's death, Rachel lost her father. Thus, she was left an orphan with two younger brothers. An uncle, a medical man, and his wife, residing in Denham, both being strongly attached to Rachel and having no children of their own, adopted her as a daughter. She was dearly loved and treated with much parental kindness.

Before coming to Honidon, John Fielding had been a local preacher in the Methodist Connexion Church at Halifax. Three years after he married Rachel, his maternal uncle and godfather, James Dyson, owner of several estates in Bedfordshire, expressed a desire for one of his nephews to occupy one of them to fill the need for a tenant. John, being fond of agriculture, was induced to accept.

About the middle of May 1794, the Fieldings with their children arrived in Honidon where a new scene of things presented itself. They had exchanged a populous town (Halifax) for a lonely village (Honidon); a large, commodious house for a small, inconvenient cottage; a circle of friends and relatives for unknown neighbors; and the immediate neighborhood of a Methodist church for a place four miles distant from one.

Honidon became the birthplace of eight of the Fielding children. It was in such a setting that Mary Fielding was born and reared quite happily on a quaint country estate belonging to her father's well-to-do uncle who was their landlord.

Consequently, Mary grew up used to the ways of English

[3]Ann Fielding Matthews, "Memoir of Mrs. Rachel Fielding of Honidon, Bedfordshire," *Wesleyan—The Methodist Magazine,* (Aug. 1830), pp. 514-522; also data from County Records Office, Bedford, England.

country life away from the conventional English towns. On this estate, there were farm animals and fowls with buildings to shelter them closely clustered and adjacent to the cottage of the custodian. For the children, there were opportunities to participate in all manner of activities which acquainted them with the work on a farm. The farm's gift to the children, besides a practical education, included fond memories of romps through green fields and pastures, walks by quiet brooks, excursions in the two-wheeled cart to cultivated plots and, farther, to neighboring markets with loads of produce.

Being newcomers and people with some book-learning, the Fieldings were at once under critical scrutiny of their less erudite neighbors. Everything had to be done in accordance with approved methods to suit these critics. Any departure from established modes of farming invited ridicule from those about them. So the Fieldings, for a certainty, had quite an adjustment to make. However, they enjoyed the prestige of their uncle's name. Come what may, it is certain that the parents placed great store in the mental and spiritual development of their children even though such things were held in disdain by some of the local landsmen.

John Fielding, like any tenant farmer, had his work cut out for him. Hard work was his lot early and late. Being a religious man, he worked and prayed. His daughter Mercy, in her later years, stated, "My father was a religious man. In fact, sometimes he was praying when I thought he ought to be out working."[4]

John's wife had no easy time of it on the farm, bearing most of her children there and performing the manifold duties required of a farmer's wife. She had certain misgivings about the farming venture in the first place, as will be seen. However, through it all, she retained her refinement of spirit which pervaded the home and brushed off on her children to give them grace and social acceptability in the best of circles.

[4]Courtesy of Robert I. Burton.

In the aforementioned memoir, Ann Matthews recounted that it was an ordeal for her parents to make up their minds to leave Halifax. Her mother was in possession of as much of this world's goods as she desired, surrounded by friends and relatives, where she had a fair prospect of a tranquil life.

When the opportunity came to be a tenant farmer, John Fielding undertook a journey to Honidon to appraise the situation. When he got there, he found it by no means a desirable place in which to take up his abode for life, so took his departure forever, as he thought. But on opening the Bible, his eyes fell upon a passage which appeared so remarkably appropriate that he could not but consider it as the voice of God indicating His will that Honidon should be his future residence. Still, when he arrived home, he could not give Rachel a very favorable report of the land he had gone to see. To satisfy herself, Rachel sent a servant to look at the farm. The report that he brought back tended very much to increase her settled opinion against leaving her home in Halifax.

After much deliberation and many difficulties which arose, including Rachel's objection, John Fielding's attention was arrested by another passage in the Bible exactly parallel to that which he had met with before, and so forceful was its impact upon his mind that he no longer doubted that he had a providential call to settle in the new place. He immediately determined to act accordingly and made preparations for the move of his family. This was a heavy trial to his wife who encountered difficulties to which she had hitherto been a stranger. The move was accomplished.

In regard therto, Ann Matthews stated:

> My dear mother was at first almost overwhelmed with anxiety, and would gladly have returned to Yorkshire. But notwithstanding her discouragement and painful apprehension it was here that her Christian graces, being put to trial, were proved to be the work of Him who has promised, "As thy days, so thy strength shall be."
>
> Many times did she in after life, when recounting her mercies, reckon this among the chief of them; although it gave her such pain, and exposed the family to so many difficulties.

> Not being acquainted with the customs of the place, they were often imposed upon and subjected to many disadvantages; and my father's landlord being his only paternal [really maternal] uncle, and his God-father, he had reason to expect from him, at least kindness and fore-bearance, instead of which he frequently received from him harsh and severe treatment. Economy, diligence, and frugality were rendered, indispensably necessary in order to the bringing up of a large family.[5]

It would appear that there was an element of providential intercession that brought about such a divergent change in the lives of the Fielding family. There really seemed to be no reason for moving to Honidon. Life in Halifax, their home town, was comfortable and quite satisfactory. What was to be gained by deliberately leaving something good and walking into something that presaged only hardships for all? The situation was akin to early America when urban folk picked up and left the old home grounds to seek out a new home on the frontier.

A strong, impelling force operated on John Fielding. Credit is his due, for when he finally made up his mind to move, nothing could dissuade him. He undoubtedly saw an opportunity to better his situation. If the crops did well, his share would bring a return greater than what he could earn in the city. Probably, a greater persuasion was the opportunity he saw for his evangelical work in the Honidon area. He was a preacher of the Word. The towns around their new abode were likely places for Methodist proselyting. This, he could do of an evening and on the Sabbath.

As it turned out, the farm was a training ground that prepared certain members of the family for important events which were to occur far in the future. They learned how to accommodate their lives to an agricultural environment and depend upon the soil for a living. In short, they learned how to be farmers with all that the term connoted—hard work, soiled hands, animals to care for, economy to be exercised in

---

[5]Matthews, *op. cit.*, p. 516.

spreading seasonal income over months with no returns, and the finding of practical solutions for unexpected problems.

Mother Fielding, the city girl, proved her mettle; she showed that she could adjust to a coarser existence. She applied her intelligence and exercised a guiding hand in the management of affairs. Her life had fulfillment in many ways. She was blessed with a wonderful family. While they may not have had means, the farm's dividend to the family was good health. The children thrived and developed in wisdom and maturity. Rachel, with her large family around her, was a complete woman. She and John had much on the credit side; they had made no mistake in coming to Honidon. The farm had given them a rich, abundant life.

Rachel Fielding was deserving of much praise and commendation. She managed her affairs well and exercised economy. She was good to the poor and relieved their wants beyond her means. She took a large share of the care of the family upon herself. This left her husband more at liberty for his religious and pulpit engagements. In the words of Solomon, she did him good, and not evil all the days of his life. (cf. Proverbs 31:12)

Her conduct toward her children was kind and tenderly affectionate, though seldom manifested by a caress, or ill-judged commendations. She showed her love by her precepts, and her firmness in opposing gratification of every desire which she knew to be harmful to their best interests. She was a prayerful woman and took part in leading prayer in the Rectory at Colmworth. While her husband was easy going, she was businesslike and capable. She was a mother-doctor and inoculated the babies of the village; people looked up to her.

In the above account is revealed considerable understanding of the character of the mother of the Fielding children. Each one was much like her—inclined and sensitive to the sacred Word. This is manifest not only in the memoir of Ann Matthews, but also, in the words of Mary, Mercy, John, James, and Joseph, which unfold later.

Rachel Fielding's life was marked by strenous activity which may have hastened her death. According to Ann, the disorder that took her mother was not well understood, even by the medical profession. About a fortnight before her demise, she was seized with a painful sensation at the heart while walking. On the Friday evening previous to her passing, she attended a church class meeting where she spoke and prayed. On the last Sabbath of her life, she led the 7 o'clock prayer meeting at the Rectory. Afterward, she persisted in going home but returned to the church in the afternoon where she received from the hands of her son-in-law, Reverend Timothy R. Matthews, "the dying memorials of her Lord and Savior."

Other attacks followed. A medical man was sent for, but to no avail. She was, toward the end, seized by a very severe pain. After about two hours, the pain abated. She was left alone for a few moments. Then one of her daughters, hearing her breathing rather hard, went in softly to her side, thinking she might be asleep. But the change was in progress. "We cried to God for help," wrote Ann, "and wept aloud; but her soul was too near its exit to be affected by our grief. The vital flame just quivered in the socket; the spirit was returning to God who gave it; and while her aged partner was bending over her and her children weeping around she sweetly fell asleep. . . ."[6]

After thirty-four years of vigorous farm life, Rachel Fielding went to a well earned rest at the age of sixty-one. She died a staunch Methodist leaving behind a large circle of friends. A funeral sermon was preached over her mortal remains the following Sunday at the Methodist Chapel in St. Neots by the Reverend James Golding.[7]

In passing, it can be rightfully said that the Fielding children would not have been so fine without the influence and teaching in their lives of their highgrade mother. In her,

---

[6] *Ibid.*, p. 521.
[7] *Ibid.*, p. 522.

we get a look at the "clay" from which Mary Fielding Smith was molded.

As a member of this devout and cultivated family, Mary was well-educated, in her own right, and properly reared. She was a devotee of John Wesley (1703-1791), English clergyman, founder of Methodism and a Protestant reformer whose teaching and noble character had touched her deeply in an idealistic way. She joined the Methodist society when she was very young. This helped her gain an understanding of the scriptures which gave her a foundation for her later reception of Mormonism.

Mary's formal education is evident in the rhetoric and style of two of her letters. Her clear thoughts and facile use of words reveal a good mind and able pen. In her preparatory years, she was trained in all the arts of homemaking. Besides this, she became a cultivated person and knew something about literature, art, music (she was reputed to be a lovely singer), and etiquette. She earned her own way in her twenties and thirties and learned how to manage and be thrifty with her money. She developed a mind of her own and showed initiative and self-control which later made her so self-reliant and resourceful.

An apple does not fall far from the limb, and so it was with Mary. She was in the image of her refined mother, having learned the things her mother had acquired in school and in a home of culture, and having read the books her mother considered choice, including Matthew Henry's *Commentary* and the *Christian Pattern.* Mary was acquainted with a variety of good books, authors, and verses. Her Bible was her refuge. She took comfort in the Psalms. Later in the wilderness, she would find courage and support in them. "To sweetness of disposition, she added strength of mind and power of instant decision. But over all the strength and firmness of her soul she drew the veil of modest womanhood so closely that only her very own realized how great was her gift, how supreme were her powers."[8]

Were we to stop here, we would carry a pretty fair impression of Mary. However, the description might fit any well-brought-up Victorian lady, but hardly does it do justice to her. She was also a pioneer in every sense of the word, resolute, unflinching, tough-minded in the face of opposition, and tempered like fine steel. She was nurtured not to the soft life, but to the hard way, tinged with the aesthetic.

The Fielding home was much more than a place to eat and sleep. It was also a place where character was molded. Christian sobriety prevailed in accordance with Methodist discipline directed against worldly pleasures. Pursuit of education by members of the family had its place. Books on subjects required by English schools were in evidence. A Latin and Greek textbook formed a part of the background of a son aspiring to become a member of the cloth. At times there were scripture readings and singing of hymns. Certainly, with son James studying for the ministry, there were times when the home was a gathering place for a coterie of young intellectuals, where vigorous debate ensued on tenets of various faiths.

James Fielding proved to be an uncompromising adherent to the straightlaced dogmas of Methodism—even feeling the need for a reformation among the faithful. This man, who gained influence, was destined to lasting fame more from his opposition to Mormonism than through his work as a legitimate Protestant minister and reformer. We learn more of him in the following:

> The Rev. James Fielding (of Preston, England), Mary's brother, was quite a religious reformer, and of sufficient ministerial reputation and force to become the founder and head of a Congregational Methodist Church. Originally he was a minister of the regular body of that powerful sect, but becoming convinced that modern Methodists had departed from their primitive faith, and that their church no longer enjoyed the Holy Ghost and its gifts, which measurably attended their illustrious

[8]Gates, *op. cit.*, p. 123.

founder and his early disciples, the Rev. Mr. Fielding inaugurated a religious reform in the direction intimated. It was an attempt to revive in his ministerial sphere the spiritual power of the Wesleyan movement; nor did he stop at this, but sought to convince his disciples of the necessity of "contending earnestly for the faith once delivered to the Saints."[9]

Further evidence of the evangelical character of the Fielding family and the respectability in which it moved are manifested in the marriage of Ann Fielding to the Reverend Timothy R. Matthews. The following excerpt opens another window through which we may obtain a larger view of the Fielding world:

> Other branches of the family also became prominent in the religious reforms of England that arose about the time of the establishing of the Church of Latter-day Saints in America. One of the Fielding sisters (Ann) married no less a personage than the Rev. Timothy R. Matthews, who figured nearly as conspicuously as the Rev. James Fielding in the early history of the British mission. This Rev. Timothy Matthews was at first minister of the Church of England, and is said to have been a very able and learned man. With the famous Robert Aitken, whom he called his "son," he attempted reformation even in the established Church; or rather, these innovative divines denounced the "apostasy" of that Church, and prosecuted a semi-apostolic mission. It was eminently successful, Robert Aitken and himself raising up large congregations of disciples in Preston, Liverpool, Bedford, Northampton and London. These disciples were popularly called Aitkenites and Matthewites. Quite relevant is all this to the history of the Latter-day Saints in England, for the congregation of the Rev. James Fielding, Rev. Timothy R. Matthews, and Rev. John Richards (father of Jennetta), gave to the apostles (Mormon) their first disciples abroad, and these ministers themselves were their instruments in establishing the British Mission.[10]

The stalwart one of the Fielding men proved to be Joseph, the fourth son. This man with many abilities was to become a bright instrument through whom much good would be accomplished. He was possessed of humility but at the same time a venturesome spirit. His restless nature refused to be contained by the shores of his native land. The opportunities

[9]Edward W. Tullidge, *The Women of Mormondom* (New York, 1877), p. 250.
[10]*Ibid.*, p. 251.

of the New World beckoned to him, and he responded. Without the formal education of James Fielding, he was to rise above his better-educated brother. Joseph, like Joseph in Egypt, flowered in another land and brought blessings to his family and countrymen. Through him, his sisters, Mary and Mercy, also found homes and destinies in the New World of America.

Chapter II

Family with a Mission

In March 1832, Joseph Fielding and his sister Mercy emigrated to Toronto, Canada.[1] Mary Fielding, who was six years older than Mercy, followed in 1834. In Toronto, they made the acquaintance of John Taylor, a well-educated and eloquent Methodist preacher. He had gathered around him a sturdy congregation of independent, religious worshippers. They believed in the necessity of revelation, gathering of Israel, and the gifts of the Holy Ghost.

Then an unusual thing happened to them. A Mormon missionary by the name of Parley P. Pratt, one of the ablest intellectuals attracted to the Mormon leader, Joseph Smith, arrived in Toronto with a message of new revelation and the restoration of the Gospel. His words, carrying the ring of truth, hit the high-minded group of John Taylor with upsetting force. However, they soon recovered and accepted the new faith.[2] The three Fieldings were baptized in May 1836.[3] Concerning these events in Canada, Pratt stated:

> The work soon spread into the country and enlarged its operation in all that region; many were gathered into the Church, and were filled with faith and love, and with the Holy Spirit, and the Lord confirmed the Word with signs following. My first visit to the country was about

---

[1]"She [Mercy Fielding] came with one of her brothers to Canada to assist him in the care and cultivation of a gentleman's farm, and meanwhile to procure land for themselves. Hardly had they arrived when the gentleman died, and thus the two were left alone in a strange country . . . members of wealthy families opened their houses to her, and from one to the other on protracted visits she went until her brother secured a farm to work upon shares. The terms were advantageous, and in a very short time, comparatively speaking, he and his sister were independent of other help."—"Temple Workers," *Young Woman's Journal,* IV (Apr. 1893), p. 290.

[2]At Toronto there was a society of Methodists who were dissatisfied with all the churches. They met together twice a week to discuss religious topics. Mrs. Walton, the lady with whom Elder Pratt boarded, invited him to a meeting. There he met John Taylor and his wife, Leonora Cannon Taylor, who were members of the

nine miles from Toronto, among a settlement of farmers, by one of whom I had sent an appointment beforehand. John Taylor accompanied me—this was before he was baptized—we rode on horseback. We called at Mr. Joseph Fielding's, an acquaintance and friend of Mr. Taylor's. This man had two sisters, young ladies, who seeing us coming, ran from the house to one of the neighboring houses, lest they should give welcome, or give countenance to "Mormonism." Mr. Fielding stayed, and as we entered the house he said he was sorry we had come, he had opposed our holding meeting in the neighborhood; and, so great was the prejudice, that the Methodist meeting house was closed against us, and the minister refused, on Sunday, to give out the appointment sent by the farmer.

"Ah," said I, "why do they oppose Mormonism?" "I don't know," said he, "but the name has such a contemptible sound; and, another thing, we do not want a new revelation, or a new religion contrary to the Bible." "Oh," said I, "if that is all we shall soon remove your prejudices. Come, call home your sisters, and let's have some supper. Did you say the appointment was not given out?" "I said, sir, that it was not given out in the meeting house, nor by the minister; but the farmer by whom you sent it agreed to have it at his house." Come then, send for your sisters, we will take supper with you, and all go over to meeting together. If you and your sisters agree to this, I will agree to preach the old Bible gospel, and leave out all new revelation which are opposed to it.

The honest man consented. The young ladies came home, got us a good supper, and all went to meeting. The house was crowded; I preached, and the people wished to hear more. The meeting house was open for further meetings, and in a few days we baptized Brother Joseph Fielding and his two amiable and intelligent sisters, for such they proved to be in an eminent degree. We also baptized many others in that neighborhood, and organized a branch of the Church, for the people there drank in truth as water, and loved it as they loved life.[4]

---

society. Through the teachings of Elder Pratt, all the members of the group were converted, Mrs. Isabelle R. Walton and her sister and daughter being the first to be baptized which took place in Toronto Bay.—Samuel Russell (grandson of Isaac Russell), "Laying the Foundation of the Church in Canada," *Church News—A Section of the Deseret News,* Salt Lake City, July 31, 1937, pp. 1 and 8.

[3]During this time, the beginning of Elder Pratt's work in Canada, it had been arranged for him to preach in the Wesleyan Church at Chestleton Settlement, but a prejudiced group forced them to withdraw. They then retired across the street and held their meeting in a maple grove on land occupied by Joseph Fielding. Half a mile west of the meeting house and settlement was a little stream called Black Creek. Thither Mr. Pratt repaired and baptized Isaac Russell, John Taylor, Joseph Fielding, his sisters Mary and Mercy Fielding, John Goodson, John Snyder, etc.—*Idem*

[4]Joseph Fielding Smith, *Life of Joseph F. Smith* (Salt Lake City, 1938), pp. 121-122. Hereafter referred to as Smith, *Life of JFS.*

Thus, in the rural area where the Fieldings had a farm, a chain of events was set in motion which had far reaching consequences for the Fielding family and the Mormon cause. Elder Pratt's words, spoken with skill, found favorable response in the hearts of his new friends. The impact was positive. It changed their lives and gave their names special distinction.

The conversion of the three Fieldings, together with John Taylor, and others, was a noteworthy achievement for the Mormon missionary. He had cause to rejoice and very good reason to look upon his success with great satisfaction. His efforts won for the Latter-day Saints a group of fine people with good minds and force of character. John Taylor would one day become president of the Church. The newcomers to the Mormon fold were favored in having a man of Pratt's caliber come to them. His sermons made Bible sense, and the minds of his newly-won converts, cultured in Christian ideology, proved highly receptive to them. He esteemed the quality of the new members which moved him to pay the Fielding sisters, in particular, the above gracious compliment as to their intelligence and amiability.

The Fieldings, in keeping with the counsel of the Church leaders, proceeded with plans for moving to the Mormon headquarters at Kirtland, Ohio. A year later, in the spring of 1837, the move was accomplished. The new Kirtland Temple had been completed by the Saints and dedicated, May 27, 1836.

In Kirtland, the Fieldings had an opportunity to meet the Mormon leaders and to mingle with members of the Church. They were made welcome and given a hand in getting located. The two sisters made a good impression and were favorably regarded by the other members.

> She [Mary] was beautiful to look upon. When she and her equally handsome sister, Mercy, came to Kirtland in 1837, trim, straight, dark-haired and dark-eyed, with delicately blooming cheeks and finely molded, graceful figures, clad in dainty silks of modern grace, they were the observed of all observers. Their refined and stately ways made them

a shining mark in Kirtland society. Wherever they went they were spoken of as those "Lovely English girls."[5]

The three Fieldings had come to the center of Mormon religious and secular activity. What transpired around them was evaluated on the basis of their pre-conditioning in the Methodist faith. Mary noticed that everybody worked for a living. There was no privileged clergy. Certain simple forms of recreation were not considered sinful. Events, such as socials, dramatic productions, or a cotillion dance, were opened with prayer. The Mormon Word of Wisdom proscribed tea, coffee, tobacco, and strong drink. There were no rich, and every effort was made to make the poor comfortable. Nearly everyone went to church, and anyone could be expected to be called on to pray or preach.

The striking Temple in their midst was awe-inspiring to Mary. The tempo of her religious and social life quickened to a marked degree requiring certain adjustments in her habits, mode of living, and thinking. Still, it was an exciting time in her life, for in Kirtland many things happened to her. In fact, a very important event occurred in the lives of each of the Fieldings, as indicated in the following:

> In the following spring [after their conversion] the Fieldings gathered to Kirtland. Soon the youngest of the sisters, Mercy Rachel, was married by the Prophet to Elder Robert B. Thompson, one of the Literati of the Church, who was appointed on a mission to Canada with his wife. At the same time Joseph Fielding was appointed on a mission to England, to assist the apostles in that land. But Mary remained in Kirtland, and on the 24th of December, 1837, she was married to Hyrum Smith.[6]

* * *

It was Joseph Fielding's earnest desire after coming into the Mormon fold that the way would be opened for the new religion to go to his native country, particularly to his own family. He confided to his journal: "My sisters and myself had written to them once on the subject, but I was afraid to

[5]Gates, *op. cit.*, p. 123.
[6]Tullidge, *op. cit.*, p. 250.

Joseph Fielding
Courtesy of Church Historian's Office

Black Creek, Toronto, Canada, where Mary Fielding and others were baptized, May 1836. The two men shown are: Joseph Fielding Smith and David A. Smith. Picture taken in 1939 while the latter was president of the East Canadian Mission. —Courtesy of Edith Smith Patrick.

write to them more lest I should not do it with that wisdom which the subject required, and so might do harm instead of good. I now felt much delighted and perhaps too sanguine as to the prospect of those glorious things which gave me such pleasure, would also be very delightful to them."[7]

He had some desire to be one of those who would go to England, but felt that he was ill-qualified for such an important mission. Yet, he knew that the Almighty used the weak things of the world to confound the strong. While he was thinking about it, Elder Pratt told him that he believed that he should go if he wished it. Joseph did wish it but was much afraid. He desired deeply to receive providential direction in the matter.

Earlier, at a conference in Churchville, Canada, John Taylor had prophesied with much power upon several brethren present. Concerning Joseph Fielding, he declared that the Spirit would be upon him, and he would lift up his voice in his native land. Joseph's reaction to this was: "I have not heard a prophecy delivered more manifestly by the Spirit of God than this was. From this I began to believe that the Lord had called me to go to England. At a meeting in Toronto also, this was confirmed by Elder Pratt and others. In short, there apeared to be but one opinion on the subject. This together with my way having been opened so unexpectedly, fully satisfied me of my call, and I was ordained a priest."[8]

When Mary Fielding stood on the pier at Fairport, Ohio, June 13, 1837, and waved goodbye to her brother Joseph and the other missionaries, her tears of sorrow at parting gave way to joy, for the new covenant was being taken to the people, including her own, in her motherland. Her heart was full

---

[7]Joseph Fielding, Journal, Bk. 1, p. 9—one of five books reproduced by Josephine Burton Bagley (granddaughter), W. Lester Bagley, Rae Barlow Barker (great-granddaughter), and Howard Barker, Salt Lake City. On microfilm, 181 pages (Dec. 1843 to Mar. 1859) in Genealogical Society Library, Salt Lake City. Hereafter this prime source will be referred to as Fielding.

[8]*Ibid.*, p. 10.

Note: While Joseph Fielding felt that he had been called to be a missionary, a call, to be official and valid, had to come from Joseph Smith, President of the Church.

of expectation that her brothers and sisters in England would accept the message and come into the Church, where the family could be together. Those who were with her to see them off likewise sensed the importance of the occasion, for this was the commencement of the first missionary work by the Mormon Church in a foreign land.

Included with the missionaries on board the boat moving out into Lake Erie were Mary's sister Mercy and her husband, Elder Robert B. Thompson, who were leaving on a mission to Canada.[9] Seeing Mercy leave, as well as her brother Joseph, made it doubly hard for Mary. She and Mercy had been good company for each other in the new land of America. As the boat moved away, they all waved until it was out of sight. This was probably not the first time that Mary had bade farewell to Joseph and Mercy when they sailed away. Five years earlier, these two had departed from their homeland for Toronto. Mary undoubtedly saw them off at Liverpool and, perhaps, helped them financially to reach America, where she joined them two years later.

Now, at the dock of Fairport, Mary not only felt a great sense of loneliness but also, deep concern for the missionaries going to distant England. They were without funds and short of clothing. The lunches that had been prepared for them by loved ones and friends would not last long. Where would they find food and lodging without means? They were leaving when affairs in Kirtland were bad and money extremely scarce. All these sobering realities made for a subdued mood in the group and a sad farewell. Knowing their situation, Mary entreated heaven to open the way for them, that all would go well, and they would have a prosperous journey.

Earlier in the day, when the time came for the departure of Elders Kimball, Hyde, and Richards, and her brother Joseph on this first leg of their trip to England, they were joined by a

[9]Orson F. Whitney, *Life of Heber C. Kimball* (Salt Lake City, 1880), p. 122, quotes Kimball, thus: "'We were also accompanied to Buffalo by R. B. Thompson and wife, who were on their way to Canada, where he intended to labor in the ministry.'"

few friends and relatives, including Mary, for the ten mile trip to Fairport to see them off.[10] Elder Kimball was sick and did not have a dollar to his name. He had started without "purse or scrip." Then Mary Fielding stepped up to him and graciously pressed five dollars into his hand.[11] It was a godsend and paid his and Elder Hyde's passage to Buffalo. The kindly deed melted their hearts. They did not forget this timely, gratuitous act. In afteryears, Heber C. Kimball rendered equally timely assistance to Mary. So, in addition to her letters with the Gospel message to her loved ones, Mary Fielding helped with her means in opening up the British mission.

* * *

The opening of a foreign mission in England was prompted by the grave situation that had developed within the Church in Kirtland because of the hostilities of the apostates. Something had to be done to save the seven-year-old Church and vindicate Joseph Smith as the Prophet of God in the eyes of the Saints and public. Joseph received the answer. According to Heber C. Kimball, on Sunday, June 4, 1837, the Prophet came to him, while he was seated in the front stand above the sacrament table on the Melchizedek side of the Kirtland Temple, and whispered: " 'Brother Heber, the Spirit of the Lord has whispered to me: 'Let my servant Heber go to England and proclaim my Gospel, and open the door of salvation to that nation.' "[12]

The above was also linked with a prophetic utterance of Elder Kimball himself concerning the mission he was about to fulfill. In the spring of 1836, he called at the home of Parley P. Pratt and, being filled with the spirit of prophecy, blessed Elder Pratt and wife. He prophesied that sister Pratt would be healed of consumption, with which she had been afflicted for six years, and would bear a son—this after ten years of marriage.

---

[10]According to Whitney, *Ibid.*, p. 122, the others were: Brigham Young, Levi Richards, Vilate Kimball, and Rhoda Greene.

[11]*Idem*

[12]*Ibid.*, p. 116.

> Thou shalt go to Upper Canada, even to the city of Toronto, the capital, and there thou shalt find a people prepared for the fullness of the Gospel, and they shall receive thee, and thou shalt organize the Church among them, and it shall spread thence into the regions round about, and many shall be brought to the knowledge of the truth and shall be filled with joy, and from the things growing out of this mission shall the fulness of the Gospel spread into England, and cause a great work to be done in that land.[13]

It happened as predicted. Parley's wife got well and bore a son, Parley P. Pratt, Jr. Elder Pratt went on a mission to Toronto, with the singular result already related. And now, the spreading of the Gospel to England was about to be fulfilled. So, in essence, the way was paved by the Spirit through members of the Fielding family found in Toronto, and for that matter in England, for the commencement of missionary work abroad.

To be called on a mission to his native land and participate in the historic introduction of Mormonism there was a great thing for Joseph Fielding and his sisters. Before his departure, he had the experience of being in the company of the Church leaders, getting to know Joseph Smith, and hearing his counsel and advice. The Prophet Joseph met with the missionaries in serious council. Besides Joseph Fielding, there were: Apostles Heber C. Kimball and Orson Hyde and Dr. Willard Richards. Three others from Canada were to join them in New York. The Prophet gave them special instruc-

---

[13]*Ibid.*, p. 135.

When Elder Pratt arrived in Toronto, he needed a place to stay. Mrs. Isabelle R. Walton said to Mrs. John Taylor: "Tell the stranger he is welcome to my house. I have a spare room and food in plenty. He shall have a home at my house and two large rooms to preach in just when he pleases. Tell him I will send my son John over to pilot him to my house while I go and gather my relatives and friends to come this very evening and hear him talk.' " Subsequently, Elder Pratt said to Mrs. Walton: " 'I was directed to this city by the Spirit of the Lord, with a promise that I should find a people here prepared to receive the Gospel and should organize them in the same. But when I came and was rejected by all parties, I was about to leave the city; but the Lord sent you, as a widow, to receive me, as I was about to depart, and then I was provided for like Elijah of old, and now I bless your house and all your family and kindred in His name. Your sins shall be forgiven you, you shall understand and obey the Gospel and be filled with the Holy Ghost, for so great faith have I never seen in any of my own country.' "—Samuel Russell, *op cit.*, pp. 1 and 8.

tions. He told them, in particular, that when they arrived in England, to adhere closely to the first principles of the Gospel and remain silent concerning the gathering, the "Vision,"[14] and the *Book of Doctrine and Covenants* until such time as the work was fully established, and it should be clearly made manifest by the Spirit to do otherwise.[15] After being set apart by the laying on of hands, the missionaries were ready to leave. They were to have astounding success in their work.

> But the name of Fielding, after those of the apostles, was principal in accomplishing these results. The sisters Mary and Mercy, with Joseph, half converted by their letters, the congregation of their reverend brother in Preston, before the advent there of the apostles. In their brother James' chapel, the first apostolic sermon in foreign lands was preached by Heber C. Kimball, and it was one of the Fielding sisters (Mrs. Watson), who gave the Elders the first money for the "gospel's sake" donated to the church abroad.[16]

* * *

When the missionaries arrived in New York City, they found the brethren from Canada: Goodson, Russell, and Snyder.[17] During the next few days, they prepared to go to sea, acquiring additional funds to cover their fares and to procure a stock of provisions for the voyage. They engaged passage to Liverpool, Second Cabin, on the merchant ship *Garrick*, 900 tons, and on July 1, 1837, departed for Liverpool. Nineteen days later, July 20, 1837, the *Garrick* anchored in the River Mersey, opposite Liverpool.[18]

To behold the green shores of England was a thrill for the missionaries, particularly for the Englishman, Joseph Field-

---

[14]Sec. 76, *The Doctrine and Covenants of the Church of Jesus Chirst of Latter-Day Saints*—containing revelations received by Joseph Smith, the Prophet; with additions by his successor in the presidency of the Church; 1928 ed. Hereafter this source will be referred to as *D&C*.

[15]*History of the Church of Jesus Christ of Latter-Day Saints, Period I*: "History of Joseph Smith, the Prophet, by Himself," (Salt Lake City, 1905 edition), II, 491-492. Hereafter this source will be referred to as Smith, *HC*.

[16]Tullidge, *op. cit.*, p. 252.

[17]This brought the number of missionaries to seven: President Heber C. Kimball, Apostle Orson Hyde, Elder Willard Richards, Elder Isaac Russell, Seventy John Goodson, Priest Joseph Fielding, and Priest John Snyder.

[18]Whitney, *op. cit.*, pp. 124-130.

ing. Little did he realize when he left those shores that he would return again so soon. Many wonderful experiences were in store for him. Also, he would soon be seeing his brother James who lived in Preston, thirty miles north of Liverpool. He hoped that James, as well as the rest of the family, would be favorably inclined and come into the fold.

Although Joseph Fielding had been in the Church only a short time, he had acquired a good knowledge of the Gospel. He had studied hard and added to his knowledge of the Bible. Earlier, he had been active in the Methodist Church at Honidon and had done a good work there. Also, he had been a leader of the Bible class in Canada.[19] He was naturally in tune with the ideals and teachings of Mormonism.[20] In addition to the first principles of the Gospel, he was strongly impressed by the renewing of the everlasting covenant that God had made with the prophets of old and of the gathering of the children of Israel. Joseph Fielding was a humble man with an amiable nature which enabled him to get along well with others. His new role was significant. He was returning as the advance nuncio to people he knew, his family and friends, his countrymen, to bear witness of the restored Gospel.

Before the missionaries, lay a civilization more than 1,000 years old, the land of Magna Carta but, notwithstanding, a

---

[19]In a letter from Ann Fielding Matthews, Mar. 22, 1833, from Priory Bedford, England, to her brother Joseph Fielding in Toronto, Canada, she stated: "Nothing we have heard from you since you left has given us so much pleasure as that which gave us the account of your accession to the same office you held while with us and O my dear Joseph what an important office is that of leading of souls. . . . Do you impress upon the members of your class the necessity of a clean heart? . . . I had rather that you were labouring thus than that you were hoarding up an independency of a thousand a year."—Courtesy of Josephine Burton Bagley.

[20]Something of Joseph Fielding's nature is found in Bernice Burton Holmes' "Great-Grandfather Joseph Fielding," MS, as follows: "Here [Canada] he established a farm, and with a team of oxen, and the primitive pioneer tools of the time, he tilled the soil and cleared the ground, his two sisters keeping house for him and aiding him in every way possible that they could. One day he was smoking as he followed behind his two plodding oxen and the plow they were pulling. Suddenly the thought came to him that it was a very silly thing to smoke in the sight of God with that pipe. Surely this habit was not pleasing to Him. He knew nothing of the scientific reasons against smoking but he decided at that moment not to smoke. He leaned over the plow and dropped the pipe in the furrow and it was covered by the brown earth as he walked on."

land of intolerance and indifference. Here was a land with many interesting things to see—old cities, towns, and hamlets; old buildings and streets; sailors, soldiers, and colonizers; a land of royalty, fine ladies and gentlemen. It was an island of cold aloofness, a keen sense of superiority, and class distinction. It was also a kingdom of great power, wealth, and egotistical nationalism, but, still, a land of abject poverty and carping cynicism.

Yet, old Albion was a land of dignity with a fine and ancient culture—Chaucer, Shakespeare, Byron, Shelley, and Keats; realm of the Common Law, Blackstone, and Old Bailey; land of majestic cathedrals and abbies; home of parliaments and prime ministers; bastion of learning, scholars, and philosophers; a picturesque fairyland given enchantment by old castles, palaces, art galleries, and theaters. But England was about to see the introduction of a new culture, as proclaimed by the missionaries from America, which would touch and change the lives of many.

The missionaries were much affected by the sight of things strange and foreign to them as they approached the great harbor of Liverpool. They stood at the rail and gazed in silence—moved deeply in their spirit. They faced the reality of their mission, the purpose of their coming. Elder Kimball spoke his feelings in these words:

> When we first sighted Liverpool I went to the side of the vessel and poured out my soul in praise and thanksgiving to God for the prosperous voyage and for all the mercies which He had vouchsafed to me, and while thus engaged, and contemplating the scene presented to my view, the spirit of the Lord rested down upon me in a powerful manner, while I covenanted to dedicate myself to God, and to love and serve him with all my heart.[21]

While the passengers were leaving the *Garrick* and going on a small steam-type boat for shore, Elders Kimball, Hyde, Richards, and Goodson jumped into a small boat and were rowed toward shore. When within jumping distance, Elder

[21]Whitney, *op. cit.*, pp. 130-131.

Kimball sprang from the boat, as if impelled by some superior force, and alighted on the steps of the dock, to be the first to set foot in England with the Gospel. He was followed quickly by Elders Hyde and Richards, all three of whom did not have a farthing on earth at their command. In the meantime, John Goodson, having a heavy purse of silver in his hand, waited until the vessel touched shore.[22]

The brethren tarried awhile in Liverpool to get their "land-legs" before commencing their missionary activities. They found lodging in the home of a widow. They needed the benefit of a warm bath, laundry service, and the shears of a barber. As missionaries, they had to look presentable. Furthermore, it was well for these strangers in England to become somewhat adjusted to a new environment and different customs, even to the left-side movement of traffic. They would have to learn how to use the many knives, forks and spoons they would find by their plates at meal time. They would have to watch their grammer and manners. Henseforth, they would be under critical scrutiny at all times.

As all new visitors to a foreign country, the missionaries were curious to see the sights. There was much to see in Liverpool. It was an important maritime trade-center. Ships of many nations entered and left the port. The Union Jack, flying from the masthead of numerous ships, gave evidence that Britannia ruled the waves. On the streets could be seen many nationalities, people from far-away places, crews from foreign ships, visiting businessmen, and tourists, giving the city a polyglot character.

The missionaries took in everything with a keen eye. Their mission was to win souls to the Kingdom. The people were their stock-in-trade and their chief interest. They beheld them as children of their Father in Heaven. But the newcomers deplored the extremes of wealth and poverty. The cries of the poor for alms distressed them. Those with scanty

[22]Smith, HC, *op. cit.*, II, 498.

clothing aroused their sympathy. As a result of this experience, the rich repelled them, and the poor had their love. As missionaries in England, they sought out the poor and the humble to receive their message.

The brief sojourn of the missionaries in Liverpool proved to be an uneasy lull before the storm, during which the powers of darkness were scouting them and probing for weaknesses. The Elders became the objects of attrition—the enemy taking advantage of any human susceptibilities to deter them. They experienced homesickness, depression of spirit, and gnawing worry. Being in a strange land without any money was a frightening and humbling experience. However, they emerged from this critical period of anxiety strengthened and galvanized for the struggle that lay ahead.

Satan knew that this part of his kingdom was being invaded by men with power to crush him. Therefore, they must be kept under surveillance. The conflict with the powers of darkness thus became joined in Europe as an extension of the struggle in Kirtland and at Far West.

Most of the wakeful hours of the missionaries in Liverpool were spent in council and in calling for divine assistance and direction. They felt a good spirit which buoyed them and gave them strength. They tarried nearly three days, the time culminating in a veritable pentecostal endowment of spirit from on high that girded them with confidence, erasing all moments of weakness, homesickness, gloom, depression, and a feeling of inadequacy. Elder Kimball stated: "Our trust was in God, who could make us as useful in bringing down the walls of Jericho; and in gathering out a number of precious souls. . . ."[23] Thus having put on the whole armor of God, they were ready to go forth, but where? " 'Go to Preston,' " said the Spirit of the Lord, " 'and to Preston they went accordingly.' "[24]

Their deliberations on where to begin their missionary

---

[23]Whitney, *op cit.*, p. 133.
[24]*Idem*

work undoubtedly included Liverpool. This city would make a good base of operations. It was a logical place for an office to handle mission business, including the processing of incoming and outgoing missionaries. As for Preston, the fact that Joseph Fielding had family connections in that place was not the only thing that prompted the missionaries to go there. Many good souls were waiting to hear their message. However, the missionaries did not know this but the Lord did. It proved to be the right place.

Chapter III

Home in America

With the marriage of Mercy Fielding and her departure with her husband on their mission to Canada, together with the departure, at the same time, of her brother Joseph on his mission to England, Mary Fielding was left to make her way alone in Kirtland. This meant finding employment to earn sufficient means to provide food, clothing, and shelter. This was by no means an easy task. Work was scarce and the pay meager. Converts were arriving daily, creating a surplus of manpower. There were few positions open to women.

However, Mary had an education and could teach school, tutor, or fill the role of an English nanny. Undoubtedly, she had gained some experience along these lines in England before coming to America. It was not possible to be choosy. Any respectable work was welcome, whether she got paid in cash, room, or board for her services. Few people had any money and, no doubt, she often worked for room and board. When it was her good fortune to receive a few coins in pay, she husbanded them carefully.

Life was rugged for her the summer and fall of 1837. She experienced many trials and hardships, not to mention anxiety of mind and loneliness. Being by herself in a new world and environment was most difficult. There were few compensations beyond the sustaining strength of the Church. Mary had a testimony of the Gospel, and it was precious to her. She also had a deep and abiding faith in God; in Him, she put her whole-hearted trust. This was to remain a distinguishing characteristic to assist her through many soul-testing crises which would arise.

Mary had an opportunity to see what a difficult task it was, administratively, for the Church leaders to keep harmony and unite all newcomers into a cohesive group. She learned that bitter opposition existed in the hearts of non-Mormons in the area and in a number of apostates. She learned how vicious mob action could be and the peril it posed for the Mormon leaders. She became all too aware of the type of hostility and danger that would hound them and cause her and so many others so much suffering.

During this period, letters from loved ones meant much to Mary. Whether the letter was short or long, her custom seemed to be to answer in some length. She had much on her heart and mind, and her pen gave welcome relief to some of her pent-up feelings. Her style of writing was eloquent and her thoughts clearly expressed. Her skill in the use of words, her phrasing, her story telling made for a highly interesting letter.

It was her custom to invest her letters with religious feeling. Any references to herself were casually couched and without undue elaboration. She did not dramatize nor go into excessive description. However, she left much to be read between the lines. Her language was devoid of frivolous vein, revealing primness and propriety.

Her few months of residence in Kirtland were at a time when the Saints were called upon to endure great affliction. In the latter part of 1837, certain dissenters united for the overthrow of the Church during the absence of the leader Joseph Smith. They publicly renounced the Church and claimed themselves to be the "old standard" calling themselves the "Church of Christ" and excluding the word "Saints."[1] Brigham Young, one of the loyal apostles, incurred their wrath by declaring openly that he knew Joseph Smith was a prophet and that he had not transgressed and fallen as the apostates had declared.

---

[1]Smith, *HC, op. cit.*, II, 528-529.

This incident and a mob action against Joseph Smith and Brigham Young affected Mary Fielding to the extent that she dwelt upon it at some length in a letter to her sister Mercy in Canada. This letter reveals much about her.

She began her letter by stating: "I have this day received a very short note from you, and am glad to learn by Brother Babbitt that you are well and comfortably situated. He tells me he is expecting soon to return to Canada, so that it is unnecessary for me to say much, as he can inform you of the state of things here verbally better than I can by writing, but still I can hardly refrain from sending a few lines." But Mary went on to say a good deal. She seemed in need to express herself, or better, to talk with someone.

In the next few lines, she disclosed what she was doing, but that her employment was about to expire. She appeared not to be worried, still she was concerned and obviously in need of a greater measure of security. "I am teaching school," she stated, "which I took for one month, the time expires tomorrow when I expect again to be at liberty, or without employment, but I feel in my mind pretty much at rest on that subject. I have called upon the Lord for direction and trust He will open my way. I hope you will remember me at the Throne of Grace."

Her next all too brief sentence disclosed that she had endured much and that life had been hard: "I have no doubt but you have many trials, but I am inclined to think you have not quite so much to endure as I have." She refrained from exposing the exact nature of her trials, and we are left wondering about them. Certainly, they were significant, but, still, she exercised forbearance and withheld them from her sister. She simply continued: "Be this as it may, the Lord knows what our intentions are, and He will support us and give us grace and strength for the day, if we continue to put our trust in Him and devote ourselves unreservedly to His service."

Undoubtedly, a large part of Mary's trials at this time were of the spirit, stemming from the severe ordeals the Church was experiencing. But despite it all, she had achieved peace of mind which, most certainly, flowed from her implicit faith that all would be well.

In the next statement, she goes to the heart of the trouble in Kirtland: "I do thank my Heavenly Father for the comfort and peace of mind I now enjoy in the midst of all the confusion and perplexity and raging of the devil against the work of God in this place, for although there is a great number of faithful, precious souls, yea, the salt of the earth, yet it may be truly called a place where Satan has his seat; he is frequently stirring up some of the people to strife and contention and dissatisfaction with things they do not understand."

It will be seen from the next part that Mary had a knowledge of the scripture. Accordingly, she was able to find a parallel in the Bible that fit the situation in Kirtland. She referred to the story of Korah, who led a rebellion against the leaders of ancient Israel. The earth opened up and swallowed him and his kind. Whether the Lord would do the same with the rebellious element in Kirtland, she could not tell: "I often have, of late, been led to look back on the circumstances of Korah and his company when they rose up against Moses and Aaron. If you read the 16th chapter of Numbers you will there find the feelings and conduct of many of the people, and even the elders of Israel in these days exactly described; whether the Lord will come out today in a similar way or not, I cannot tell. I sometimes think it may be so, but I pray God to have mercy upon us all and preserve us from the power of the great enemy, who knows he has but a short time to work in."

She went on to name the modern day Korah, the leader of the aforementioned apostates: "We have had a terrible stir with Wm. Parrish the particulars of which I cannot here give you at length. We are not yet able to tell where it will end. I have been made to tremble and quake before the Lord and to call upon Him with all my heart almost day and night, as many others have done of late."

Her thoughts went next to the House of the Lord and the voice of prayer there. She gave credit to prayer for the fact that the Church had been able to endure and, also, ascribed to it the source of her expectations. Surely, the Temple was a refuge to Mary and, within its sacred precincts, her earnest longings ascended on high: "I believe the voice of prayer has sounded in the House of the Lord some days, from morning till night, and it has been these means that we have hitherto prevailed, and it is by this means only that I for one expect to prevail."

Her words became beatific, expressing a sublime happiness and love of God which transport the spirit of the reader: "I feel more and more convinced that it is through suffering that we are to be made perfect, and I have already found it to have the effect of driving me nearer to the Lord and so suffering has become a great blessing to me. I have sometimes of late been so filled with the love of God, and felt such essence of his favor as has made me rejoice abundantly indeed. My heavenly Father has been very gracious unto me both temporally and spiritually."

This outpouring of feeling is a story of Mary in itself. Her few words are eloquent testimony of her feeling for the Lord in gratitude for special blessings which have enthralled her soul. We may only surmise the nature and extent of them but, whatever they were, they filled her being with joy.

Some of her feelings of gratitude may be attributed to her finding work, as related further in her letter: "Since I commenced this letter, a kind sister has proposed my going to stay for a while with her to take charge of two or three children who have been in my school; they purpose giving something besides my board, and I think this will suit me better than a public school, if it is but little. I expect to go there in a day or two, and hope to be quite comfortable as I know the family to be on the Lord's side. The mother is a cousin of Brother Joseph's, and took care of him when a child. Their name is Dort."[2]

The mob action, referred to earlier, against Joseph Smith

[2]With reference to the Dort family, David Dort married Mary (Polly) Mack, daughter of Stephen Mack, a brother of Lucy Mack Smith.—Records of Genealogical Society, Church of Jesus Christ of Latter-day Saints.

and Brigham Young, forms the climax of Mary's letter. Her account of it, as set forth below, reflected the critical situation of the Church in Kirtland:

I felt much pleased to see Sister Walton and Snider who arrived here on Saturday about noon, having left Brother Joseph Smith and Brigham about twenty miles from Fairport to evade the mobbers. They were to come home in Dr. Avard's carriage, and expected to arrive about 10 o'clock at night, but to their great disappointment they were prevented in a most grievous manner.

They had got within four miles of home, after a very fatiguing journey, much pleased with their visit to Canada and greatly anticipating the pleasure of seeing their homes and families, when they were surrounded with a mob and taken back to Painsville and secured, as was supposed, in a tavern where they intended to hold a mock trial, but to the disappointment of the wretches, the housekeeper was a member of the Church, who assisted our beloved brethren in making their escape, but as "Brother Joseph" says, not by a basket let down through the window, but by the kitchen door.

No doubt the hand of the Lord was in it, or it could not have been effected. The day had been extremely wet and the night was unusually dark and you may try if you can to conceive what the situation was. They hardly knew which way to start as it had by that time got to be about ten o'clock. The first step they took was to find the woods as quickly as possible where they thought they should be safe, but in order to reach there, they had to lie down in a swamp by an old log, just where they happened to be. So determinedly were they pursued by their mad enemies in every direction, and sometimes so closely, that "Brother Joseph" was obliged to entreat "Brother Brigham" to breath more softly if he meant to escape. When they would run or walk they took each other by the hand and covenanted to live and die together.

Owing to the darkness of the night, their pursuers had to carry lighted torches, which was one means of the escape of our beloved sufferers, as they could see them in every direction while they were climbing over fences or traveling through bush or cane fields, until about 12 o'clock. After traveling on foot along muddy, slippery roads until near three in the morning, they arrived safely home before sunrise, and thank God it was so.

Notwithstanding all that he had to endure, he appeared in the House of the Lord throughout the Sabbath, in excellent spirit, spoke in a very powerful manner, and blessed the congregation in the name of the Lord; and I do assure you the Saints felt the blessings upon him.

Brother Rigdon, through his great weariness, and a small hurt, received from a fall, did not attend the House, but is now well. I suppose all these things will only add another gem to their crown. I did not think of taking up so much room in relating these circumstances, but I have been as brief as possible.

After reporting other news, Mary concluded her letter with a few family matters: "I expect to hear from you soon and also from England. I hope I shall not be disappointed. Tell me if you and Brother Thompson have any idea of coming to Kirtland this fall. If the field of labor remains open there and unless a change should take place in the state of affairs here for the better, I should not advise it, however much I desire to see you here. Scores of men are out of employ here in the summer and how it will be in the winter I cannot tell. But I fear for Kirtland. Oh, that we as a people may be faithful, for this is our only hope, and all we have to depend upon."

She ended her letter with an expression of love and thanks to others for their manifested kindness, in these words: "Give my kind love to Brother Thompson and all other friends, particularly Brother and Sister Law. I thank them for their kindness to you. I thank Brother Thompson for his last kind letter. I shall be pleased with another. I remain, your very affectionate sister, Mary Fielding."[3]

The foregoing introduces Mary and brings her intimately to the reader. The kind of a person she was is revealed. Moreover, she ceases to be somewhat legendary and becomes very real. One might say that she was saintly before becoming a Latter-day Saint. Yet, superimposed, glows a special thing in her life, the new faith she had espoused.

She was afraid for Kirtland. The aforementioned mob action left no question in her mind that the danger from mobbers was very real. She read into it a portent of things to come. But hardly could she discern that the hot breath of mob spirit and mob action would be aimed at her household to shape the future trend of her life. She would be spared, but grief and

[3]Gates, *op. cit.*, pp. 124-127.

sorrow caused by mobs would be heaped upon her to bring her agony of heart. They would hem her in; they would take from her the object of her deepest affection; they would drive her from her home into an untried land. Because of them, she would be no stranger to terror. A desperate struggle lay before her.

Chapter IV

Mary and Hyrum

A number of things had a bearing on bringing Mary Fielding to the new world of America, the chief one being that she was unattached in her homeland and quite free to do as she pleased. In addition, she had kinsmen in America for whom she had special affection and to whom she could come. Subsequent to her arrival, a new and vital factor brought her to Kirtland, that of becoming a member of the Church. Here, her situation soon altered, as already related, leaving her separated from all her loved ones.

With the marriage of Mercy, Mary remained the only one of the Fielding sisters who had not married. This fact and the knowledge that she was in her mid-thirties were not consoling. Yet, Mary might have married in England. There was someone there who had liked her, a man by the name of Dover who was a lay-preacher in the Methodist faith in Bedford and a person known especially to her sister Ann Matthews. It appears that Mary did not like his attention and took herself away. Her sister Ann, exhibiting a strange form of piety, thought it very likely that Mary was providentially removed, interpreting it thus because it freed him to be more at liberty in the Methodist cause.[1] Hardly could anyone foresee that it was providential for a better reason: to fulfill a greater role that lay in store for her. Mary, it seems, went to Preston (perhaps with her sister Martha) from whence, later, she left to go to America.[2]

---

[1]Ann Matthews' letter, *op. cit.*, Mar. 22, 1833.

[2]In Fielding, Bk. 1, p. 56, it is recorded: "This [St. Neots] was our place of worship, but soon after my brother James left his business to go to Preston as a preacher . . . and one or two of my sisters with him, one of whom came to America to me (Sis. Mary)."

After the departure of Mercy and Joseph from Kirtland on missions, Mary passed through a very difficult period of her life as indicated earlier. However, it was a period of great spiritual uplift for her. She drew nearer to the Lord during her isolation from her people. She felt the power of Satan raging in the midst of the Saints. She was made to tremble and quake and call upon the Lord with all her heart, day and night. As a member of the Church, she did not lack for friends. Yet, they could not substitute for her own family. In such a situation, her thoughts naturally went to her loved ones. She was vulnerable to homesickness and, perhaps, experienced a bit of nostalgia for her native England but, evidently, not to induce her to return there. Her mother had died in 1828 and her father in 1836. So there was no impelling reason, even if she entertained the thought, to return to the place of her birth. But she needed roots. She needed to belong somewhere and to be busy and happy.

A realization of these things, including a home and family, came to her in Kirtland. Again, a combination of events brought them to her. Fall came, and with it the chill winds off Lake Erie. Children were back in school. Mary was busy as a private tutor. Then, an event occurred that saddened the Mormon community. Jerusha Smith, a prominent matron of Kirtland and wife of Hyrum Smith, died on October 13, 1837, leaving five small children.[3] Hyrum was away in Far West, Missouri, at the time. The community mourned her deeply.

Her mother-in-law, Lucy Mack Smith, wrote of Jerusha: "About one year after my husband returned from this mission [to New England], a calamity happened to our family that wrung our hearts with more than common grief. Jerusha, Hyrum's wife, was taken sick, and after an illness of perhaps two weeks, died while her husband was absent on a mission to Missouri. She was a woman whom everybody loved that was

---

[3]The ages of Hyrum Smith's children other than the new baby Sarah, were: Lovina ten; John, five; Hyrum, Jr., three; and Jerusha, one year and nine months. A daughter, Mary, born after Lovina, had died at the age of three.

acquainted with her, for she was every way worthy. The family were so warmly attached to her, that, had she been our own sister, they could not have been more afflicted by her death."[4]

Jerusha died eleven days after the birth of her sixth child Sarah who was born on October 2, 1837. Certainly, it was an agonizing thing for the young mother to die with her husband away and to leave him and her children. Her heartache, without the comforting presence of her husband and with the precious faces of her children closing from view, far exceeded her clinical pain. As the crisis approached, Jerusha said to her little ones, " 'Tell your father when he comes that the Lord has taken your mother home and left you for him to take care of.' "[5] While one might find a trace of bitterness in this statement, the meaning was clear that Jerusha's chief concern was for the proper care of her children. In other words, her dying wish to Hyrum was that he take good care of them.

The death of fair Jerusha imposed unexpected responsibilities upon the Smith family. Hyrum and Joseph were both away at the time. So it devolved upon Father Smith and other members of the family to make the funeral arrangements and give Jerusha a good burial. Mother Smith, out of her boundless love, was available to assist all she could in Hyrum's home in the emergency. Persons living in the home, who received their board and keep, also assisted, including Aunty Grinnels.[6] She devoted herself to the care of the baby. Mother Smith could sense deeply the big void that was left in the home by the loss of Jerusha. Aunty Grinnels could manage for awhile, but five children needed the tenderest care and understanding of a mother.

To find his beloved Jerusha gone upon returning from Missouri was a painful shock to Hyrum. His grief and suffering touched the hearts of all who knew him. Joseph noticed

---

[4]Lucy Mack Smith, *Joseph Smith the Prophet,* ed. Preston Nibley (Salt Lake City, 1958), p. 246.

[5]Smith, *HC, op. cit.,* II, 519.

[6]Hannah Woodstock Grinnels, b. Nov. 3, 1793, Killingsworth, Conn., daughter of William and Elizabeth Woodstock.—Courtesy of Mary Porter.

his grief and felt deep, brotherly concern for him. The Prophet loved his brother, and Hyrum's soreness of heart was reflected in his own heart. Joseph gave Hyrum's situation sober thought, then, in due course, received the answer on what was best for him, as expressed in the following: "The Prophet Joseph, realizing the necessity of the situation, informed Hyrum that it was the will of the Lord that he marry again and take as a wife a young English convert, Mary Fielding by name . . . ."[7]

Mary Fielding, as we have noted earlier, had an opportunity to take charge of two or three children in the home of the Dort family. The coming of this family to Kirtland was the outgrowth of a visit of Mother Smith, together with her son Hyrum, and others, to her people in Michigan.[8] There, she labored hard to convey to her kinsmen an understanding of the Gospel. Of her immediate kin in that place, she succeeded in gaining the hearts of only the Dort family.[9] It pleased her when they came to Kirtland.

Mary Fielding, undoubtedly, had met members of the Smith family in a formal way at Church or social functions. Now, as a tutor-nurse in the Dort home, she had the opportunity to become acquainted with them more intimately. Mother Smith, on visits to her niece Mary Dort, would notice the neat and competent English lady and what a fine job she was doing with the Dort children. So, through good report and character, Mary found favor and was accepted within the Smith family circle.

In due course, and following his brother's counsel, Hyrum sought the hand of the lady whom it was providentially appointed that he should marry. This unusual circumstance,

---

[7]Smith, *Life of JFS, op. cit.*, p. 120.

[8]Lucy Mack Smith's brother, Stephen Mack, was a prosperous businessman in Pontiac, Michigan. He owned various stores, mills, a bank, and the townsite of Pontiac which he founded.—Archibald F. Bennett, "Solomon Mack and His Family," *The Improvement Era*, LIX, 30-32; from Tunbridge Town Record Bk. A.

After the death of Stephen Mack, Lucy Mack Smith visited his widow and four married daughters and their families. She found them in comfortable circumstances. —Lucy Mack Smith, *op. cit.*, pp. 211-216.

[9]*Ibid.*, p. 216.

wherein the Lord revealed whom a person should marry, has few parallels. Subsequent events were to prove the rightness of Joseph's pronouncement in behalf of his brother. Mary, definitely, was the proper person for Hyrum. However, it must not be assumed that the marriage was one of convenience for either of them. Hyrum would not have wanted it that way. Neither would Mary's fine sensitivity have permitted it. Marriage was something she had looked forward to for a long time and which she regarded as very sacred. It had to have feeling and heart-meaning. Hyrum was a handsome man and Mary a lovely woman. His gentlemanly and courtly proposal was the type that she had always anticipated. It provided the basis of lasting affection between them.

So, in Kirtland, marriage came to Mary when she was thirty-six years old and Hyrum one year her senior. It occurred the day before Christmas, 1837. Undoubtedly, the Prophet Joseph Smith officiated in the presence of loved ones in the quiet of the Kirtland Temple but in the absence of any of her people. It would have been nice if some of her brothers and sisters could have been there to share her moment of happiness at the altar. But is was a marriage without fanfare or festivities. Anything of this sort would have been out of place in view of the short time that had elapsed since Jerusha's passing. However, the next day, surely the Christmas in Hyrum's home was a special one. The children would have the best of care again.

Chapter V

Mary's Trek with Her Husband

Mary's first goal in taking over the management of Hyrum's household was to get acquainted with the children, as well as the two older people whom Hyrum had taken in, and gain their confidence. She went about it intelligently, realizing it required patience, skill, and tact. She was assuming the role of a stepmother which called for an out-going spirit, the giving of herself, and the exercise of her Christian graces. She had the help of Aunty Grinnels in bridging the first days of strangeness and the natural shyness of the children. Gradually, Mary managed to fit herself into the household rather than have them fit into her ways and expectations.

Mary's chief consideration was to please her husband. She accomplished this best by engendering a good spirit in the home and maintaining an atmosphere of peace and good cheer. She endeavored to have a well-ordered home, with an eye to the children's schooling and spiritual development. Gradually, she achieved a full assumption of her important role as the wife of one of the general authorities of the Church. This meant a full understanding of his high and special calling and a readiness to face every contingency with courage and faith.

Her experience in managing and tutoring the children of others had prepared her well for her new role. This, coupled with the fact that she was mature and had some comprehension of the needs of children and how to handle them, enabled her to concern herself with the needs of each child individually at his age level. She formed a real love for the little brood and understood and mothered them all. They were not only Hyrum's children but God's choice spirits. Mary was a religious woman, and her heart was full of appreciation for her many blessings, including a ready-made family and a faithful husband. Her quiet love overflowed to bridge the difficulties that arose.

Ten-year-old Lovina was the only one of the five children who was of school age. She probably had attended school in Kirtland and learned to read and write. It fell to Mary to assist her in continuing her schooling even to the extent of tutoring her at home. Lovina was an intelligent, pretty child. Time only would assuage her heartache over the loss of her mother. It was necessary for Mary to show her special deference and be very considerate of her to pave the way to complete rapport between them.

At the time of the transition of the home to Mary's management, little John had turned five. Mary undoubtedly saw to it that he got started in the methods of the English beginner schools, step by step, getting used to routine discipline, teaching him to read by phonetics, moving on to writing and art. In due course, this routine might have been repeated for each of the children, with sewing added for the girls. Besides the three R's, Mary imparted to the children what their mother would wish them to have, refinement in speech and manners. Considering the peripatetic life of the family during the next few years, such instruction as Mary could give the children would be a lasting foundation for further learning.

Hannah Grinnels, who was sometimes called Aunty Grinnels or Grandma Grinnels, had been in the family for some time assisting with the housework and serving as a nurse in times of sickness and confinement. The care of the new baby Sarah, before and after Jerusha's death, fell upon Hannah. Many were concerned for the tiny infant, but Hannah brought the baby safely through the early critical period of her life. She hovered over the little one and watched her thrive and grow. At the time Mary Smith came into the home, the baby was going on three months and doing nicely. This care and attachment extended into months, then years, and finally established the tradition among the descendants of Sarah Smith Griffin that "She was raised by an old lady by the name of Grennels [sic] who lived with the family."[1]

Another dependent in the home was an old man by the name of George Mills who was given shelter by Hyrum Smith about 1833. "Old George," as he was sometimes called, had been a soldier in the British-Canadian Army. He had never learned to read or write. Quite often, he acted upon impulse more than the promptings of reason which at times made it difficult to get along with him.[2]

Old George was a handy man about the place. He kept the wood pile replenished and saw to it that the wood box in the house was kept full. He also worked about Hyrum's farm taking care of the garden and looking after the farm animals. He looked up to Hyrum and was loyal to him. This old soldier and handyman stayed pretty close to the family. When a move occurred, he went along, too. He was not a Latter-day Saint, but this made no difference with Hyrum and his family. He was among the first pioneers to reach Utah.

Hyrum had the propensity for taking in people who had no where else to go nor means to sustain themselves. All the Smiths were like this. Joseph threw his home open to indigents and other friends. Father and Mother Smith had always set the example.[3] So, if Hyrum took in widows with children, which he did, and kept them for indefinite periods, it was the Christian thing to do. Later on, in Nauvoo, he invited other poor people to stay permanently. It was something Mary would have to accept. And this she did; the needy under her roof always had a home; she did not forsake them.

Hyrum's house in Kirtland was a large two-story structure which had an extension to the rear where the kitchen and store-

[1] "Autobiography of Charles Emerson Griffin," MS, Escalante, Utah, Mar. 18, 1883.—Courtesy of Leah Porter Griffin, a great-granddaughter.

[2] Gates, *op. cit.*, pp. 132-133.

[3] Lucy Mack Smith, *op. cit.*, pp. 231-232; wherein she stated: "How often I have parted every bed in the house for accommodation of the brethren, and then laid a single blanket on the floor for my husband and myself while Joseph and Emma slept upon the same floor, with nothing but their cloaks for both bed and bedding."

room were located. The house had dignity, and Mary felt good in it. She now had a place of her own where she was mistress. It brought her the security that she needed. She now belonged and had roots. It was a joy to arrange and decorate the rooms. The house was not pretentious, but it was better than the average home in Kirtland and imparted a feeling of respectability. Mary could remain here and be happy. Indeed, the home was a blessing to her. From the moment she moved in, she was deeply grateful for it and her new estate.

It was a new way of life for her. She moved in a choice circle of friends and acquaintances. She was close to the governing council of the Church. She learned more of the dangers and problems that beset the brethren. Quite often, she answered a knock on the door to find the Prophet Joseph there. Sometimes, his face would light up with a smile, but, more often, it was tense and sober. He came to confer with Hyrum or to find seclusion. Mary came fully to realize the heavy burdens that rested upon Joseph and Hyrum. So far, the ferocity of the apostates and local mob had not focused on her husband, but she worried when he was away from home. Brigham Young had been compelled to leave Kirtland on December 22, 1837, because of the hot fury of the mob spirit which prevailed in the apostates who threatened to destroy him.

The true situation was recorded by Joseph Smith, as follows:

> January, 1838. A new year dawned upon the Church in Kirtland in all the bitterness of the spirit of apostate mobocracy; which continued to rage and grow hotter and hotter, until Elder Rigdon and myself were obliged to flee from its deadly influence, as did the Apostles and Prophets of old, and as Jesus said, "when they persecute you in one city, flee to another." On the evening of the 12th of January, about ten o'clock, we left Kirtland, on horseback, to escape mob violence. which was about to burst upon us under the color of legal process to cover the hellish designs of our enemies, and to save themselves from the just judgment of the law.[4]

[4]Smith, *HC, op. cit.*, III, 1.

The Prophet Joseph's mother added other facets about their departure and that of Joseph's family in these words: "That night he was warned by the spirit to make his escape, with his family, as speedily as possible; he therefore arose from his bed and took his family, with barely beds and clothing sufficient for them, and left Kirtland in the dead hour of the night."[5]

At the time of flight, the weather was extremely cold. The fleeing men were obliged to go ahead on horseback, their families catching up with them a few days later. The two men secreted themselves in their wagons to elude the grasp of their pursuers, who, armed with pistols and guns, continued their pursuit of them for two hundred miles from Kirtland, seeking their lives.[6]

Hyrum Smith remained in Kirtland until the latter part of March after Joseph's departure. There was certain Church business that he had to discharge as Joseph had directed. In the next few weeks, Hyrum made quiet preparations to leave. He checked with his folks and brothers William and Don Carlos to make sure they would also be able to get away. They wouldn't be able to leave until a little later. However, just as soon as Hyrum carried out certain business with the Seventies pertaining to their evacuation from Kirtland, he would be on his way.

In the meantime, Mary Smith busied herself with the packing. The furniture and farm implements would move by water through the Ohio and Erie Canal to the Ohio River, down the Ohio and up the Mississippi to Quincy, Illinois. Several wagons and teams were needed to transport the family, their food, bedding, and personal effects. Plantings of all kinds of fruit, garden seed of every kind, and a variety of grain seed were needed in Far West, as well as choice breeds of stock. It is certain that Hyrum procured many of these things to take along.

---

[5]Lucy Mack Smith, *op. cit.*, p. 248.
[6]Smith, *HC*, *op. cit.*, III, 2-3.

Besides Hyrum's immediate household, Robert B. Thompson and his wife, Mercy, recently returned from their mission to Canada, traveled with them. Concerning this, Mercy recorded the following: "We remained there [Canada] until March 1838 when we were appointed to journey with Hyrum Smith . . . to Far West, Missouri. We arrived there in May where my daughter Mary Jane was born on the 14th of June, 1838."[7]

Hyrum's final official act for the Church before departing from Kirtland was in meeting, by invitation, with the Council of Seventies. The purpose of the meeting was to draw up a constitution for the organization and government of the Camp of Seventies; also, rules of conduct and procedures to govern the Seventies during their journey, in a body, to Far West. Being called upon, Hyrum opened the meeting with prayer. Under his guidance, the Council proceeded to draft the outlines of a constitution. It was ready for adoption at their afternoon meeting. Hyrum imparted practical advice about organizing the camp. He instructed the Seventies to request the assistance of the High Council in carrying the plan into execution.[8]

After Hyrum had finished with the Council, he asked the Seventies to excuse him, and he retired from their meeting. He was now prepared to leave for the West. When he reached home, Mary could tell at once by his expression that his mind was free and that they would, for sure, soon be on their way. Everything was in readiness to depart. It took considerable planning and financing for Hyrum to provide transportation for ten people, besides himself, and all their luggage. Several wagons and teams required teamsters. Since there were only three men in the group, the women would have to assist with the driving. This meant handling the lines and operating the heavy brakes when necessary. To say the least, an amazing

[7]Mercy Fielding Thompson, Centennial-Jubilee letter, Dec., 20, 1880, deposited in Relief Society Jubilee box, Salt Lake City, for opening April 1, 1930. Hereafter referred to as Thompson Centennial letter.

[8]Smith, *HC, op. cit.*, III, 94-95.

experience lay ahead for the ladies and children. But Hyrum's efficiency inspired confidence; they would learn many things from him and feel secure.

When Mary Smith took her place by her husband in the lead wagon to begin their journey, she entered upon what might be called an apprenticeship. In the days that followed, she learned all the rudiments of pioneer travel. Under the supervision of her husband, she put her hands to do what she had never done before. Much of it was man's work, requiring physical strength and exertion. Even in the areas where women excel, she was to pick up many pointers and techniques associated with "roughing it." Little did Mary realize that the trip for her would be a grand rehearsal for things to come, when Hyrum would not be by her side, and when she would be alone with her family on a much longer and more dangerous trek. So what she learned was preparatory, a training mission for this English lady, that would one day qualify her as a "journeyman" and give her the confidence to tackle the impossible for a woman. Yes, as if by providential design and foreordination, this trip was to be a "turnkey" experience in the life of Mary Smith.

It was a spring day when the wagons started to move out of Kirtland, with Hyrum and Mary setting the pace. There was warmth in the air; nature was beginning to come alive. The village of Kirtland was attractive in its spring attire—situated the way it was overlooking the East Branch of the Chagrin River. It was surrounded on the north, east, and west by rolling woodland. On the top of a broad eminence, the beautiful, new Temple gleamed in the morning sunlight. White vapor rose from the roof-tops of the houses below on the flat. Kirtland was a choice place, made dear by the labor of love the Saints had put into it. It would not be easy to forget. For the Mormons, much history had been made there. In the beginning, there were only a few converts, but in seven years over 1,000 members had converged on the area and established homes.

While Mary Smith had been in Kirtland only a few months, the period was memorable to her. Here, she had been initiated into the full Mormon creed and community spirit. To her was shown the strength and weaknesses of men—how high they rose under the Spirit and how low they fell when they lost it. She learned something of mob action and deviltry. She had seen the missionaries, including her brother, under special appointment, go forth to open the first foreign mission—in her motherland. She had done her part with her letters to her people in laying a foundation for the conversion of many souls. In Kirtland, her cup at times had been bitter, then sweet, and finally overflowing with joy and happiness. Consequently and unquestionably, Kirtland would always have meaning for her. But now in parting, she turned her face westward prepared for what lay ahead. For the next few weeks, the sky would be her roof. She dreamed of another home, peace, and security for them all beyond the western horizon.

Hyrum had good cause to be emotionally moved by the departure. As the wagons passed out of town, a panorama of events unrolled before his memory. He had just come from telling his parents goodbye. He felt some anxiety for their safety. He recalled how the Gospel had been brought to Ohio by Parley P. Pratt, Oliver Cowdery, and Peter Whitmer, who were on their way to take the Gospel message to the Indians. They found Sidney Rigdon, a Campbellite minister, at nearby Mentor, Ohio. Rigdon was soon baptized. The work flourished. It was in January 1831, as Hyrum remembered so well, when he and Joseph came to Kirtland. The town was laid out and homes built. In the winter of 1832, at Hiram, Joseph and Sidney were tarred and feathered. This had been a terrible shock to Hyrum and the Mormon community.

Then in 1833 work on the new Temple had commenced. On the 5th of June a lad by the name of George A. Smith, Hyrum's cousin, hauled the first load of limestone. Hyrum recalled that he and Reynolds Cahoon had started the trench for the foundation after the corner stakes had been set and the white cord stretched between them. Hyrum had removed the first shovelful of dirt. They finished the foundation with their own hands. To be the first to work on the Temple to the Most High was an honor for them. Hyrum had taken great pride in the construction of the building, as any man does in his own handiwork. From the foundation, he had witnessed a magnificent edifice rise story by story to become the finest edifice in the land. The Saints had been called upon to make great sacrifices in service, money, and provision to make the Temple possible. They had worked diligently in the face of extreme austerity to complete the structure. The sisters had brought treasured glassware, crockery, and dishes to be crushed and the fine pieces mixed with the plaster to go on the outside so that the building would sparkle in the sunlight. There had been some difficulties. Enemies loitered about at night to do damage to the rising walls which made it necessary to post guards. Also, raising the final money to finish the Temple, with only six days left before dedication, had not been easy. Hyrum's father and Uncle John Smith had been given a special assignment to do this, as indicated in the following.[9]

Kirtland May 21st 1836
This may certify that John Smith and Joseph
Smith Sen are autherised to collect donations
for the finishing the hous of the Lord
also to lone moneys to pay debts that
have all ready been contracted to build said
hous

Reynolds Cahoon
Hyrum Smith
Jared Carter

[9]Courtesy of Mrs. Mabel Irene Boyd, Colchester, Ill., granddaughter of Arthur and Lucy Smith Millikin. Mrs. Boyd, eighty, has the original painting of her great-grandmother Lucy Mack Smith—picture painted as she sat in a rocking chair.

Hyrum would never forget the dedication of the Temple—particularly the acceptance of it as manifested by the outpouring of God's spirit upon it during the services. He knew of the special events that had occurred and the important keys that had been conferred upon his brother Joseph and Oliver Cowdery.[10] These things gave the House a sacred aura. As Hyrum looked upon the noble edifice for the last time, his heart was full. He felt badly to have to leave it. He turned his eyes away. Somewhere in the West, they would build another House of the Lord.

Hyrum would never forget Kirtland for other reasons, one of which was the memory of Jerusha. This was a spiritual souvenir. However, he carried with him another souvenir which he might have avoided had he been more careful. It was a scar on his left arm from a bad wound four or five inches in length, caused when he accidently fell and cut himself on his sharp axe. Doctor Williams sewed up the wound and dressed it. His brother Joseph was concerned and felt to thank God that it was no worse. He wrote: "I ask my Heavenly Father in the name of Jesus Christ to heal my brother Hyrum, and bless my father's family, one and all, with peace and plenty, and eternal life."[11]

Hyrum's wagon-train headed southward from Kirtland. The route was practically the same one taken by him the fall before, when he returned from Missouri, and the one with which he was the most familiar. He knew the villages along the way and where isolated Mormon families were to be found. He knew the character of the roads, the good and bad stretches, and where they would have difficulty in crossing streams, swamps, muddy flats, and debilitating prairies.

Leaving when they did, they ran into many spring showers and a variety of weather. They hit plenty of mud after a downpour on the prairies. This made for gruelling travel and miserable living. Hyrum, sometime later, said: "I left Kirtland,

[10] *D&C* 110:1-13.
[11] Smith, *HC, op. cit.*, II, 393-394.

Ohio, in the spring of 1838, having the charge of ten individuals; the weather was very unfavorable, and the roads worse than I had ever seen, which materially increased my expenses, on account of such long delays upon the road. However, after suffering many privations, I reached my destination in safety. . . ."[12]

Delays because of weather prolonged the journey and caused a shortage of supplies forcing them to purchase additional provisions along the way. Getting about in stormy weather was particularly distressing to the women whose long skirts and petticoats touched the ground, subjecting them to water and mud. It was difficult to dry things. Consequently, their wet clothing had to dry on them.[13]

When they reached the Ohio and Erie Canal, which connected Cleveland on Lake Erie with Portsmouth on the Ohio River, Hyrum was in a position to use water transportation. "I sent on by water all my household furniture," he said, "and a number of farming implements, amounting to several hundred dollars, having made purchases of several hundred acres, upon which I intended to settle."[14] With lightened load, travel would be faster.

The route took them through Ohio, Indiana, and Illinois to Quincy on the Mississippi River. Over the river in Missouri, the road led to a town called Louisiana, then west to Paris,

---

[12]*Ibid.*, III, 373.

The ten people were: Mary Fielding Smith (wife), Lovina, John, Hyrum, Jerusha, Sarah (children), Hannah Grinnels, George Mills, Robert B. Thompson, and wife Mercy.

[13]Lucy Mack Smith, who made the trip from Kirtland to Far West with her husband and sons William and Don Carlos and their families, described the weather they encountered, thus: "Sometimes we lay in our tents through driving storms; at other times were traveling on foot through marshes and quagmires. Once in particular, we lay all night exposed to the rain, which fell in torrents, so that when I arose in the morning, I found my clothing was perfectly saturated with the rain. However I could not mend the weather by a change of dress, for the rain was still falling rapidly, and I wore my clothes in this situation, three days; in consequence of which I took a severe cold, so that when we arrived at the Mississippi river, I was unable to walk or sit up. After crossing the river, we stopped at a negro hut, a most unlovely place, yet the best shelter we could find. This hut was the birth-place of Catherine's son Alvin [Salisbury]."—Lucy Mack Smith, *op. cit.*, pp. 251-252.

[14]Smith, *HC*, *op. cit.*, III, 373.

Moberly, and Chillicothe. The last leg of the road lay northwest to Gallatin, then to Far West, Caldwell County, their destination. The total distance traveled was 870 miles. In perspective, it was some 160 miles short of the distance traveled later by the Saints from Winter Quarters, on the Missouri River, to the Salt Lake Valley.

It had been a tremendous adventure for Mary Smith. She had seen much of America's vast heartland, virgin country awaiting the coming of settlers and the plow point. At first, in Ohio, the country was rather hilly with some beautiful flats on the creeks. Farther along, the country became more diversified with hills, valleys, and timber areas interspersed with vegetation and grassy sod. Spring flowers, extending into the distance, and occasional wildlife broke the monotony of travel. The country in Indiana leveled out, with many shallow watercourses to cross.

Through Illinois, the land was painfully flat. Mary noticed its amazing emptiness. The sight of so much land across the endless landscape became dispiriting. There were no hills to give a little variety. A lonesome farmhouse, now and then, broke the dreary sameness. There was not a tree to shade a cabin door. The few settlers appeared divested of any pride in their surroundings. After a rain storm, the roads became a ribbon of mud. Surely for anyone to stop in the midst of this was to be cloistered in misery by vastness. This was the famed Illinois prairie which, to cross, taxed the endurance of the Smith party — man and beast.

When the travelers approached Far West, they saw that the terrain was thickly covered with grass and weeds among which was plenty of wild game, such as, deer, turkey, prairie hens, and wolves. Occasionally, the travelers caught a glimpse of trees in the distance outlining a water course. The landscape had pleasant diversity; it was choice country. They had nothing to fear but rattlesnakes which were native to the area, but not very numerous. However, there were other kinds of snakes which they would come to fear more.

The meaning of the trip to Far West and its importance in Mary Smith's future is quite clear. It made her familiar with long-distance travel by wagon-train. She had learned what to expect from day to day and the need to go prepared for any eventuality. She was now an experienced veteran of the long trail — no longer the novitiate. She had learned the right way to dress for such a journey; the diet to sustain health and good morale; the preservation and preparation of food in all kinds of weather; cleanliness and its importance to a sense of well-being; the care of a baby and how to travel with children; comfort stops; tents and how to handle them; animals and their care; and how to meet unexpected difficulties as they arose. However, the trip had been taxing, and she had good reason not to feel well, but she came through it safely and thoroughly seasoned to the rigors of the long trail. She could undertake such a journey on her own if ever it should become necessary. To know of this great experience in Mary's life is to gain a new insight into her background and an appreciation of the extensive groundwork laid for her later achievements. Under the guiding hand of her husband, she had received a rigid training which established in her the confidence to cope with bigger difficulties that lay ahead.

Far West had still greater meaning for Mary. She became aware of the dangers ahead. A hostile climate existed as in Kirtland. There would be organized "wolf hunts" directed against the Mormon settlers. She saw the hard look of the pro-slave Missourians who resented Yankee newcomers. The Saints, as a minority group, would feel the wrath of those in power, as other such groups had done before them, in other times and places.

Chapter VI

Stormy Relations

The stirring happenings in Kirtland and the exodus of the Saints to Far West did not push into the background what was transpiring for the Church in England nor diminish the anxious concern felt for the newly arrived missionaries there. This bold project was highly important to the Prophet Joseph Smith and very close to his heart. It was a long wait between reports during which suspense mounted for the Church leaders and also for Mary Smith. She waited avidly for news and the latest information. Any word received, by anyone, was quickly exchanged and most welcome.

Mary's immediate interest was in how her brother Joseph was making out in his great adventure and what his reception by their kinsmen might be. The first news was exciting. She relived the voyage, the landing of the missionaries in Liverpool, their stay there, and the commencement of the work in Preston. To learn that things were going well was cause for great rejoicing. She caught the significance of the whole venture. Still, she was not prepared for its impact on her kinsmen and future family relations as well as its effect in opening the British Mission. Family turmoil would be connected with developments resulting from the missionary effort.

The missionaries arrived in Preston, England, about 4 o'clock in the afternoon of July 22, 1837. Bands were playing and thousands of men, women, and children were parading the streets. The occasion was election day; a festive mood abounded. Queen Victoria had come to the throne three days before the landing of the missionaries and had called a general election for members of Parliament. As the foreigners stepped from the coach, they noticed a large flag hoisted out of a window over their heads. The banner bore the inscription, "TRUTH WILL PREVAIL". Joseph Fielding recorded in his Journal: "This we took as from the Lord; this is our motto: Truth shall prevail".[1]

The missionaries found a room in Wilfred Street at the home of a widow. In the meantime, Joseph Fielding went to find his brother James who lived at 18 Edward Street. "My brethren procured comfortable lodging," stated Joseph, "and I for a time lodged with my brother."[2] At the address sought, Joseph found James, his sister Martha Watson, and her husband, Reverend Watson, from Bedford. They gave him a warm welcome. Joseph had returned with the prestige of the traveler who had crossed the great waters and seen the New World. They noticed certain changes in him; he was older but lean and hard from years of outdoor toil. His ruddy cheeks had the glow of health and his eyes a twinkle. His smile was quick and lovable. He exhibited a new confidence and poise born of achievement and added knowledge. Joseph had left England to make his fortune in America. He was back, not with silver and gold, but with a humble message.

He was given the best chair in the room. The others leaned forward and listened eagerly to all he had to say — to the news he brought of Mary and Mercy, as well as his description of life in America. Gradually, he got around to speaking about what they wanted to hear most, the new religion which had been declared from Heaven. He explained what he was doing in England — that he was there as a missionary to bring the message of the restored Gospel or new covenant to the people of England. Coupled with this, he told them he was with several fellow missionaries who were in town.

Joseph conducted himself with care. It was important that he fill his role ably as an intermediary and make a good impression for the sake of the cause he represented. This he did very

[1]Fielding, Bk. 1, p. 17.
[2]*Idem*

well, thus establishing a climate for the entree of the other missionaries. His kinsmen saw a new Joseph, a man with a sense of dedication and self-confidence. James listened intently to his brother. He was impressed and, at the same time, curious to learn more of the astounding things his brother spoke about with sureness. He wanted to meet Joseph's friends and see what they were like. Accordingly, he extended a cordial invitation to them by Joseph to come to his home that evening.

The invitation cheered the missionaries. At the appointed time, Apostles Kimball and Hyde, Elder Goodson, and Joseph Fielding were kindly received by Reverend James Fielding. The discussion or interview lasted until a late hour. The visitors were careful to avoid tension. The wrong word might be harmful to their cause. A good spirit prevailed. Martha Watson was touched by it to the extent that she sent each of the missionaries a half crown the next day. For his part, Reverend Fielding invited the missionaries to Vauxhall Chapel to attend his Sunday service the next morning.

The newcomers were in their places at the appointed hour. While Reverend Fielding held forth at the pulpit, the Elders hoped that the way would be opened for them to preach. Their desires were fulfilled. At the close of the discourse, Reverend Fielding, of his own accord, announced that the visitors from America would preach in his chapel at 3 o'clock that afternoon. The news spread and, at the hour, a large congregation had assembled to hear the preachers from across the sea.

Elder Kimball was the first to speak. He declared that an angel had visited the earth and committed the everlasting Gospel to man. He called their attention to the first principles of the Gospel and gave a brief history of the nature of the work which the Lord had commenced on earth. Elder Hyde then bore testimony to what had been said. The message was received by many, who cried: "Glory to God!" and rejoiced that the Lord had sent His servants to them.[3] Thus, on the

---

[3]Whitney, *op. cit.*, p. 137.

first Sabbath after their arrival, the key was turned and a new Gospel dispensation opened in England.

At the end of the meeting, Reverend Fielding was in good spirits and announced that the visitors would speak again that evening. Elder Goodson occupied the pulpit, after which Joseph Fielding bore witness to the truth. At the conclusion of this meeting, Reverend Fielding announced that the Elders would preach the following Wednesday night. Come Wednesday, the chapel was filled to overflowing. Apostle Hyde was the speaker, and Elder Richards added his testimony. Many were pricked in their hearts, being convinced of the truth, and began to praise God and rejoice exceedingly.[4]

At this point the powers of darkness intruded. The beachhead that the missionaries had established was about to be expanded. Then came opposition. Suddenly Reverend Fielding, who had kindly invited the Elders to preach in his chapel, became aware that a number of his flock believed on their word and desired to be baptized. His heart hardened, and he shut the doors of his chapel against further use by the missionaries. His excuse was that they had violated an agreement with him and had preached the doctrine of baptism for the remission of sins.

Reverend Fielding was a proud man who had his position as a minister to maintain. To see his congregation forsake him and his teachings for those of the foreign evangelists was more than he could stand. It was a damaging blow to his ego and extremely humiliating. Also, how would he live if he lost his flock and their contributions in the plate each week? The adversary provoked him with such thoughts. He responded willingly, turning passionately against the preachers from America, including his brother Joseph.

However, this did not deter missionary activity in Preston. Invitations were received to preach in private homes. The ingredients of conversion took hold of those who heard. They

---

[4]*Idem*

believed on the testimonies of their humble teachers. Once faith entered, the next step, repentence, followed naturally as night follows day; then came the consuming urge to go into the waters of baptism for the remission of sins and the gift of the Holy Ghost. When faith became operative, the Gospel structure rose, precept upon precept, to an enlargement of their souls. These steps produced results.

Several persons applied for baptism. This was arranged for the following Sunday morning in the river Ribble which flowed through the city. Satan was now aroused. While he had succeeded in closing the doors of Vauxhall Chapel, he hadn't succeeded in preventing the spread of the new message. The Old Serpent would show his power. This he did in an awesome and terrifying manner which almost cost Elder Kimball his life.

About daybreak, Sunday, July 30, 1837, Isaac Russell, who had been appointed to preach on the Obelisk in the quaint Preston Market Place that day, and who slept in the second floor of their lodging on Wilfred Street, went up to the third floor loft where Elders Kimball and Hyde were sleeping. He called upon them to pray for him, that he might be delivered from the evil spirits which were tormenting him to such a degree that he felt that he could not live long unless he obtained relief.

Sensing the gravity of the situation, Elders Kimball and Hyde immediately arose and laid their hands on him and prayed earnestly that the Lord would have mercy on His servant and rebuke the evil spirits. While thus engaged, Elder Kimball was suddenly struck with great force by some invisible power and fell senseless to the floor. It was a frightful moment. The first thing that he recollected was being supported by Elders Hyde and Russell while they beseeched the Lord in his behalf.

They laid him on the bed, but relief was not forthcoming. His agony was so great that he could not endure it. He arose, fell on his knees, and prayed. Then, he arose and sat on the bed while the brethren distinctly saw the evil spirits. By legions they foamed and gnashed upon them with their teeth for the space of many minutes. Elder Richards came and was present the latter part of the time. The scene grew more terrifying, as told by Elder Kimball.

We gazed upon them about an hour and a half (by Willard's watch). We were not looking towards the window, but towards the wall. Space appeared before us, and we saw the devils coming in legions, with their leaders, who came within a few feet of us. They came towards us like armies rushing to battle. They appeared to be men of full stature, possessing every form and feature of men in the flesh, who were angry and desperate; and I shall never forget the vindictive malignity depicted on their countenances as they looked me in the eye; and any attempt to paint the scene which then presented itself, or portray their malice and enmity, would be vain.

I perspired exceedingly, my clothes becoming as wet as if I had been taken out of the river. I felt excessive pain, and was in the greatest distress for some time. I cannot even look back on the scene without feelings of horror; yet by it I learned the power of the adversary, his enmity against the servants of God, and got some understanding of the invisible world. We distinctly heard those spirits talk and express their wrath and hellish designs against us. However, the Lord delivered us from them, and blessed us exceedingly that day.[5]

This terrifying experience, opened to the minds of the Elders in vision, revealed to them the awful kingdom of Satan which stood arrayed against them and the work of the Lord. The Prophet Joseph Smith later told Elder Kimball: "When I heard it, it gave me great joy, for I then knew that the work of God had taken root in that land. It was this that caused the devil to make a struggle to kill you."[6]

About 10 o'clock on Sunday morning, after the encounter with the adversary, the brethren repaired to the river according to previous appointment and, in the midst of several thousand people who came to witness the unusual event, they baptized nine individuals. As they were about to be led into the water, Reverend Fielding went into a frenzy. Earlier, he had been to

[5]*Ibid.*, pp. 144-145.
[6]*Ibid.*, pp. 145-146.

the Elders' lodging and, confronting Elder Kimball, forbade him to baptize them. " 'They are of age,' " answered Heber, " 'and can act for themselves; I shall baptize all who come unto me, asking no favor of any man.' "[7]

Upon hearing this, Reverend Fielding trembled and shook as though he had had a chill. Thereafter, he became a bitter opponent of the missionaries. He broke with his brother Joseph, whom he had welcomed with open arms, and influenced other members of the Fielding family in England against him. This was the beginning of a tragic schism in the family that never healed.

On Monday, July 31, 1837, the Elders met in solemn council to consider enlarging their field of activity. Elders Richards and Goodson were appointed to go to Bedford and Russell and Snyder to Alton. Following the discharge of this business, they called upon the Lord in prayer until morning when the brethren, who were to leave, took their departure, August 1. Thus, from Preston, the work branched out to new areas which resulted in further success.

Elders Goodson and Richards arrived in Bedford on August 2 and were joyfully received by the Reverend Timothy R. Matthews to whom they had letters of introduction from Joseph Fielding, his brother-in-law. They were invited to preach in his chapel that evening to his congregation. The Elders gratefully accepted and made the most of it. They were also permitted to lecture in the basement of the chapel each evening which they did with flattering results.

Many, including Mr. and Mrs. Matthews, were convinced. Mr. Matthews himself bore testimony to his congregation and invited them to accept baptism at the hands of the Elders. The time was set for his baptism; but before it arrived, contrary to positive counsel, Elder Goodson read to Mr. Matthews and some of his followers the vision of Joseph Smith and Sidney Rigdon (Doctrine and Covenants, Section 76), which these new friends apparently were not yet prepared to receive. Mr. Matthews did not appear for baptism at the appointed time and place, but received the ordinance elsewhere, and soon after denounced the

[7]*Ibid.*, p. 147.

missionaries saying that their doctrines were false. He then began to preach those very doctrines on his own account.[8]

The prohibition against reading the "Vision," it will be recalled, stemmed from instruction given by the Prophet Joseph Smith before the Elders embarked for England. He knew that the word on the three degrees of glory would be too heavy for persons capable, at first, of only receiving "milk." Mr. Matthews, although a man of the cloth, was not ready for the things disclosed in the new revelation. Elder Goodson's unfortunate disregard of counsel had harmful effect for the Mormon cause in Bedford. It resulted in controversy which turned the current feeling against the missionaries in all that region.

Deep sadness and no little consternation came to Mary Smith when she learned of her people's rejection of the new covenant. Gradually, she became aware that the name Fielding was synonomous with mounting opposition to the Mormon missionary effort in Great Britain. In truth, her kinsmen stood identified as the vanguard of anti-Mormon feeling against the new Church. They denied it, spoke against the Elders in public and print, and marshalled an opposition that gave no quarter. Their poison spread from town to town, sect to sect, minister to minister, citizen to citizen to prejudice a nation. Despite it all, the missionaries from America rolled-up one success after another. Joseph Fielding grew under the opposition, and his sisters in America remained steadfast and true. Perhaps the heart of no family was wrung so hard as that of the Fieldings by an issue, both sides manifesting sincere conviction. Only time would reveal an edge of one or the other.

---

[8]Richard L. Evans, *A Century of Mormonism in Great Britain* (Salt Lake City, 1937), pp. 39-40.

With further regard to the violation of instructions by Elder Goodson: "Soon after this Brothers Goodson and Snyder departed for Liverpool, from whence they sailed for America on about the 1st of October. Urgent business was given for this action. Elder Goodson took with him two hundred copies of the *Book of Mormon* and *Doctrine and Covenants,* despite Heber C. Kimball's request that he leave them, and despite his offer to pay for them. These, writes Elder Kimball, he burned soon after he reached Iowa Territory, at which time he apostatized and left the Church." —*Ibid.,* p. 40.

Chapter VII

Far West Ordeal

While Joseph Fielding was having many soul-stirring experiences on the missionary firing-line in England, his sisters in America were passing through a severe ordeal. Mary Smith, in particular, was called upon to suffer great affliction of body and spirit. But during it all, Joseph and his brothers and sisters in England had no knowledge of it. For considerable time, they did not know that Mary had given birth to a son nor that, subsequently, she was ill nigh unto death. Whether this knowledge would have softened the hearts of her unbelieving, non-Mormon kinsmen is debatable. In their poor condition of spirit and smug little world, they would hardly have been capable of genuine sympathy, free from any tinge of reproach, owing to the fact of Mary and Mercy having become Mormons.

Still, it would have been well if they had known. Perhaps, it would have given them something beyond themselves to reflect upon — evidence of what their loved ones in the New World were willing to suffer for the Gospel's sake. Surely their sisters' magnificent demonstration of fidelity to the Church would have given them pause — a chance to reexamine their own ill-founded judgments and to discover their shortcomings. Mary and Mercy could not write because of the dire calamities that were befalling them, coupled with their stark preoccupation with survival in a struggle of life and death.

When it was all over, and they were in a place of safety, Mary finally wrote to Joseph — a moving, beautiful letter giving a summary of the events through which she had passed. In retrospect, mighty were those events — cataclysmic in scope — which left their imprint upon her and all others who passed through them, but which brought to the sufferers nobility of soul.

When Mary Smith first arrived in Far West from Kirtland, she sized up the situation and went to work to make a comfortable home for her husband and family. The house (still to be completed) in which they were to live, definitely needed the efforts and touch of a woman to adorn it fittingly and make it livable. Although Mary was enceinte, she eagerly undertook the task and, with the help of her family, achieved many desirable improvements. The frontier house became a home — a humble retreat. It would be the birthplace of an infant who would become an important man. Mary came into her own as the directing force of the domicile. She was the central figure, the guiding mind in managing the household, and all domestic activities revolved around her. Schedules of duties were established, and the adults and larger children had their assigned tasks. Thus, various chores got done on time and in good order. Her husband was a public figure and, as such, was away from home a good deal of the time. He confidently left the details of running the home in Mary's hands. In this, Hannah Grinnels and George Mills were a big help to her.

During the next few months, Mary's joy was supreme in the knowledge that she was to become a mother. After the realization of it dawned, her energies were directed toward creating the things her baby would need. She worked intently at fashioning tiny graments and baby blankets. Her pleasure was evident on her countenance as she finished them, then laid them carefully away in her chest, touching them lovingly with her finger tips as she moved her hands along to smooth them before closing the lid. Her heart was full, and she praised the Lord for looking upon her and granting her the blessing of motherhood so late in life. As her time approached, the doctor lady was engaged. Sometime in November she figured. Mary's sister Mercy and Aunty Grinnels were available to assist in any way. A few months earlier, Mercy had given birth to a daughter, and Mary helped take care of them.

However, Mary looked with some trepidation upon what the immediate days might bring. Dangerous mob actions hostile to Mormon interests kept occurring. Refugees from outlying communities, whose homes had been burned, were making their way to Far West. The lack of housing forced them to set up makshift shelters. As the homeless increased in number, feeding them became a problem. Their miserable plight aroused the sympathy of the community and increased the problems of the Church leaders.

As related earlier, the young Church had moved to Far West to escape persecution in Kirtland, but the Saints fared no better at the hands of the Missourians. In fact, the harassment increased many fold. A dangerous struggle ensued between the new Mormon settlers and their hostile neighbors. Missouri was a slave state, while the Mormons had declared that all men should be free. This was the cause of the earlier expulsion of the Saints from Jackson County, Missouri (1833-1834). And now, the Governor, high military officers, judges, ministers, and frontier riff-raff combined against the Mormons.

The immediate cause of the new difficulty was a skirmish with an armed mob under the leadership of Captain Samuel Bogart, a Methodist preacher. He had taken three Mormon men prisoners. At the instance of Judge Elias Higbee of Far West, Lieutenant Colonel George M. Hinckle sent a Mormon militia company to free the prisoners. The mob was dispersed and the men set free. There were casualties on both sides. However, the Saints suffered an irreparable loss in the death of Apostle David W. Patten. Following this, the ill-advised and prejudiced Governor of Missouri, Lilburn W. Boggs, issued his infamous extermination order on October 27, 1838, which declared that the Mormons must be treated as enemies and exterminated or driven from the State.

Three days later, the town of Far West was approached by a mob-militia force under Major General Samuel D. Lucas and Brigadier General Alexander W. Doniphan. The Saints, upon seeing them coming across the prairie, hoped and prayed that they had come to give them protection. To their horror and dismay, they learned that the army, 2,200 strong, had really come to destroy them and burn the town. Hastily, the Saints moved wagons into positions, tore down buildings, and set up a defense manned by approximately 150 men (the enemy considered the number to be greater). This forced the army to hold up and camp outside the town.

The Mormon commander, Hinkle, sent a messenger, Charles C. Rich, with a white flag, to request an interview with General Doniphan. As Rich approached the army, he was shot at by the perverse Bogart who had come up with the troops. Rich requested Doniphan to spare the people and not suffer them to be massacred until morning. The General agreed to this. He stated that he had not received the Governor's order but expected it at any hour. Rich returned to the town and reported. Hinkle immediately dispatched a second messenger, with a white flag, to request another interview with Doniphan for the purpose of touching his sympathy and to get him to use his best efforts to preserve the lives of the people. The messenger returned with word that several Mormons had already been killed by soldiers under General Lucas.

The next morning, Hinkle sent a third messenger into the camp for another interview with General Doniphan. The messenger brought back word that the Governor's order had arrived, and it was to exterminate the Mormons, but the General had stated that he would be damned if he obeyed the order; however, General Lucas might do what he pleased. Then it was learned that the order was only a copy, and the original was in the hands of Major General John B. Clark who was expected with a force of 6,000 men.

Immediately after this, a messenger reached Far West bringing news of the massacre of the Saints at Haun's Mill, where upward of twenty Mormons were killed and wounded by a mob-militia. In the meantime, Far West was surrounded by a strong enemy guard which harassed the citizens. The latter were shot at while attempting to leave town to get food from their fields. The news of Haun's Mill left the people of Far West shuddering and fully aware of their awful plight. The Church leaders met in solemn council. The tension reached into every home.

Mary Smith saw the anxiety in her husband's face; yet he tried not to alarm her. The hour called for great stamina and mighty faith. They strengthened each other, and both were fortified with a calm courage. Together, they steeled themselves and put their trust in the Almighty.

In the evening of the next day, after arrival of the army, Colonel Hinkle went to the camp of the enemy. He returned and asked for an audience with Joseph Smith, Parley P. Pratt, Sidney Rigdon, Lyman Wight, and George Robinson, stating that the officers of the army wanted to consult with them. Hinkle assured the men that the officers had pledged their sacred honor that they would not be abused nor insulted but would be given protection and returned in safety after the consultation was finished.

Unaware that Hinkle had turned traitor and foul play was afoot, the Mormon leaders started immediately with him. As they approached the army camp, they were met by General Lucas with a strong detachment of men which the Mormon leaders thought were come to give them safe escort into camp. But to their surprise, Lucas ordered his men to surround the Mormons. Hinkle then informed General Lucas that the prisoners were the men that he had agreed to deliver. Upon which, Lucas drew his sword and said, " 'Gentlemen, you are my prisoners.' "[1] At this point, the main army marched out to meet them. Thus, the prearranged scheme went off like clockwork.

As the prisoners were marched through the camp, the whooping, yelling and shouting of the army was so hideous and loud that it could be heard by the Saints in town. When the wretches saw the Mormon prophet, they burst into wild

[1]Smith, *HC*, *op. cit.*, III, 413.

glee. Mary, Hyrum, his parents, and all who heard the racket were horrified. Their feelings were indescribable. It sounded as if all the demons of the pit had suddenly broken loose in a fit of fiendish triumph. The black-hearted brutes, filled with venom and lust for blood, thirsted to strike with murderous passion. Like hungry animals, they licked their chops and waited to pounce upon and devour their prey. They were on the verge of taking the lives of the prisoners after which they would wipe out the inhabitants of Far West.

The lines were now drawn. In one camp were Satan and his servants, while in the other were the servants of the Lord. The forces of evil had just scored a coup by capturing several of the high command of the Saints through a ruse. It remained now to see how the battle would shape up and how the enemy would be defeated. It was a strange sort of war in which few shots were fired. Verily, a higher power was in command, and the evil plans of the Missourians were to be thwarted.

The Saints could only wait, remain calm, and have faith. Mary, for one, summoned all her courage. She sensed that the enemy would strike at her home. Sooner or later, they would be coming for Hyrum. After the hideous outburst in the army camp, Mary and Hyrum were plunged into agony of heart, fearing for Joseph's life, his fellow prisoners, and the Saints in general. Even at that moment, Joseph might be dead. Hyrum had no immediate way of finding out what Joseph's fate might be. Therefore, his anguish was deep, and he suffered acutely. He was out and in, during the night, consulting with other top leaders. He called upon his parents and found his father prostrate with grief, the broken-hearted man thinking that the army had killed his son Joseph. He did not wish to live any longer. During the night, with the assistance of Elias Smith and others, Hyrum hurriedly dug a hole in the back yard of the Dawson home and buried the printing press on which his brother Don Carlos intended to begin printing the Times and Seasons.[2]

---

[2] *Ibid.*, IV, 398.

When back at home, Hyrum walked the floor, then sat, then walked some more until a late hour. Mary tried to comfort and reassure him, although she needed reassuring herself. Hyrum's inner conflict was nigh overpowering. He felt that he should be by Joseph's side, if he were still alive, yet his wife and family needed him in the worst way. Mary stoically endured the ordeal of the night. She urged Hyrum to get some sleep. She tried to snatch a little herself. In her mind was the overriding question: "Would they come for Hyrum?"

Outside in the town, the homes were silent and dark. Fear gripped the hearts of the inhabitants. Powerful prayers ascended from each cottage for the safety of their beloved leaders, that their lives might be spared, as well as their own, on the morrow. Surely, no more earnest words were ever uttered, as the pervading cloud of doom hung ominously over the beleagured town with death in prospect for everyone.

The hours ticked slowly by without further incident. But the next morning, soldiers from the camp took up positions in the town. They boldly entered the homes of the Saints on pillaging forays. After depriving families of firearms, the mob continued to hunt the brethren, day and night, like wild animals, and shot several. They ravished the women and killed one near the city. In the days that followed, the Saints could not leave town for food, so they lived on parched corn. The wretches left in their wake a stunned and frightened people.

The next day after Joseph and the others were taken, a detail of armed men approached the home of Hyrum and Mary Smith about noon. After the command to halt was given, there came the sound of musketry as the squad executed, Order Arms! Colonel Hinkle, the Mormon betrayer, was with them. He opened the door and called for Hyrum to come outside. Hyrum did so and was made a prisoner.

Mary witnessed the scene and reeled under the impact of the awful moment. Fear seized the other members of the household, the color draining from their faces. The shock passed through the home like an electric current leaving each one trembling and afraid. Hyrum remonstrated with Hinkle and protested that he could not go, that his family was sick, and that he also was sick. Hinkle said that he didn't care, that Hyrum would have to go. The prisoner's cloak and hat were brought. The guard surrounded him and marched him toward the army camp. Hyrum asked when they would permit him to return. There was no answer. He was forced along at the point of bayonets to the prisoner compound. There, to his great joy, he found Joseph and the other prisoners safe and well. Hyrum lay on the ground that night in November weather with only his mantle for a covering.

In the night, Colonel Hinkle came to Hyrum and told him that he had been pleading his cause before the military court but was afraid he would not succeed. He told Hyrum that the court was then in session. It consisted of thirteen or fourteen officers, Circuit Judge Austin A. King, and Mr. Thomas C. Burch, District Attorney; also Sashiel Woods, a Presbyterian minister, and about twenty other ministers of different religious denominations in the area. Hinkle then dropped the bomb shell. He told Hyrum that these men were determined to shoot the prisoners the next morning in the public square of Far West. Hyrum made no reply.

The Great Judge has a way of bringing to nought the plans and schemes of evil men which are inimical to His interests. This happened in the court session. In the group, there emerged a man of honor—a lone dissenter to the evil plan that had been hatched. The Lord used him to confound the others and defeat their murderous designs. At the critical moment, General Doniphan, moved upon by a high impulse, spoke up and declared that he would not go along with the rest in their decision to shoot the Mormon leaders. He meant business and, in the morning, backed it up by ordering his brigade to leave the camp. Before his departure, he came to the prisoners to shake hands and bid them farewell. He told them that they had been sentenced by the court to be shot that morning, but that he would have nothing to do with it, that he considered it to be cold-blooded murder. This courageous action of General Doniphan frustrated the whole plan to kill the prisoners.

Another court-martial was called which ordered the prisoners to be taken to Jackson County to be executed. Before the decision was put into effect, the prisoners, with much difficulty, persuaded the officers to give them permission to go see their families and get some clothing. Under a strong guard of five or six men to each prisoner, they were marched to their homes. When Hyrum reached his home, the brutal guard would not allow him to enter nor to speak with anyone of his family under pain of death. The foul-mouth sergeant ordered Mary Smith to get him some clothes within two minutes. If she failed, he would be marched off without them. Hyrum later recorded: "I was obliged to submit to their tyrannical orders, however painful it was, with my wife and children clinging to my arms and to the skirts of my garments, and was not permitted to utter to them a word of consolation, and in a moment was hurried away from them at the point of a bayonet."[3]

The unfeeling guard, with hideous oaths and threats, commanded Mary to take her last farewell of her husband for his die was cast and his doom sealed, and she need never think that she would see him alive again. In the critical condition of her health, this heartrending scene and what followed came near ending her life. However, her reserve of vigor and inner strength sustained her in the terrible ordeal.

During the awful moment, with Hyrum standing with bayonets at his back, Mary was called upon to endure a devastating shock to her nervous system as well as extreme anguish of soul. The children were terrified at seeing their

---

[3]*Ibid.*, III, 415.

Parley P. Pratt was a witness to the scene before Hyrum Smith's door. He stated: "As I returned from my house towards the troops in the square, I halted with the guard at the door of Hyrum Smith, and heard the sobs and groans of his wife, at his parting words. She was then near confinement; and needed more than ever the comfort and consolation of a hsuband's presence."—Parley P. Pratt, *Life and Travels of Parley P. Pratt* (Salt Lake City, 1938), Third Edition, p. 190.

father being so badly treated by brutish men who threatened him harm. The sight of him standing in manacles before his door, rumpled, unshaven, and pale from his ordeal definitely was enough to unnerve completely a wife whose first child was about due. They could not speak. He could not give her an encouraging word, touch her hand, wipe away her tears, nor give her a parting kiss. The scene was rare drama, silent drama, filled with torture and pain for both of them expressed in the anguished gaze of two people whose hearts were breaking for each other. Thus bedeviled, Hyrum read the suffering in Mary's soul, knowing her situation, anxiety of mind over her coming travail, family wants, and her great need for him at this time. They might not see each other again. It was an intense experience they were called upon to endure. What may we say of the evil persecutors whose tongues dripped with profanity and obscenities? Poor ignorant men. Ahead of them lay an eternity of pondering their part in the evil incident.

Mary watched the guard take Hyrum away. She was helped to her room where she wept quietly alone. She struggled with all her might to compose her grief and obtain relief from the pain in her bosom. It seemed that her heart would break. She could only plead with her God to protect Hyrum and return him to her.

Chapter VIII

Mary Visits Liberty Jail

Hyrum Smith and his fellow prisoners were taken to Independence and then to Richmond, Missouri, where they were turned over to the custody of General Clark who had the signed copy of the extermination order from the Governor. He had all the prisoners chained together. He put them on display and allowed them to be subjected to abuse and insults from those who came to look. He went so far as to select men for a firing squad to shoot the prisoners, and handed out guns to them for that purpose, telling them that they would have the honor of shooting the Mormon prisoners the next morning at 8 o'clock. However, the General, who was somewhat of a lawyer, discovered that he did not have jurisdiction over civilian prisoners. As a consequence, after a few days, they were turned over to civil authority. They were charged with many trumped-up crimes and denied witnesses to disprove them.

During the dark moments of their incarceration in chains, and while the public was filing through to see them, the brethren were cheered by the appearance of two familiar and noble faces. Brigham Young and Heber C. Kimball (the latter recently returned from England) appeared on the scene and, unrecognized by the guards, filed into the place where the prisoners were kept and passed by with the curious public. No one was permitted to hold conversation with the prisoners. But the two Mormon visitors did say, "How do you do." They hardly needed to say more. Their presence let the prisoners know that they were not forgotten nor deserted. Silent messages passed between them. Their presence told the Prophet

Joseph that the two men were on the job and would shepherd the flock in the crisis. To see the faces of their two friends reassured the prisoners and raised their spirits.

A few days after Hyrum Smith was marched away from his door the second time, there was a scurry in the home. The doctor lady made a quick call for hot water. Mary went far into the "valley" and brought forth a fine son, November 13, 1838. Kind hands administered to her needs and helped her through her ordeal. However, she lingered in sickness and pain and failed to regain her strength. She remained bedfast, her situation aggravated by a cold and a fever that developed. Her sister took charge of the baby and nursed him along with her own. The days extended into weeks, then months. Mary lay pale and weak; she was unable to wait on herself. She fought to stay away from the "brink" and remain alive. Christmas was cheerless for the family. The weather was cold as well as the house which was impossible to heat throughout. She was sustained by the words: "Yea, though I walk through the valley of the shadow of death I will fear no evil: for thou art with me; thy rod and thy staff they comfort me." (Psalms 23:4)

Adding to her suffering, her privacy was invaded by some ruffians led by the notorious Methodist preacher Bogart. They ransacked the home and scattered things about. They helped themselves to Hyrum's papers from his trunk which they broke open. Under English Common Law, a man's house was his castle. He was justified in killing anyone who made a forced entry. Bogart and his hoodlums, however, committed their deviltry with impunity. Besides their plundering, they nearly caused the death of Mary's new born baby. The details of this incident were given years later by Joseph F. Smith:

> I being an infant, and lying on the bed, another bed being on the floor was entirely overlooked by the family (my mother being very sick, the care of me devolved upon my Aunt Mercy and others of the family, during the fight and excitement.) So when the mob entered the room where I was, the bed on the floor was thrown on the other, completely

smothering me up, and here I was permitted to remain until after the excitement subsided. When thought of, and discovered, my existence was supposed to have come to an end; but subsequent events have proved their supposition wrong, however, well founded.[1]

Heaven watched over Mary's household during this difficult time. There were many privations, the most serious one being a shortage of food. The beseiging army lay waste the corn fields of the Saints. The lack of good, nourishing food undoubtedly prolonged Mary's recovery. In the crisis, Hannah Grinnels took charge of the children. Old George Mills obtained wood for fuel and conducted himself cautiously while performing many useful tasks. Mercy was a constant and efficient nurse. Everyone was kind and did all they could to assist the distressed family, although, they, also, had been impoverished by the plundering of the militia.

Meanwhile, after a farcical investigation by a pretended court presided over by Circuit Judge King and District Attorney Burch, the Mormon prisoners at Richmond were ordered to be taken to Liberty, Clay County, and placed in jail.[2] When asked the charge, the answer received by the prisoners was that it was because they were Mormons. The judge made out an order and committed them to jail on the false charge of treason. A blacksmith came and put chains on their ankles and wrists. They were taken to Liberty in a large wagon. There, they were held in close confinement in the jail. Hyrum's bed was the square side of a hewn white-oak log. The food was anything but good or decent.

There is no question that the terrible happenings in Far West nearly cost Mary her life. Man's inhumanity in the form of heartless persecution and depraved outrages to human dignity were compounded in the soul of this gentle lady. She had been reared in an orderly society. In her native land, a man was innocent until proven guilty. Not so here in the

---

[1]Smith, *Life of JFS*, *op. cit.*, p. 124.

[2]Those imprisoned in Liberty jail were: Joseph Smith, Hyrum Smith, Lyman Wight, Caleb Baldwin, Alexander McRae, and Sidney Rigdon. The last named person was admitted to bail because of poor health.

midst of mob rule. If a person were a Mormon, he was considered just plain guilty no matter the charge brought against him. Rude people, crude people, full of hatred and vengeance repelled Mary and galled her soul.

The Saints were forced to leave Missouri. However, they won a moral victory. Their leaders escaped death and the Saints, extermination. The hostile army that came up against Far West to destroy it was diverted from its objective by the hand of Providence. The seizure of the Mormon leaders by the army proved to be a diversionary move in favor of the Saints. Once the generals had the leaders fast in their power, they became so engrossed in phony trials, legal procedures, and the matter of jurisdiction that extermination proceedings got sidetracked. In its place an arrangement emerged whereby the Saints were allowed to save their lives. General Clark marched on Far West from Richmond with 1,600 troops and forced them to sign away their property and promise to leave the State. The Saints made a gallant retreat and consolidated their position on the banks of the Mississippi in Illinois.

* * *

During the critical period that followed Mary Smith's confinement, she made an unusual journey to Liberty jail to visit her husband. This was accomplished with the help of her sister Mercy and her brother-in-law, Don Carlos Smith.[3] Mary had been kept informed as to Hyrum's desires and well-being. He wanted to see his new son, so Mary felt that she must visit him no matter the cost.

The anticipation of the visit lifted her spirit and gave her added will to get well. Yet it was risky. Any doctor would have advised against it, considering the delicate state of her lungs and body. However, her spirit said, "Go," and perhaps this fact aroused her and helped save her life. The trip would get her away and give her a change. The very thought brought a note of cheer to her. She was indeed fortunate to have her

[3]Smith, *HC, op. cit.*, IV, 398.

wonderful sister to help with the baby. Together, they planned the trip in detail. There would be no inns along the way where they could obtain warm food; therefore, they would have to get along the best they could with what food they could take with them. Each of them had a child to consider; they must be nourished and kept warm.

January passed by and, come February (1839), they were ready. A bed was placed in the wagon. Mary was gently carried from the house and placed on it. She was made warm and comfortable. On her arm was placed her baby son nearly three months old. The other baby, Mary Jane Thompson, was going on eight months. Mercy continued to nurse both babies. Emma Smith and her son Joseph accompanied them. The weather was biting cold. The shaggy horses, in their winter fur, responded stiffly to the urging of the driver, Don Carlos Smith, and the travelers were on their way.

Forty miles of frozen, uneven road lay ahead. If they made twenty miles a day, they would do well. They suffered much from the cold. Perhaps they had misgivings about the whole venture. It was hardly safe to be traveling beyond the confines of the settlement because of the prevalence of mobbers and renegades on the prowl. In the evening of the second day, the wagon stopped before Liberty jail. Don Carlos, numb with cold, descended from the wagon, approached the jail door and requested permission for his party to see the prisoner, Hyrum Smith.

The heartless guards were on the alert because of a rumored jail break, but the entreaty in the eyes of the person at the door overcame their objections to having visitors. The big iron key turned in the grating lock and Mary, with the light of expectancy in her eyes, moved haltingly through the prison portal, her whole being tingling with emotion at being able to see her husband again. Mercy followed with the infants. The heavy door closed behind them on rasping hinges, shutting out the world. Their feelings, as they entered the foul place, were intense. They experienced a sense of horror on realizing that they were locked up in that dark and dismal den fit only for criminals of the deepest dye, as Mercy described it later.

Into the gloom of the prison walked a living light. There she stood—a bit bewildered—her frail figure trembling and bearing slightly forward. She must stand; Hyrum must see her stand. Then, there was Hyrum coming toward her. Deep and heartfelt happiness enveloped them. A touch of the hand, a warm embrace, a smile, a spoken word were as blessed manna to their hungry souls. It had been such a long time since they had seen each other. Hyrum led her gently to his prison area and seated her tenderly, solicitous of her comfort. She was mindful of him and looked closely to see if he were all right except for his chains. She noticed his thin cheek bones and heavy beard.

"How are you, Hyrum," she asked.

"Just fine, and how are you, Mary?"

"I am quite all right now," she replied.

There, in the dismal den, according to Mercy, they also saw Joseph the Prophet—the man chosen of God in the dispensation of the fulness of time to hold the keys of His Kingdom on the earth, with power to bind and loose as God should direct—confined in a loathsome prison, for no other cause or reason than that he claimed to be inspired of God to establish His church among men.

For Mary, the meeting was ample reward for the hardships of the journey. In descending to the dungeon, she experienced the true meaning of joy. The impact of the visit upon her and Mercy was tremendous—something they would not forget the rest of their lives.

"The night was spent in fearful forebodings," stated Mercy, "owing to a false rumor having gone out that the prisoners contemplated making an attempt to escape which greatly enraged the jailer and the guards."[4]

Hyrum's new son, whom he saw for the first time, was

---

[4]Mercy Fielding Thompson, "Recollection of the Prophet Joseph Smith," *Juvenile Instructor* (Salt Lake City, 1892), XXVII, 398.

the center of attraction as the smiling prisoners crowded around to peer down at him in the candle light while his blankets were being removed. Both babies, so unusual in such a place, evoked genuine pleasure that brought relief to prison boredom. There was much for the visitors to tell, and the night passed rapidly with little sleep for any of them.

The reunion of Mary and Hyrum Smith within the walls of Liberty jail carried with it an element of heroic drama. It was an unusual occasion supercharged with tension. The line between the forces of evil and the forces of good in the confines of the jail-house was thin and precarious. The wrong gesture on the part of a prisoner could cause a finger to tighten on a trigger. The jail's stale odor left its impact on the senses to linger in memory. The absence of light was heavy like the evil that held sway. The prisoners in their fetid surroundings languished in cramped quarters not dissimilar to the dungeons under the arenas where the early Christians awaited death at the hands of the Romans. This was the setting in which Mary and Hyrum met. Accordingly, it was a unique event in the annals of the period. True, Emma Smith and the wives of some of the other brethren had visited their husbands the previous December, and Emma again now. But none did so under such hazardous circumstances as did Mary. Her life had nearly ebbed away. Yet, heroically, she made the supreme effort to see her husband once more even if it should cost her her life.

The visit was the tonic that Mary needed. It provided a silver lining to the dark cloud of doom that settled over her life the day Hyrum was marched away at bayonet point. It had been truly a happy reunion. Conceivably, in the dim candle light of the jail, a proud father, joined by his brother Joseph and other prisoners, took the new infant and gave him a name and a blessing. The given names, Joseph Fielding, were for Mary's missionary brother, then in England, for whom she had deep affection. It is also conceivable that the eminent prisoners anointed Mary and administered to her that she might regain her health for, not long after this visit, she began to get well. The next morning, following a nerve tingling night, the visitors were constrained by the jailer to take their leave.

On the return trip, Mary and Mercy had much to think about. They carried away a mental picture of the jail's nauseous interior that was fixed in their consciousness for life. Mary, tucked again in her bed in the wagon, left the jail town with a heavy heart. She lay speechless and overwhelmed by the experience of the past night. Yet, with it was a sense of exhilaration stemming from the hours behind bars with the elite of men in the camp of the enemy. Hyrum's long embrace and comforting words at parting soothed and sustained her. She wept silently, her tears dropping to the pillow on which, also, rested the head of her little son. But she now had new courage. She had received new mental direction. She must live for Hyrum and her baby. She and Mercy battled the ache in their throats, as the wagon moved slowly away from the town with the ironic name of Liberty. They rode in silence, neither of them able to talk for thinking.

Mercy left the following recapitulation of the experience:

> About the first of February 1839 by the request of her husband, my sister was placed on a bed in a wagon and taken on a journey of about 40 miles to visit him in prison, her infant son Joseph F. then being about 11 weeks old. The weather being extremely cold, we suffered much on the journey. We arrived at the prison in the evening. We were admitted and the doors closed upon us. A night never to be forgotten. A sleepless night. I nursed the darling babes and in the morning prepared to start for home with my afflicted sister, and as long as memory lasts will remain in my recollection the squeaking hinges of that door which closed upon the noblest men on earth. Who can imagine our feelings as we traveled homeward, but would I sell the honor bestowed upon me by being locked up in jail with such characters for gold? No! No![5]

Mary Smith, also, made reference to her husband's imprisonment in a letter that she wrote to her brother Joseph

[5]Thompson Centennial letter.

after reaching Illinois, following her flight from Missouri. However, she made no mention of her visit to Liberty jail, and this is understandable. Mercy, as she said of the visit, found it beyond her power to describe. If this were the case with Mercy, far more difficult would it be for Mary to write the details and her feelings about it. It was a poignant memory which she locked deep in her heart.

She had seen first hand how it was in the prison and how innocent men were made to suffer by the circumstances of wrongful imprisonment. The saving element for her was the opportunity to see her husband, even in a miserable jail where he had reason to be embarrassed to have his wife see his degradation. The dramatic occasion outweighed the jail's mean interior. The hours with Hyrum were special to her. Time would not erase the impact of the jail scene nor the honor of being locked up with him behind bars.

It is hard today to grasp the fact that such a miscarriage of justice ever occurred in any state of the union, whereby innocent men could be deprived of their freedom for so many months without due and legal process of law. The travesty was cause for Mary to carry strong resentment of Missouri's style of jurisprudence and justice.

Chapter IX

Flight from Persecution

At the time of the visit of Mary Smith to Liberty jail to see her husband, the evacuation of the Saints from Missouri had begun. Under the able direction of Brigham Young, they were moving out in increasing numbers. Mary had undoubtedly discussed with Hyrum the matter of her leaving. He would want her to get away as soon as she felt physically able, and, certainly, he helped her by his counsel and advice. Upon returning home, she set things in motion to join the Saints in leaving Far West. Of this, Mercy Thompson subsequently recorded: "Shortly after our return to Far West we had to leave our cold, unfinished house and start in lumber wagons for Illinois, my sister again being placed on a bed in an afflicted state. This was about the middle of February, the weather extremely cold. I had still the care of both babies."[1]

Their departure was escape from the hell imposed by the armed hoodlums who made the homes, streets, and sidewalks of Far West unsafe for the inhabitants. As the wagons moved out, the frigid house, that had been their refuge and the birthplace of a son, was abandoned permanently to the enemy. It held the silent gaze of the family until it was shut from view.

They also gave up all their livestock, farm implements, furniture, and farm land.[2] Fortunately, more than one wagon

---

[1]Thompson Centennial letter.

[2]In his statement of suffering and damages sustained in Missouri, Hyrum Smith said: "In the meantime my family were suffering every privation. Our enemies carried off nearly every thing of value, until my family were left destitute. My wife had been but recently confined and had to suffer more than tongue can describe; and then in common with the rest of the people had to move, in the month of February, a distance of two hundred miles, in order to escape further persecution and injury.

was available to effect the removal of everyone in the large family. In her preparations, Mary had the benefit of what aid Don Carlos could give her. Although he was engaged in making preparations to leave with his own family, as well as that of his father and mother and other kin, he was in a position to keep a watchful eye on the progress of Mary's family to leave. When the time came to depart, he was available to lift her onto her bed in the wagon and see her safely away. Don Carlos waited until a wagon became available to carry his parents and sisters Catherine Salisbury and Sophronia McCleary and their families. As for him, he and his family traveled in a buggy.[3] However, they all got away in February 1839.

The Saints, except for a few who left the Church and stayed behind, carried out the terms imposed by Lucas and upheld by Clark in the public square of Far West. They had surrendered their arms and land and made haste to leave the state as soon as circumstances would permit. The scenes that took place when the time came for carrying out the harsh terms beggared description. In Caldwell and Daviess counties, ". . . they were turned out of their homes into the prairies and forests without food, or sufficient protection from the weather."[4] It was winter time, transportation was totally insufficient and, yet, notwithstanding silent appeals for delay, ". . . some thousands of these unfortunate creatures of all ages, sizes, condition, and of both sexes, were driven from their homes, and compelled to cross almost the entire northern part of the state before they could hope to find a resting place."[5] As a rule, they were poor and had only the small farms from

The loss of property which I sustained in the state of Missouri would amount to several thousand dollars; and one hundred thousand dollars would be no consideration for what I have suffered from privation—from my life being continually sought—and all accumulated suffering I have been subjected to."—Smith, *HC,* III, 373-374.

[3]Lucy Mack Smith, *op. cit.,* p. 294.

[4]Brigham H. Roberts, *Comprehensive History of the Church* (Salt Lake City, 1930), I, 515-516; from History of Caldwell County, National Historical Co., 1881, p. 142.

[5]*Idem;* from American Commonwealths, Missouri, Lucien Carr, 1888, pp. 183-184.

which they were driven; but the pressure put upon them was such, or their anxiety to get away so great, that not infrequently a valuable farm was traded for an old wagon, a horse, a yoke of oxen, or anything that would furnish them with the means of leaving. Many of the Mormon men, women, and children, the sick and aged were compelled to walk for lack of transportation. Some died along the way.

Bad weather made life miserable for the refugees in general. The roads were very bad; numerous chuck-holes threw a heavy burden on the teams. This made travel a torture. The refugees were scattered out like black dots against the white background of the snow-covered terrain. The Smiths had plenty of company, as fellow evacuees were ahead and behind them on the dreary road.

In the absence of quite a number of fathers, the burden fell upon the women to do the work of men. For Mary Smith, the large number in her charge posed a real problem of providing sufficient supplies for so many mouths to last the journey. However, their biggest need was for a measure of insulation from the terror they had known. The adults had to be of good courage and suppress their fears in order to make the children feel secure. To be leaving the hostile environs of Far West brought relief to them all. Gradually, as distance was put between them and the mobocrats, the emotional tension in their lives began to subside.

The homeless Saints were not a pretty picture. Their poverty was quickly apparent. Tragedy hung over them like a cloud and loomed darkly in their faces. Their silence was akin to shock. Their gauntness bespoke their hunger. The terror that had been theirs showed in the galvanized, straight ahead look in their sunken eyes. Their situation gave evidence of people who had been picked clean of their property and substance. It was obvious that they had been dealt with harshly. The picture was one of humans in a trance, with cowed spirits and hopeless outlook.

Accordingly, the scene that the rag-tag Saints presented

in flight was tragic. They were strung out across the bleak prairie for miles in every kind of conveyance: white-tops, buggies, carts, and wagons. Some were mounted, some afoot carrying packs on their backs. The wayfarers lacked personal items for their individual comfort such as warm mittens, stockings, underwear, and coats. Crude wagon boxes made of rough planks rested on bare bolsters without cushioning springs. With nothing to absorb the shock, travel was hard and jolting. Patched, makeshift wagon covers were a common sight. A family was lucky to have a bit of canvas to keep out wind and storm. The teams were below par in strength and moved along weakly. In the main, provender for them consisted of frost-covered bunch grass and weed stalks. Inside the wagons, the victims sat huddled closely for warmth. Flatirons heated by camp fires imparted comfort to the feet and hands of the travelers during extremely cold weather.

The rough roads made travel an ordeal for Mary Smith, since she had to keep to her bed during the trip. The sideward motions of the wagon, sometimes excessive, tossed her back and forth inducing fatigue and soreness. This prevented her from relaxing. Sleep and quiet at night were a balm to her exhausted body. She had time—too much time—to think of her husband in that miserable jail at the mercy of brutal guards. Each mile of travel took her farther away from him causing her distress of spirit. When would she see him again? Not knowing and the uncertainty of the future robbed her of the calm needed for her recovery.

* * *

The preservation of Mary Smith's life and that of her son after his birth in Far West, when her life flickered in the balance, was due, in no small part, to the untiring care and administration of her inimitable sister Mercy. The Far West episode, the trip to Liberty jail, and the exodus from Missouri fell heavily upon her shoulders. She, too, stood alone, as her husband, Robert B. Thompson, had been forced to take cover for his life.

Without Mercy's assistance, Hyrum's household might have disintegrated after his imprisonment. The visit to Liberty jail and the removal to Illinois might not have succeeded as well as they did without her help. Mercy stood at her sister's side nursing and comforting her and caring for her wants as well as those of her children. She mothered them all, prepared food for many over a fire at camping time, and assumed a heavy responsibility in the care of two nursing babies. Mercy's star, which had begun to rise after Hyrum's imprisonment, reached its zenith on the long journey from Far West. She was an angel of mercy, indefatigable, self-sacrificing, kind, and loving. Through it all, she endured bitter cold which suggests that she did not have sufficient warm clothing for her needs. Verily, she established herself as a truly choice person, worthy of the highest commendation and a sure place in the ranks of superior women. The times called for great courage on her part, a courage which matched that of Mary Smith.

Of her hardships at Far West, she stated the following in her Centennial letter:

> To describe the suffering and privations we endured while there would be past my skill and would make this sketch too lengthy. Some few things, however, I will relate. My husband with many of the brethren being threatened and pursued by a mob fled into the wilderness in November leaving me with an infant five months old. Three months distressing suspense I endured before I could get any intelligence from him during which time I stayed with my sister who having given birth to a son, Nov. 12 (while her husband was in prison) she took a severe cold and was unable to attend to her domestic duties for many months. This caused much of the care of her family which was very large to rest upon me. Mobs were continually threatening to massacre the inhabitants of the city. At times I feared to lay my baby down lest they should slay me and cause it to suffer worse than death.[6]

These searing experiences remained soul-shaking. In fact, they seem to have taken precedence in her memory over the moving experiences associated with her later expulsion from Nauvoo and crossing the plains to Utah. Although that dan-

[6]Thompson Centennial letter.

gerous time in Far West was the most trying, it was, it seems, the most soul-satisfying. Throughout her life the events remained fresh in her mind to become faithfully recorded by her aging hand, as she added these lines: "We arrived at Quincy about the end of the month. My husband had engaged a room for our accommodation, but my sister being obliged to be with me on account of the babe the whole of Brother Hyrum's family of 10 remained with us until April when Brother Hyrum arrived in Quincy, Illinois. He soon made arrangements to move his family. I went along to Commerce leaving my husband in Quincy who followed in a few weeks and was employed by Joseph Smith as a private secretary which office he held until his death which took place August 27, 1841."[7]

* * *

When Mary Smith set foot on the Illinois bank of the Mississippi River with her family, she was deeply grateful for her deliverance from Missouri; also, for the great ribbon of water that flowed protectively between her and that accursed land. With her little ones, she gave thanks for her rescue from the clutches of demons in human form who had shown them no pity. The great fear of impending harm and disaster gradually left her. Also, her mind and spirit were freed from the gnawing anxiety that had gripped her so long. The nights and days that followed were without terror. She could relax and sleep soundly which enabled her to regain her health and strength. Yet, while she had been through one crisis after another—about as much as a mortal could bear—she was neither bitter nor vindictive. She considered it a privilege, as she said, to have been counted worthy to suffer these things. Her great desire now was for Hyrum to come home.

Kind friends took her in and provided for her needs upon her arrival in Quincy. She had good food in sufficient quantity for the first time in months. In retrospect, it was something of a miracle that she had passed through so many

[7] *Idem*

privations and sickness and survived. The last ordeal, the slow tortuous trip out of Missouri, had been bearable only because it meant escape from bondage.

Something of the conditions encountered on that trip may be gathered from the account given by Mother Lucy Smith. She and her husband, with Don Carlos and others, found the going pretty rough. One time, they traveled two and a half days in rain and felt that, if they were compelled to go much farther, they would die. They were given timely assistance by a kind man who did all he could to help them, as they stopped overnight with him. Of this occasion, Mother Smith wrote:

> After spending the night with this good man, we proceeded on our journey, although it continued raining, for we were obliged to travel through mud and rain to avoid being detained by high water. When we came within six miles of the Mississippi river, the weather grew colder, and, in the place of rain we had snow and hail; and the ground between us and the river was so low that a person on foot would sink in over his ankles at every step, yet we were all of us forced to walk, or rather wade, the whole six miles.
>
> On reaching the Mississippi, we found that we could not cross that night, nor yet find a shelter, for many Saints were there before us, waiting to go over into Quincy. The snow was now six inches deep and still falling. We made our beds upon it and went to rest with what comfort we might under such circumstances. The next morning our beds were covered with snow and such of the bedding under which we lay was frozen. We rose and tried to light a fire, but, finding it impossible we resigned ourselves to our comfortless situation.[8]

The experiences of Mary Smith and her family were not dissimilar. While her group did not travel with Don Carlos' group, they passed through comparable hardships due to the inclement weather. She was, no doubt, specially conveyed by kind friends the last few miles through the sub-marginal ooze. She suffered no aggravation of her illness. However, her sickness persisted after her arrival in Quincy. A week later, this report by Don Carlos went to his brothers in Liberty jail: "Hyrum's children and Mother Grinolds [sic] are living at

[8]Lucy Mack Smith, *op. cit.*, pp. 296-297.

present with father; they are all well. Mary . . . has not got her health yet, but I think it increases slowly. She lives in the house with old Father Dixon; likewise Brother Robert B. Thompson and family; they are probably a half mile from Father's. We are trying to get a house, and to get the family together; we shall do the best we can for them, and that which we consider to be most in accordance with Hyrum's wishes."[9]

Another report reached Hyrum in a letter from Edward Partridge, stating in part: "Brother Hyrum's wife lives not far from me. I have been to see her a number of times; her health was very poor when she arrived, but she has been getting better. . . ."[10]

During April 1839, the second month following Mary Smith's arrival in Quincy, she was joined by Hyrum who, with Joseph and the other prisoners (after removal from Liberty jail, Clay County, to Daviess County), had been permitted by the guards to escape while being transferred on a change of venue from Daviess County to Boone County.[11] Thus a dismal period of her life ended on a note of joy for Mary Smith. She regained her strength. Happiness came into her life once more. Her mind could now turn to things that she had put off doing so long, including the writing of a letter to her brother Joseph in England.

---

[9]Smith, *HC, op. cit.,* III, 273.
[10]*Ibid.,* 272.
[11]*Ibid.,* 320-321.

Chapter X

Mary's Letter of Rejoicing

At midyear, 1839, Mary Smith was settled with her husband and family at Commerce, Illinois, some forty miles north of Quincy. Their living was somewhat primitive, but their situation had greatly improved. Father was home, about the house, taking care of things which made everyone happy. The children crowded around him, tugged at his hands, and clamored to go with him when he left the house on an errand. As for Hyrum, his heart was full, and he rejoiced to be with his family once more.

He and the others, who managed to escape their captors in Missouri, had had the use of two horses to help them reach home. They took turns riding and walking a distance of 200 miles. They had to be careful and avoid recognition by the enemy. Their beards were good disguises. In nine or ten days, they reached their families.

Hyrum needed the best of care when he arrived home. His body was broken down and his health much impaired from the afflictions and fatigue he had suffered. He was unable to perform any labor for some time. Mary saw his needs and set to work to rehabilitate him. He was in immediate need of warm, nourishing food. A hot bath and clean clothing made him feel human again. With kind care and plenty of rest, he started to mend. Gradually, he was able to put out of his mind the memories of Liberty jail. He was aware of what Mary had endured for him and the cause. He would be eternally grateful to her. His gratitude and love extended to Mercy and Hannah for their untiring and heroic efforts in caring for his family and helping to bring them through the terrible trials in Missouri.

Mary, who, until recently, had required care and attention herself, was now able to give it. Her health had returned. The state of her spirit was magnificent. She had cause to be resentful and angry toward those who had been brutal to Hyrum, the children, and her. Instead, she was full of good spirit and cheerfulness which was a tribute to her stamina and force of mind.

Her little son Joseph F. was going on to ten months. He was the best tonic in the world for her. She was now able to care for him, to love him to her heart's content and watch him grow. His happy smile brought a smile of joy to her face. He was trying to stand and, soon, he would be walking. Her pride in him was effusive. She thought of her brother Joseph and wished that he could see her little ones. She must write to him. Then a letter from him was received by Heber C. Kimball. Mary had a chance to read and be cheered by it and the report of the success of missionary work in England, although she was saddened by other news.

Finally, she sat down and commenced to write. Her letter must be ready to go with Elder Kimball who was about to return to England. From her pen came an unusual letter, humble in tone, dispassionate, and touching only lightly on the ordeal of her accouchement and subsequent suffering. There was no breath of self-pity. It contained no recrimination, rancor, nor malice, mirroring the mind of a person who could focus her thoughts on a high plane. Her recital of events, general in nature, indicated that she had locked in the recesses of her mind the grim details of her trials at Far West. Her effort was an epistle of thanksgiving for her deliverance from her painful affliction — an outpouring of her heart in rejoicing. Her life and that of her husband had been spared. The family was together again. For these things, her heart was full. Certainly, when her brother read the following words, he was deeply moved.

Commerce, Ill., North America
June, 1839

My very dear brother—

As the Elders are expecting shortly to take their leave of us again to preach the gospel in my native land, I feel as though I would not let the opportunity of writing you pass unimproved. I believe it will give you pleasure to hear from us by our own hand; notwithstanding you will see the brethren face to face, and have an opportunity of hearing all particulars respecting us and our families.

As it respects myself, it is now so long since I wrote to you, and so many important things have transpired, and so great have been my afflictions, etc., that I know not where to begin; but I can say, hitherto has the Lord preserved me, and I am still among the living to praise him, as I do today. I have, to be sure, been called to drink of the bitter cup; but you know my beloved brother, this makes the sweet sweeter.

You have, I suppose, heard of the imprisonment of my dear husband, with his brother, Joseph, Elder Rigdon, and others, who were kept from us nearly six months; and I suppose no one felt the painful effects of their confinement more than myself. I was left in a way that called for the exercise of all the courage and grace I possessed. My husband was taken from me by an armed force, at a time when I needed, in a particular manner, the kindest care and attention of such a friend, instead of which, the care of a large family was suddenly and unexpectedly left upon myself, and, in a few days after, my dear little Joseph F. was added to the number. Shortly after his birth I took a severe cold, which brought on chills and fevers; this, together with the anxiety of mind I had to endure, threatened to bring me to the gates of death. I was at least four months entirely unable to take any care either of myself or child; but the Lord was merciful in so ordering things that my dear sister could be with me. Her child was five months old when mine was born; so she had strength given her to nurse them both.

You will also have heard of our being driven as a people, from the State, and from our homes; this happened during my sickness, and I had to be removed more than two hundred miles, chiefly on my bed. I suffered much on my journey; but in three or four weeks after we arrived in Illinois, I began to mend, and my health is now as good as ever. It is now little more than a month since the Lord, in his marvelous power, returned my dear husband, with the rest of the brethren, to their families, in tolerable health. We are now living in Commerce, on the bank of the great Mississippi river. The situation is very pleasant; you would be much pleased to see it. How long we may be permitted to enjoy it I know not; but the Lord knows what is best for us. I feel but little concern about where I am, if I can keep my mind staid upon God; for, you know in this there is perfect peace. I believe the Lord is overruling all things for our good. I suppose our enemies look upon us with astonishment and disappointment.

I greatly desire to see you, and I think you would be pleased to see our little ones; will you pray for us, that we may have grace to train them up in the way they should go, so that they may be a blessing to us and the world. I have a hope that our brothers and sisters will also embrace the fullness of the gospel, and come into the new and everlasting covenant; I trust their prejudices will give way to the power of truth. I would gladly have them with us here, even though they might have to endure all kind of tribulations and affliction with us and the rest of the children of God, in these last days, so that they might share in the glories of the celestial kingdom. As for myself, I can truly say, that I would not give up the prospect of the latter-day glory for all that glitters in this world.

O, My dear brother, I must tell you, for your comfort, that my hope is full, and it is a glorious hope; and though I have been left for near six months in widowhood, in the time of great affliction, and was called to take joyfully or otherwise, the spoiling of almost all our goods, in the absence of my husband, and all unlawfully, just for the gospel's sake (for the judge himself declared that he was kept in prison for no other reason than because he was a friend to his brother), yet I do not feel in the least discouraged; now though my sister and I are here together in a strange land, we have been enabled to rejoice, in the midst of our privations and persecutions, that we were counted worthy to suffer these things, so that we may, with the ancient saints who suffered in like manner, inherit the same glorious reward. If it had not been for this hope, I should have sunk before this; but, blessed be the God and rock of my salvation, here I am, and am perfectly satisfied and happy, having not the smallest desire to go one step backward.

Your last letter to Elder Kimball gave us great pleasure; we thank you for your expression of kindness, and pray God to bless you according to your desire for us.

The more I see of the dealing of our Heavenly Father with us as a people, the more I am constrained to rejoice that I was ever made acquainted with the everlasting covenant. O may the Lord keep me faithful till my change comes! O, my dear brother, why is it that our friends should stand out against the truth, and look on those that would show it to them as enemies? The work here is prospering much; several men of respectability and intelligence, who have been acquainted with all our difficulties, are come into the work.

My husband joins me in love to you. I remain, my dear brother and sister,[1] your affectionate sister,

Mary Smith[2]

---

[1]Hannah Greenwood Fielding, wife of Joseph Fielding whom he married in England.

[2]Smith, *Life of JFS, op. cit.*, pp. 143-146.

Chapter XI

Family Sorrow

Through the months while Joseph Fielding was away in England, Mary Smith took great pride in having a missionary brother. When a letter from him arrived, she drank deep of its missionary zeal and spirit. News of family was looked forward to and absorbed with keen interest; but all was not well in England. Joseph had been rejected by his loved ones. Gradually, Mary learned the distressing details which pyramided into a dramatic story.

The first intimation that differences had developed between the missionaries and her brother James caused Mary deep concern. She and her sister Mercy discussed the matter and wondered what it might portend for the future. They commiserated with Joseph; he was in a difficult position. The sisters had entertained high hopes that the other members of the family would come into the Church and be gathered to Zion. The changed situation caused them uneasiness of spirit. In fact, they were about to experience a painful family tragedy that would bring a termination of cordial relations and involve the family in a bad split. Progressively, deep sorrow in news from England and renewed persecution in America became the pattern of their lives.

When Reverend Fielding closed the door of his chapel to the missionaries, he also closed the door of his home to his brother Joseph. He passed the word to other members of the family, and a united front of opposition was formed against Joseph causing him great soreness of heart. He saw little of James after that.

All of Joseph's people in England, except Martha Watson,

took him to task. James had lost most of his flock. In his hostility, he bitterly denounced Joseph, for it was he, as he thought, who had brought the missionaries to Preston. His sister Ann Matthews sympathized with James over his loss and excoriated Joseph for it. She and her husband, the Reverend Timothy R. Matthews, labored greatly in their letters to point out the "errors" of Mormonism and save Joseph. Even brothers John and Thomas Fielding came to the defense of James.

The Fielding family, which had always been welded together in a strong bond of love, was rent in twain by the religion from America called "Mormonism." They could not understand their beloved brother Joseph and sisters Mary and Mercy and what had happened to them. As for Joseph, he labored diligently in an effort to help them understand the message that he bore. For their part, they could not be moved to see any element of Joseph's point of view.

The following August, 1837, after Joseph arrived in England, he and James had an exchange of words which signalled the parting of the way for them. Joseph lodged with James and ate with his sister Mrs. Watson—if he ate. The Reverend became much opposed to the missionaries. One morning, as they were sitting down to breakfast, he proceeded to say some hard things about them and the Book of Mormon. Joseph was much grieved and could not eat. He arose from the table, took the Book in his hand and declared to all, James in particular, that what had been told them was the truth, that the Book was of God, and that he would have to repent. After that, when they met, James would scarcely speak to him. Joseph found lodging elsewhere. Sister Martha remained very kind. She was delighted to feed Joseph and give him money according to her means. She got his washing done at her expense and was careful to avoid saying anything against the missionaries.

As a result of the impasse that developed between the two brothers, Joseph felt very lonely. James' rejection of him and his message weighed heavily upon his mind. However, on a few occasions, they saw each other and also exchanged letters. Both exhibited fluency and force in what they wrote. James felt that Joseph was under a delusion and in Satan's grasp.

On the occasion of the breakfast table incident, James had lost his temper. In a letter, he made a grudging attempt to apologize. He told Joseph that it was not his business to declare in plain terms that the Book of Mormon was the word of God; that this was assuming the thing. He wanted something to convince his judgment. He confessed that he felt something of what St. Paul felt at Athens when, as it was written, upon beholding the idolatrous devotions of the people, his spirit stirred within him, or, according to the original, he was in a paroxism of anger. James felt that if his feeling carried him a little too far, it was no wonder because of Joseph's dogmatic way of asserting a thing. This, he felt, was a strong argument against the truth of Joseph's principles. But he hoped that Joseph would not be offended if his remarks came with power.[1]

Then James turned to what was really bothering him, the matter of losing his flock, declaring: "Now I do not believe at all that you were sent of God to rend my little church to pieces. Were we to speak as 'plain' as you do I should boldly declare that it was not God but Satan as an angel of light [that] sent you here, however, I do not seriously declare that this is my sincere belief. I feel truly thankful to find that you give me credit for the sincerity of my prayers for you. I feel as if I could lay down my life to reclaim you."[2]

By nature, Joseph was a mild man with a kindly spirit. Yet, from the remarks of Reverend Fielding, it would appear that Joseph was perhaps dogmatic in his dealings with his brother. However, this is a doubtful appraisal in view of James' hurt feelings and Joseph's known amiability. Joseph,

[1]Rev. James Fielding's letter, Aug. 27, 1838, to Joseph Fielding.—Courtesy of Eva Burton Franz.

[2]*Idem*

convinced of the rightness of his mission, had stood up for his principles and spoken boldly, as one having authority, in rebuttal to James' remarks.

Reverend Fielding also vented his anger on Joseph because the missionaries had come to Preston to commence their work. In the same letter, he declared that if God had sent the Mormon missionaries to preach the new doctrines and covenants, without respect of person, he could not see on what grounds they could possibly justify themselves in by-passing Liverpool and coming to Preston. Had they opened their mission in Liverpool, they might have avoided the charge of working with a poor brother's materials. Their work would have some less of human character and be more like a work depending alone on the power of God for its success.

Certainly, the work of the Mormon missionaries depended much on the power of God for its success, but not alone. The Lord required them to exercise faith coupled with hard work. The elders assuredly knew that without divine help they had little chance for success. As for by-passing Liverpool and going first to Preston, would it not be like the logical prompting of the Holy Spirit to go there? The Gospel message had been sown in Preston through written communications from America. Moreover, James Fielding had been so impressed with the letters from Joseph, Mary, and Mercy that he had read them to his congregation and told the members about the restoration of the Gospel. He advised them to pray that the inspired prophets might visit them also with the truth. When the missionaries from America arrived, he voluntarily threw open his chapel for their use. Surely the prompting of the Spirit of God had also been upon him as well as his flock. James would have to answer to his conscience, for he definitely had played a part in what had transpired.

Reverend Fielding was prone to arrogate to himself the notion that he was the keeper of the souls of his communicants. If they put themselves in his hands, their salvation would be assured. He showed, in his letter, that he was piqued because

Joseph appeared more willing to put his eternal welfare elsewhere than in the hands of his brother. He declared to Joseph: "No one but God knows what I experienced during my affliction on your account—the idea of the loss of your immortal soul seemed to excell all my other afflictions—and although you may see no danger at present, I assure you I see it and feel it painfully. Sometimes I imagine after all that were it possible that your eternal welfare should rest with one of your elders or with your long tried brother and friend, you would in such extremity rather hazard your soul in my hands than theirs."[3]

James expressed a desire to have further conversation with Joseph, but he felt it should not be where he lived as Mr. Watson seemed so averse to the subject of Mormonism being talked about. James was afraid a meeting would cause uneasiness, as he and Watson were of one mind upon the subject, and it would be a pity to endanger their quiet. Furthermore, it would wound his feelings to meet Joseph at the house of any of those who had deserted him, but if he would name any other house and the time, James would meet him.

Apparently, James had no real desire to meet Joseph in further conversation. After suggesting it, he seemed to offer excuses to avoid it. In any event, he would not stoop to enter the house of a former member of his congregation. To say the least, James was in deep resentment over the ignominy he had suffered because of the disaffection of his flock to Mormonism. He would never forgive nor forget.

The above happenings were a sample of the drama that was occurring in England which tore the family apart, news of which reached Mary in America causing her deep grief and heartache. But it had only begun. Other family "big guns" were unlimbered against Joseph and, indirectly, his sisters in America.

In the meantime, the missionaries persevered and achieved

---

[3]*Idem*

unusual success.[4] Several leading men were baptized as were almost all of James' congregation. This led him to declare that Joseph's conduct in coming to Preston to oppose his brother had made religion stink in the noses of the sensible and intelligent people of the place. Accordingly, Joseph did not wonder that his brother was unfriendly. He told James that he was willing to suffer in such a cause. "Sister Martha is still kind," he wrote, "though she cannot manifest it as she would like. Sister Ann Dawson, a widow in whose house we are lodging, is exceedingly attentive and kind to us. A very diligent woman; may the Lord help her and bless her. We have not wanted for anything. The people are poor; to take them out of this country will be much like taking the children of Israel out of Egypt, and will require the same power and wisdom."[5]

Reverend James Fielding united with others in opposing the elders. He was bitter and spoke and wrote against them. The elders decreed, in the name of the Lord, that whatever was done by anyone against the work of God, it should turn aginst him. And so it was and so it would be.

Then Joseph received Mary's splendid letter. He was impressed with it and went to see James and sister Martha for the purpose of reading it to them. But Joseph was rebuffed by his brother to the extent that his mind was hurt and darkened. He did not intend to visit them again unless they sent for him.

At this time, two important events occurred affecting Joseph. He engaged in fasting and prayer with Elders Kimball and Hyde after which Joseph was ordained an Elder under their hands. Then the three washed their feet against several priests and others who had rejected their testimony and worked

[4]In eight months, there were 2,000 baptisms, Heber C. Kimball having converted about 1,500 himself.—Whitney, *op. cit.*, p. 204.

[5]Fielding, Bk. 1, p. 31.

against them.[6] Joseph recorded: "My dear brother James was included; this had been long delayed. May the Lord have mercy on them."[7]

Joseph again heard from his sister Mary — a short letter dated November 3, 1837. She was much troubled about their loved ones in England because they had rejected the message of the missionaries. Joseph prayed that the Lord would "support" her mind. Mary, in her letter, told about a dream that she had had a short time before the date of her letter. She thought that some of the Elders had been to Jerusalem and had found the garment which Christ wore while on earth. It had been brought by them and was in the old Fielding home in Honidon, where, she said, she saw her brother Joseph wearing it. She felt a great desire to have it in her hands and persuaded Joseph to take it off, which he did. As Mary examined it, she turned it inside out and found it covered with blood. This sight greatly affected her, and she, in her dream, turned with emotion to her mother and said: " 'O mother, you remember it is said they scourged his back, and here are the marks of His blood left upon His garment.' " She went on to say: " 'I mentioned this dream to Brother Joseph (Smith) who gave me this interpretation. He said it was evidence that you wore the priesthood of the Son of God, and you would have to endure His stripes.' "[8] Joseph observed and recorded that just about the time Mary had this dream, he was ordained an Elder. While the dream appeared somewhat alarming to Joseph, it greatly strengthened his faith. He felt that it would be an honor to suffer as the Savior had done.

John Fielding, the eldest brother, also labored with his pen to point out to Joseph the "error" of his ways. In a well-worded letter — written under the pressure of one from Joseph

---

[6]The term "washing feet" as used by Joseph Fielding, had the same connotation as in the Biblical sense: "And whosoever shall not receive you, nor hear your words, when ye depart out of the city, shake off the dust of your feet."—*Book of Matthew* 10:14; cf. Mark 6:11, Luke 9:5.

[7]Fielding, Bk. 1, pp. 40-41.

[8]*Ibid.*, p. 44.

—John showed that he was as stiffnecked as James, and that he also had a religious mind and a knowledge of the Bible. He admitted difficulty in replying to Joseph. He also made reference to earlier letters from America evidencing that the message had reached him before the arrival of the missionaries in England.

While John's letter was emphatic, he interjected an essence of brotherly love which seemed sincere even while he castigated Joseph, saying: "I confess and do assure you my dear brother Joseph, my views are such and my love to you and my dear sisters in the 'New World' is such as to cause me most deeply to deplore your misfortune (to say the best I can of it) in being so much deceived yourself, and being rendered so capable of deceiving others, and to pray that God in his infinite mercy may give you fully to know his will in these matters; and that he may keep me and the rest of the family steadfast and unmovable in the true faith, always abounding in the work of the Lord, knowing that 'no good thing will be withheld from those who walk unrightly.' "[9]

Then John revealed the true basis of his antagonism. James had been in touch with him and prejudiced his mind by alleging that the Mormon Elders had broken a promise not to introduce any new doctrine in exchange for the use of his pulpit. John affirmed that James' anger against the elders stemmed from this and the loss of his congregation to the Mormons — the *casus belli* that underlay the schism in the Fielding family. He wrote: "I would entreat you, if you would establish your own cause, as you have a legal right to do, not to do it upon other men's foundation (even St. Paul would not do that) but in a fair and honest way, as others do, out of the world, not exclaiming against or persecuting others who may differ from you, and who are quite as confident that they are right as you can be, and who would then feel quite satisfied that you should think for yourself, etc. While you observe

[9]John Fielding's letter, Dec. 19, 1837, to Joseph Fielding.—Courtesy of Josephine Burton Bagley.

this advice, I should, with all my family, notwithstanding any difference of opinion, feel happy to see you."[10]

John would save Joseph, which he tried to do, by pointing out the "error" of his ways; yet, there was doubt and perplexity in his mind. This led him to show his letter to Thomas Fielding who agreed with him in all that had been written. Still John was not satisfied so went to Bedford and showed his letter to his sister Ann and her husband Reverend Matthews. They agreed that Joseph was "under an awful delusion." Finally, satisfied and reinforced, John mailed his letter.

Brother John put forth a great mental effort to compose his long letter. As the eldest brother, he seemed to feel it his duty to remonstrate with his "fallen" younger brother and help save him. He had to uphold the family tradition of Christian piety and devotion to the orthodox religion and teachings of their parents. For any member of the family to depart therefrom was pure sacrilege. Yet, Mormonism, as much as he knew of it, had rocked his religious foundation and given him something to think about — something with the ring of truth but which he could not reconcile with what he had been taught all his life. John was a good man and a patron of the old Methodist church in St. Neots where the family had worshipped. Being a well-to-do man, he had given liberally of his means toward its upkeep and improvement. He wanted to see Joseph, but it appears that his letter was the last communication to pass between them. He was involved in an accident which cost him his life before Joseph got to see him.

John's effort in writing to Joseph was not entirely wasted. The letter served to provide additional background information regarding the reasons for James' resentment against the Mormon missionaries. It was read by Elder Kimball who commented on it. He categorically denied James' accusation that the elders had made a promise not to introduce any new doctrine, then broken it. He stated: "I need scarcely assure my

[10] *Idem*

friends that nothing was said to him from which any inference could be drawn that we should suppress the doctrine of baptism. We deem it too important a doctrine to lay aside for any priviledge we could receive from mortals."[11]

As further explained by Elder Kimball, the missionaries had talked to James on the subject of baptism during their interview with him. He knew well the Mormon position on it as a result of that interview and from the letters he had received earlier from Joseph, Mary and Mercy in Canada.[12] He had been conditioned to believe in infant baptism and saw the situation that he would be placed in if he obeyed the Gospel. Notwithstanding his talents, standing in the Gospel, and preaching to others, he would have to be baptized for the remission of sins by those ordained to the power. These considerations, no doubt, had their weight upon his mind.

Another member of the family who took Joseph Fielding over the coals and opposed Mormonism was Ann Matthews. She leaned toward the Church of England where her husband had been a minister before he espoused the Methodist faith and James Fielding's reform movement to become a fellow nonconformist. As the wife of a prominent churchman, she moved in a select society.[13] Like her opportunist husband, she, at first, had shown some interest in Mormonism and was ready to accept it; however, she did an about face. Several letters passed between Joseph Fielding and her. She belabored him vehemently and allowed herself not the slightest thought that

[11]Whitney, *op. cit.*, p. 142.

[12]Joseph Fielding made reference to the Fielding letters from Canada on the subject of baptism, thus: "It is a strange fact that the letters we sent from Canada were brought forward as weapons against us. My brother James had formerly highly recommended them to his people, i.e., when he received them, though he kept from them that part that treated of baptism. He has now given them into the hands of an enemy to us, who has selected from them such parts as he could make serve his turn, as he supposed."—Fielding, Bk. 1, p. 47.

[13]"Ann became the wife of that remarkable man Timothy Matthews, curate of Colmworth and Bolnhurst and from 1821 until his death in 1845 preacher at the Primitive Episcopal Church of Christ Church, Bedford, the building now known as Bromham Road Methodist Church. Matthews called his congregation together by blowing a trumpet or bugle in the streets of Bedford."—H. G. Tibbutt, "Westward Across the Atlantic," *Bedfordshire Biographies XXII, Bedfordshire Magazine*, Spring-1956, p. 46.

he might have something on his side. She condemned him and considered him fallen. This indictment also applied to her sisters in America.

The following excerpt from one of her letters reveals her frame of mind: "O my brother, let me entreat you to beware what you are about. Last week while Mr. Goodson was reading some of Mr. Cowdery's letters I remarked to him I could easily imagine that man capable of conjuring up some of the fables (to that effect). A simple man as Joseph Smith is described to be might be the tool but this affair did not originate with such a one. It is a deep laid scheme. It often makes me think of an enemy transferred into an angel of light and of the time that will be full of delusion that if possible the very elect shall be deceived. Lord keep those of us who have not fallen and recover those who have for Jesus sake. Amen and Amen.[14]

Here we have the doubting mind of one sister in the family as compared with the believing mind of her younger sister Mary, as shown in her utterance: "The more I see of the dealing of our Heavenly Father with us as a people, the more I am constrained to rejoice that I was ever made acquainted with the everlasting covenant;"[15] also, compared with Mercy's statement: "And I would not now give up my religion for all the gold in America. I know I have not followed cunningly devised fables."[16]

Ann Matthews, in the same mentioned letter, referred to an alleged anathema that Joseph had pronounced upon their brother James, although she did not say what it was: "Is it possible I ask myself that the once loving hearted Joseph who I believe would almost have laid down his life for that brother (James) can have been so far deluded by strangers in a foreign land as to be guilty of so unChristlike an act. . . . Joseph how cutting must be such accusation . . . which has been made to

---

[14]Ann Fielding Matthews' letter, Aug. 20, 1837, to Joseph Fielding.—Courtesy of Eva Burton Franz.

[15]Mary Fielding Smith's letter, June 1839, to Joseph Fielding.

[16]Thompson Centennial letter.

my face. I know not what can be the religion of your family when your brother can curse another. O Joseph if this is the case farewell forever to peace as it is."[17]

Her husband, the Reverend Timothy R. Matthews, also wrote to Joseph in the same vein, as shown by this excerpt: "I saw enough to convince me that the Elders who came down were never sent by the Lord Jesus, nor baptized by the Holy Ghost and I do pray that the Lord may open your eyes to see the awful delusion into which you have fallen and deliver you from it. You will be responsible before the judgment seat for helping forward the delusion and assuming to yourself an authority to preach and baptize which the Lord never conferred upon you by an authorized man that Joseph Smith sent out. It is a cause for deep upset both to myself and all the family that you and our dear sisters have been so fearfully deluded, but I believe that many prayers are offered for deliverance."[18]

After hammering Joseph in the above manner, Reverend Matthews took a different tack: "Think not that we love you less, yea, we love you and them that love Jesus. Further, I cannot but love you. The recollection of your work at Honidon, the kindness you manifested toward all, your amiable and loving spirit survives in my recollection, and I only wish that Joseph was safely rescued from Mormonism."[19]

Matthews had cause to be resentful. The missionaries who came down from Preston to Bedford had baptized many of his flock. He was about to be baptized himself, but had backed out after Elder Goodson disobeyed instructions and read to him the "Vision" which started a controversy. However, Reverend Matthews assumed the authority to baptize and immersed himself.

As for Joseph, despite the castigations from his kinfolk, he remained strong as an oak; the onslaught against him had

---

[17]Ann Fielding Matthews' letter, *op. cit.,* Aug. 20, 1837.

[18]Rev. Timothy R. Matthews' letter, (undated), to Joseph Fielding.—Courtesy of Eva Burton Franz.

[19]*Idem*

no effect, and he continued unshaken in his testimony and knowledge of the Gospel. Except for James and Martha, he did not get to see his relatives until some time later, as he was busily engaged in the Preston area. Besides, he had no money for side trips. But he reached them by letter, as indicated by the following excerpt from one of them in an appropriate reply to Reverend Matthews: "My real opinion is that you would have received all that has been brought to light in these last days in the mercy of God, if your mind had been perfectly free, i.e., if you had been alone and if I should cast some reflections on Mrs. Matthews in this as she is my sister, I think you would pardon me. . . . you said if you embraced the faith of this Church you must give up your former ordination. I know she has felt much attached to the Church of England . . . but I've written to her on these subjects perhaps often enough, and I do hope she has attended to my request in preserving one letter in particular and I did not intend to trouble more on the matter."[20]

Joseph further declared to Reverend Matthews that in view of world events; prophecies being fulfilled; the setting of God's hand to gather the children of Israel in fulfillment of His promise to Abraham His friend; the renewing of the everlasting covenant; the revelation of God to His church in the last days; the need for repentence; the laying of the axe to cut down every tree that did not bear good fruit: "It is hard to still my tongue or my pen if I see the least hope of success. I do indeed wish that I could reason with you face to face. . . ."[21]

Mary Smith was moved by her filial concern for them even though they had rejected the message of Mormonism. But she still hoped that the Word would get through to them, and that they would have a change of heart. However, she waited in vain for a fulfillment of that hope. Communications with them slackened to a standstill. Her brother Joseph

[20]Joseph Fielding's letter, Aug. 12, 1839, to Rev. Timothy R. Matthews.— Courtesy of Eva Burton Franz.

[21]*Idem*

was her only medium of news of them. As for Joseph, there continued to be intermittent contact with the rest of the clan in England.

Then a misfortune occurred which brought a softening of the feelings of the Fieldings in England. Joseph received a letter from James saying that John Fielding had met with an accident while using a chaff-cutting machine. A second letter from him anounced John's death. John, a successful farmer, was respected as the eldest brother. His death was common cause for them to unite in mourning his passing. The funeral had to be hurried as a mortification had set in. Sister Martha Watson left to spend a month or six weeks with John's widow. James concluded: "She [Martha] unites with me in sincere love to you and believe me to remain your ever affectionate Brother not in the Mormon faith but in the faith of the N. Testament."[22]

Despite a certain contrition of heart manifested in James' letter, there still remained a breath of the conflict that separated them. He hated Mormonism and could not resist the uncivil remark, in an otherwise friendly letter. Joseph's reaction to the news of John's death was sober and reflective. He appraised his brother objectively. He had become rich—had all he could wish for. Joseph remembered the severe letter from him saying that he (Joseph) was welcome to his home on condition that he would renounce his faith. Joseph had looked upon the letter as a poor farewell and felt that if he had gone to his neighborhood to preach, John would have been his greatest opposer.

When he was younger, Joseph had worked "as a servant" for John and had come to know him perhaps better than any of his other brothers and sisters. No doubt the long hours on John's farm with little or no pay dampened any deep affection for his rich brother. The letter from him had hurt Joseph

[22]James Fielding's letter, Nov. 23, 1839, to Joseph Fielding.—Courtesy of Josephine Burton Bagley.

who, as a younger brother, had reason to expect a friendlier tone from an older brother.

When Apostle Heber C. Kimball returned from America, Joseph was relieved of his administrative duties, freeing him fully for missionary work. He was given a special blessing by Elder Kimball to the effect that inasmuch as Joseph was faithful and hearkened unto the counsel of God and listened to His servants, the power of the Priesthood would rest upon him. He would have the power to heal the sick, cast out devils, to cause the lame to walk, the dumb to speak, and the deaf to hear. He was also told: "And the time shall come when thou shalt say to the dead, come forth, and they shall come forth . . . ."[23]

Thus fortified with these and many more prophetic promises, Joseph went forth anew, a humble missionary, to proclaim the gospel and commence a new era of his mission.

* * *

In the meantime, Joseph had met and married Hannah Greenwood, a convert to the Church. Elder Kimball had pointed her out to Joseph, when she attended one of their meetings, as the person he would marry. She was crowned with auburn hair and possessed distinctive charm.

In July 1840, after visiting several branches in various towns, Joseph returned to Preston. He learned that his sister Ann was in town and wished to see him. He called on her at James' place. As Joseph talked to her, James interrupted twice and took away the conversation. Joseph proposed that she come to see him. She was invited to spend the next afternoon with him at sister Nightingale's. Joseph called for her and the meeting took place as arranged.

The next day another meeting with her occurred. Elders Kimball, Richards, and Turley (Theodore Turley, a new missionary) were present. Elder Kimball conversed with her and carried it on in an excellent spirit. She also manifested a good

[23]Fielding, Bk. 3, p. 32.

spirit, although she could not accept the things discussed. Elder Turley spoke awhile much to the point. In conclusion, Elder Kimball bore his testimony. At Mrs. Matthew's suggestion, it was written down, both she and Elder Richards having a copy. Elder Kimball proposed closing with a prayer. A hymn was sung, and Elder Turley prayed. They parted on the best of terms. She had been exposed to a new spiritual persuasion and was perhaps impressed and influenced against her will that she was in the presence of something unusual in her life. It is quite possible that she was touched by the spirit and message of the Elders and came to understand the force that had influenced the lives of Joseph, Mary, and Mercy. There had been present and in evidence unexpected erudition in spiritual matters which commanded her respect. Ann saw that her brother did not stand alone but was part of a forceful corps of Mormon missionaries. While she manifested no desire to accept Mormonism, she did henceforth treat Joseph more considerately. The fact that he now had a wife may have softened her and made her more sisterly.

In a few days, Joseph saw her again and left a copy of the Mormon publication, *Millenial Star*. They talked in a congenial spirit. However, James was present and questioned everything and disputed at every point. Ann asked Joseph concerning some points of discipline. He explained his authority in cutting off members. If no one had the authority to so act, none had any authority at all. Ann agreed that it ought to be so with the Church of God. She felt that the Mormon system was good, and she believed her brother Joseph, Kimball, and Turley were good men, but she said that she could not accept their doctrine. She reverted to her customary spirit and wished that if Joseph found iniquity at the bottom of the work, he would not turn to infidelity, but would come to them, and they would receive him. Joseph confided to his journal: "It does not seem likely that she or my brother James will come into the Kingdom unless it is through tribulation."[24]

[24]*Ibid.*, pp. 41-42.

Still, Ann retained a warm spot for Joseph. When he visited Bedford, she and her husband invited him to lodge with them. He had further conversation with her and felt that she was of far better spirit than James. But he found that she would not consent to one principle he held. She was of the opinion that the Mormon system had merit; yet, maybe Joseph Smith might be a deceiver—perhaps a beast appearing as a lamb.

Joseph did missionary work near Bedford. After a week, he walked thirteen miles to Papworth and called on his brother Thomas and family whom he had not seen in eight years. Joseph washed his face, hands, and feet, ate dinner, then walked to Gravely to visit his brother John's family. There, many years earlier, he had lived as an employe of his brother and labored hard. Joseph found John's family in good health and engaged in the fall harvest. While they were of high station with their riches, they were pleased to see Joseph and expressed the wish that he could come and be with them again. But for the cause for which he labored, "The World of Satan" would have tried him when he saw the prosperity of the farmers, being very fond of farming himself.

Joseph returned to Papworth where he stayed with his brother Thomas. On Sunday, he went to the English church to which Thomas belonged, but it was "no food," as Joseph said. After two or three days with Thomas, he found things intolerable. Thomas would not hear his testimony nor permit him to talk with Mrs. Fielding. He did not ask Joseph to pray nor bless the food. He treated Joseph as an infidel and was rude. Joseph told him that he could not be comfortable in his house. So Joseph left Thomas, as he had done James, and for the same reason. He went back to the house of John's family in Gravely where he assisted two days with the harvest.

He then went to St. Neots and tried to find a place to speak. The following Sunday morning, he went to church at the Methodist chapel at St. Neots. This was the Fielding family's old place of worship. A flood of memories crossed his mind as he entered. This was where his father and mother had prayed; to which the family had walked four miles from Honidon every Sabbath for many years—often in bad weather—Joseph with them up to the time he left for America.

While Joseph was in the chapel at St. Neots, his heart ached so that he could scarcely sit upright. Several of the main "pillars," he observed, were fat as a stalled ox, and they did not seem to hear, but slept. They had almost a new chapel and an organ in it. This was brother John's doings; and they needed something to keep them awake.

He went often to St. Neots to see if he could get a place to preach, but each time he failed. No one there would assist him. His old Methodist friends looked shyly at him, almost as if he were an enemy. It was quite singular that on his many visits to St. Neots, he had come within four miles of Honidon and had not gone near the place of his birth, old home, and haunts of his youth. Perhaps he was afraid that it might call up too many memories. Then he decided to go there. Of the visit, he stated: "Went over to Honidon, my native place, where I was treated kindly by Mr. and Mrs. Brightman, who live in our old house. I looked over the old fields where I spent the days of my youth, with peculiar feelings. I saw how one generation passeth away & another cometh. Some of my friends say they wish I had stayed there. The farm is improved, though the house is not, but the place as a gift would be no temptation. . . . I bowed down before the Lord in a hollow in the field and renewed my vows with him, to be his forever. Left an appointment to preach in the old home on Wednesday of the next week."[25]

After Joseph had looked over the old farm, his thoughts went to Colmworth where his father and mother were buried. He made his way there. Pertaining to this, he wrote: "I called at Colmworth to see the graves of my beloved father and mother. The Priest of the parish has for his own pleasure

[25] *Ibid.*, p. 60.

LOT 2.

Consists of the Manor or reputed Manor of Honydon, otherwise Camoys, otherwise Chamois Park Grove, and all that

VALUABLE FREEHOLD ESTATE,

Situate at Honydon in the Parish of Eaton Socon, Beds., containing according to a recent survey about

8a. 0r. 16p. OF WOOD LAND, AND ABOUT

90a. 0r. 17p. of capital deep staple Arable and Pasture Land,

Divided into convenient fields, as shown on plan, coloured Pink, together with the

STUD-BUILT AND TILED FARM HOUSE,

Containing 6 rooms, together also with stabling, chaff house, wood-built and thatched hovel and cow shed, a partly brick and stud-built and thatched corn barn with nearly new thrashing floor and nag stable at end, enclosed yards well supplied with water and other conveniences, let with the property comprised in Lots 3 and 4 to Mr. Shadrach Brightman, a yearly tenant of long standing, at the very low rent of £110 per annum. The apportioned rent to be received by the purchaser of this Lot will be £103 per annum.

SCHEDULE.

	A.	R.	P.
Pasture	20	3	26
Arable	68	1	11
Wood	8	0	16
Homestead, about	0	3	20
TOTAL............	98	0	33

The timber upon this Lot has been valued for the purposes of this sale at the sum of £113 and is to be taken by the purchaser at that sum.

Sale description of farm — October 20, 1870 — where the Fieldings had once lived.

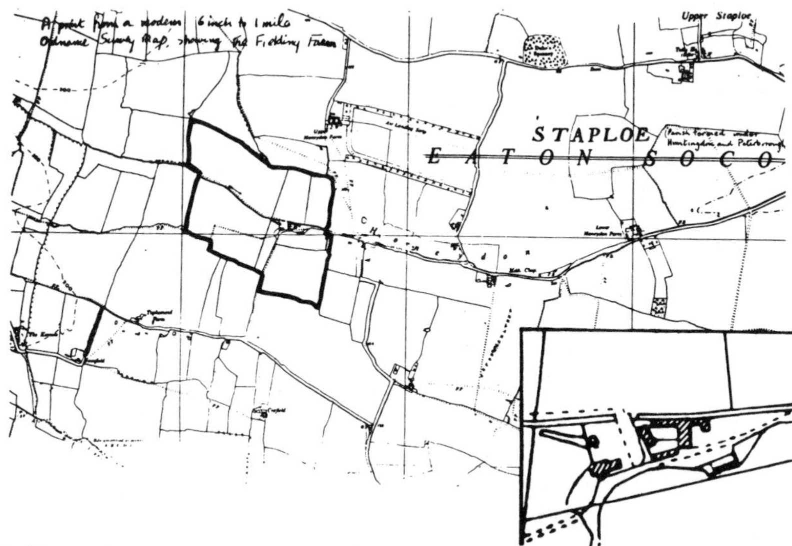

Fielding farm — area in heavy border — Honeydon, England; also, inset — lower right — showing arrangement of farmhouse and buildings.

Courtesy of County Records Office, Bedford, England.

enclosed a portion of the church yard with a quick, or thorn fence, and planted it with shrubs and flowers, and my father & mother and sister Sarah are just in the inclosure. Their grave stones look well burnished by my brother John, at least the 2 former. Mother died October 15, 1828, aged 61—and father, May 3rd, 1836, in the 77 year of his age. They died in peace, but neither of them ever heard of the fullness of the gospel. And as my friends reject it, I am glad they died before it came, lest they should have been influenced by them to reject it also."[26]

Joseph took himself away. The visit to Honidon and the old homestead and then to Colmworth to the graves of his parents touched his heart and brought a turning point in his work. The following Wednesday, he returned to his old home and, by appointment, preached to a houseful of old neighbors. The home became a seminary, as it were, where Joseph expounded the word of God. Thereafter, he returned several times to Honidon before he ceased his labors in the Bedford area. He entered upon a new phase of missionary work which proved successful. Several were baptized. Two hundred came to hear him preach, on one or more occasions, in an old barn in Gravely—the hamlet where his brother John had wielded much influence before his death—John Wheeler being the first there to be baptized by Joseph. Out of his labors, at a later date, a branch of the Church was organized in Gravely. Still, he made no headway with his brother Thomas. When Joseph went to Papworth and bade him goodbye, his brother called after him to beware of that *Book of Mormon* and that Smith. This he repeated several times. Joseph merely said that he would take care. He did not rebuke his brother but walked sadly away never to see him again. Thomas joined the opposition. Later when President James H. Flannigan of the Bedford Conference was getting the best of Mr. Poole, a

[26]*Ibid.*, p. 62.

Methodist minister, in a debate, Thomas put his hand over Flannigan's mouth and prevented him from speaking.[27]

When Joseph returned to Preston, he found that his sister Martha and her family were planning to go to America. (Word of this reached Mary Smith in America.) Joseph told Martha that she might become a member of the Church yet. She only smiled. She continued to be very nice to Joseph, and he noted that her attitude had always been right toward the Church. The day after Joseph saw her, she visited him and Hannah. She took them a quantity of preserved black currants and other things and showed them much kindness. However, Martha never realized her desire to go to America. Yet, she remained the one bright spot in Joseph's relations with his family in England.

Toward the end of Joseph's mission, Ann Matthews treated him and Hannah and their children with special kindness. In a final letter, she mentioned that she was sending some bottle caps for the babies (Rachel and Ellen) and some French cambric which she had worked. In this letter, she mentioned her children having been sick with the measles and how her little daughter had got in bed with her and prayed out loud without knowing her mother was listening. Ann seemed sort of mixed up and said that if they, as a family, emigrated it would be to the Holy Land. She made mention of Joseph's fortieth birthday, and said: ". . . and when you receive this O may your eyes be opened to see the light of God's light this year for Jesus Christ's sake. Amen & Amen."[28]

Little is known of Ann Matthews' later life, except that she was widowed at the age of forty-six and died in her eighty-sixth year. She bore six children, four sons and two daughters. She maintained her religious zeal and took pride in her family background and antecedents. According to Sarah M. (Lillie) Wright, daughter of Reverend James Fielding, Ann Matthews

---

[27]Henry Linford, Autobiography, MS, pp. 10-12.

[28]Ann Fielding Matthews' letter, Mar. 24, 1841, to Joseph Fielding.—Courtesy of Josephine Burton Bagley.

always spoke of the Fieldings as being from good stock. Lillie also said that Aunt Matthews, Aunt Watson, and Aunt Thompson were three of the most charming women she had known. The latter she knew for only a short time when she came from America to England on a visit. Further, Millicent F. Wright, a daughter of Lillie Wright, said that her mother was very fond of Aunt Matthews and described her as a saint.[29]

---

[29]Millicent F. Wright's letter, Oct. 22, 1964, from England to author.

ANN FIELDING MATTHEWS
Sister of Mary Fielding Smith.
Courtesy of Josephine Burton Bagley

FIELDING HOME, HONIDON
Birthplace of Mary Fielding Smith

Chapter XII

Mary's High Station

While her kinsfolk in England were heaping opprobriums upon Joseph Fielding, considering him fallen and deluded, Mary Smith and her sister Mercy were not spared the sharp shafts of calumny hurled at him. The three of them were considered victims of delusion and cunning fables. Mary and Mercy were not in a position to offer any rebuttal nor reinforce their brother with the power of their testimony and the strength of their spirit. However, it is quite likely that Joseph let some of them read Mary's letters. If so, they may have caught the strength of her decision and feeling of her heart in such words: ". . . blessed be the God and rock of my salvation, here I am, and am perfectly happy, having not the smallest desire to go one step backward." These words carrying the ring of conviction were such as to give the skeptic pause. The opposition may not have agreed, but they would be forced to respect the full implication of them.

In addition to Mary's great faith, a reserve of courage had sustained her in all her afflictions and crises. These two attributes, stronger than sinew, enabled her to surmount obstacles any one of which would have defeated the average person. It took the best in Mary to start from scratch to build a home and make a new life without ready means. In Nauvoo (formerly Commerce), her spirit was refreshed with new hope and promise. She watched a miracle unfold before her eyes, as the industry of a homeless people transformed the swampy shore line around the bend of the Mississippi into a desirable community. Street after street of homes came into being, extending up the slope to higher ground where a Temple was to be built. Nauvoo was to become the largest city in Illinois within the short breathing space permitted the Saints.

Besides the religious activities, a pleasant social life developed. After a few months, a proud militia group, the Nauvoo Legion was formed. There were fine horses, carriages, and military displays. Attractive homes were, in due course, constructed by many of the brethren. The sisters appeared in public adorned and dressed in the current fashions. The people, as a whole, were industrious and happy. Life could be beautiful if their enemies would leave them alone. However, the continued agitation of their old Missouri enemies caused disquieting fears that they were living under an uneasy truce.

Mary Smith was probably the busiest woman in Nauvoo, with all the demands on her time by a large family that had to be fed and clothed. Having been dispossessed of furniture and household belongings in Missouri, she and Hyrum were under the necessity of setting up housekeeping bit by bit, piece by piece. During the latter part of 1839 and well into 1840, the work continued of fitting out a home that would accommodate and make comfortable a growing family. Because of their poverty, Mary had to exercise the greatest wisdom and economy in her management of affairs to keep her family clothed and in good health. She became a good seamstress, making big and little shirts, underclothing, dresses, and trousers.[1] The preparation of food, washing dishes, fetching water, washing, and ironing, etc., kept the household busy. Aunty Grinnels bore a great deal of the labor-burden. For other close companionship, Mary had her sister Mercy who lived nearby. The two sisters thought of each other in many little ways and shared dress patterns and the latest word on

[1]Many years later, Hyrum Smith's youngest daughter wrote: "I remember one day mother had made him [father] a pair of pants and he was very proud of them. I saw him walk back and forth with his hands in his pockets. It was seldom that he was cheerful. He always looked anxious and sober."—Martha Ann Smith Harris, Centennial-Jubilee letter, Mar. 22, 1881, to her posterity. Letter deposited with others in the Relief Society Jubilee box in Provo, Utah, to be opened April 6, 1930; hereafter referred to as Harris Centennial letter.

what was in style and what the ladies were wearing in bonnets and dresses.

In due course, Hyrum Smith succeeded in acquiring a farm, which was a blessing, as it provided food for the family and some income. It was located one and a half miles east of the Temple site. The green acres of grazing and farm land provided a place for recreation. Happily, the children explored and played to their hearts' content, got acquainted with the animals, and helped out with little tasks. The place was dear to the family and became a vital part of their lives.

Mary Smith found her husband's people to be a closely united and affectionate family which revolved around Father and Mother Smith. Besides them and her husband Hyrum, there were Joseph and Emma (Hale), Sophronia and William McCleary, Samuel and Mary (Bailey), William and Caroline (Grant), Catherine and Wilkin J. Salisbury, Don Carlos and Agnes (Coolbrith), and Lucy and Arthur Milliken. All were plunged into deep mourning when Joseph Smith, Sr., died, September 14, 1840, from the effects of the exposure suffered during the expulsion from Missouri.[2] Before he died, he gave each of his children a blessing. In this and his passing, Mary fully appreciated his many virtues. He was a true Patriarch to his family and the Saints. He had the love and esteem of his family. A large throng attended his funeral out of respect and grief.[3] As the mourners gathered about the grave during the

[2]In a biography of Joseph Smith, Sr., the Prophet Joseph Smith stated: "The exposure he suffered brought on consumption, of which he died on this 14th day of September, 1840, aged sixty-nine years, two months, and two days. He was six feet, two inches high, was very straight, and remarkably well proportioned. His ordinary weight was about two hundred pounds, and he was strong and active. In his younger days he was famed as a wrestler, and, Jacob like, he never wrestled with but one man whom he could not throw. He was one of the most benevolent of men; opening his house to all who were destitute. While at Quincy, Illinois, he fed hundreds of the poor Saints who were flying from the Missouri persecution, although he had arrived there penniless himself."—Smith, *HC, op. cit.,* IV. 191.

[3]Robert B. Thompson, delivered the funeral discourse at the service for Joseph Smith, Sr. The following was his opening statement: "The occasion which has brought us together this day, is one of no ordinary importance: for not only has a single family to mourn and sorrow on account of the death of an individual, whose funeral obsequies we this day celebrate; but a whole society; yes, thousands will this day have to say, *a Father in Israel is gone.*"—Smith, *HC, op. cit.,* IV, 191-192.

dedicatory services, five tall sons with their mother, sisters, and others, mourned quietly as the departed one was laid to rest in solemn reverence. Of the five sons, four would depart this life within the next four years. So the funeral was prologue to others which would plunge the family into tragedy and sorrow. Many trials followed the Smith family in the loss of loved ones, but there were many joys bringing a measure of consolation, as a number of babies made their advent in various families.

A special cause of rejoicing at this time for the Saints was the laying of the corner stones of the Nauvoo Temple. On April 6, 1841, Mary Smith was up at the break of dawn to assist her family in getting ready to witness the important event. Hyrum, a Brevet Major General in the Nauvoo Legion, was away in Philadelphia organizing a branch of the Church. The awaited day started early with fourteen militia companies from Nauvoo and across the river in Iowa parading and carrying out military maneuvers. At twelve o'clock the ceremonies of laying the corner stones commenced. Mary, as the wife of an official of the Church, had a seat where she could see all the dignitaries. President Rigdon addressed the assembly, after which the architects, under the direction of the First Presidency, lowered the southeast corner stone to its place. The Prophet Joseph spoke these words: "This principal corner stone in representation of the First Presidency, is now duly laid in honor of the Great God; and may it there remain until the whole fabric is completed; and may the same be accomplished speedily; that the Saints may have a place to worship God, and the Son of Man have where to lay his head."[4]

The services were adjourned for an hour. After reassembly, the three other corner stones were laid. Mary Smith took in all that transpired with silent interest. Little did she realize that she would play a role in the construction of the Temple and render service therein when it was completed. Hyrum

[4]Joseph Fielding Smith, *Essentials in Church History* (Salt Lake City, 1928), p. 309. Hereafter referred to as Smith, *ECH*.

would have a major part in the construction of it. Mary would work with him as his loyal supporter.

In the months that followed, Mary had the honor of attending many official functions. She conducted herself with quite-proper English dignity. The distinctive honors that came to her as the wife of an important church official registered in her heart. Her status was extra special. After her lowly afflictions in Far West, she was regarded in new light by the community and favored with rank, recognition, and high station. But she was not worldly proud because of it—only humbly grateful for her many blessings.

* * *

Now a personal item—an announcement that originated in the confines of the Hyrum Smith home and traveled across land and sea—casually couched and incidental with a request for a bit of finery, a bit of straw, lace, and silky frivols not common on the frontier—an order in a letter going to England for pretty bonnets. Mercy Thompson, in writing to her brother Joseph, had in mind a bonnet for her little girl, one for her sister Mary, and one for Emma Smtih. Mary would have written but was preoccupied.

Nauvoo April 20th 1841

My dear Brother —

As Brother Herringshair has been detained waiting for a boat till now I thought of several things which I had forgotten before and being so hurried before I am afraid I made many blunders. Brother Walmsley wished me to say that he has got a house and work already—they are in excellent spirits. Mrs. W. wished me to remind Sister Fielding to pack her drawers full of things and bring them also all her earthenware, and I should be glad if you ask Sister Watson[5] to bring to Sister Mary and me and my little girl each one of those pretty bonnets which the English people wear so much and I should like one for Sister Emma very much. We cannot get any thing like or neat straw bonnets here for less than 6 dollars. I can pay her very easy in provisions when she comes. It really seems a pity for English people to bring money here as they might lay

[5]Martha Fielding Watson.

it out there to so much better advantage—we cannot get anything like good print here for less than 3 York Schillings per yard, common plates 1 s each, basons [sic] 1 s 6 d, good flannel 6 s & all other things in proportion.

Sister Mary would have written, but is not able being about to add another to her maternal ties—she wished to be remembered to you and all friends. Dr. Bennett & Family are still with us—we have rented a school room for one quarter expecting that you won't be here by the end of it.

Your, Mrs. R. Fielding [Thompson][6]

Joseph Fielding
Mr. Watson
1 Bingham St.
Preston, England

Mary gave birth to a little daughter, May 14, 1841, just twenty-one days after the above letter was written. She was given the name, Martha Ann, apparently for her two aunts in England. The baby was fair, resembling more her father than her mother. Mary rejoiced at this new favor to come to her—to have a baby girl of her own. She watched over her, communed with her, and rocked her to sleep to the melody of an old English lullaby. It was an auspicious time for the little one to be born—to grow and become conscious of the Nauvoo world around her, including a knowledge of her father, Uncle Joseph, and her Grandmother Smith.

* * *

The months passed rapidly, bringing about many changes in the home of Hyrum and Mary Smith. The family was cramped for space with so many under one roof. It was Hyrum's desire, eventually, to build a house for his family which would comfortably accommodate all. Not far away, a fine house, to become known as the Mansion House, was going up for Joseph, befitting his station in the Church. He would have a place to receive and entertain his many visitors and guests. The other leading brethren were building nice houses

[6]Courtesy of Eva Burton Franz.

suitable to their importance and position in the Church. Accordingly, Hyrum made plans to do likewise—perhaps on the order of the homes which Brigham Young, Heber C. Kimball, and others were about to build for themselves. Mary had the prospect of being mistress of a fine, elegant home, fittingly adorned with nice furniture, carpets, fixtures, etc. It would be a place for gracious living.

A new home would also be nice for the children, a social center, a place where they could bring their young friends and hold parties and dances. Lovina Smith was rapidly approaching courting age. A fine home would befit her budding-out status, a place to receive her young friends. Mid-teen age Lovina was very attractive, with fine eyes, high spirit, and intelligence. She was the apple of her father's eye. He observed her fondly and watched her grow and mature to become a lot like her mother. He was indulgent with her and gave in to her persuading reasons for a new dress or other object of attire. A new dress for her side-tracked all other home activities for a few days and cluttered up the sewing room while Mary cut, sewed, and fitted a special creation that suited Lovina's mood and whim. But when she was dressed, ready and radiant for a party, the family looked on with unstinted pride. She was lovely. The family loved her, and she loved her family.

On occasions, Lovina had her tantrums when something displeased her. One time after she had left for a party and all was quiet again about the house, the family pet dog, old Tige,[7] stole into her room and bedded down on some of her clothing which happened to be left on the rug beside her bed. When Lovina returned and found the dog snoozing away on her things, she stamped her foot and raised the roof. The dog beat a retreat with Lovina right after him. Of course, this waked the household and left the memory of it imprinted in

[7]With further reference to the family's pet dog, "Martha's earliest memories were going to visit grandmother, Lucy Mack Smith, and of sitting on a little stool by her side; of seeing their pet dog Tige go to the store with a note in a basket and come back with whatever her grandmother had sent for. . . ."—Richard P. Harris, "Martha Ann Smith Harris," *The Relief Society Magazine*, XI, (Jan. 1924), 12.

HYRUM SMITH — PATRIARCH
First reproduction of original painting.

MARY FIELDING SMITH
First reproduction of original painting.

the minds of the younger children to amuse and cause them to tell about it in later life.[8]

It became the vogue in Nauvoo for the prominent leaders of the Church to have their pictures painted. Mary and Hyrum were no exception. They joined Joseph and Emma, Mother Smith, and others in having a likeness of them painted or sketched by a visiting artist by the name of Maudsley who put up at the Mansion House. Hyrum donned his finest suit and Mary her best dress in which to pose. Hyrum elected to stand with a cane, which made good sense, as it gave him some steadying support during the long moments of posing. When the portraits were finished, they were the pride of the family. They occupied a prominent place on a wall of the best room, where they were observed and admired by visitors. The pictures preserved the profiles of the subjects, the style of clothes worn for best, the blue of his eyes, and the brown of hers. Hyrum, in his black coat with tails, lighter shade of trousers, standup collar, and fancy tie, made a fine looking figure. His long sideburns and starched "bosom," setting off a gold pin, were details imparting added distinction. The pin, undoubtedly, was the special pin given him by his brother Joseph.[9]

Mary, in her blue dress with a wide collar of light colored material, tight bodice, full sleeves, and skirt, was a picture of simplicity and modesty. Her brown hair, coiffed with a center part, each side brought from front to back in a twist fastened close with a decorative hair clasp, revealed Mary's best in hair grooming. The book in her hand was a picture style among the Saints at the time. The pictures of her and Hyrum were mounted separately in matching, wooden frames painted black, buff, brown, and gold according to the ornate

[8]Related by Martha Ann Smith Harris and preserved in family tradition.

[9]According to family tradition (Martha Ann's), there were three such pins. Joseph had them made for the First Presidency—one each for himself, Sidney Rigdon, and Hyrum Smith.

surface cut of the wood. Today, the pictures are priceless heirlooms.[10]

The joy that the birth and presence of the new baby Martha Ann brought into the lives of Mary and Hyrum was dampened later in the year by the sickness of Hyrum Smith, Jr., which culminated in his death on September 21, 1841 (cause unknown). He was a promising boy, 7 years, 4 months, and 28 days of age. All their untiring care, medication, and prayers failed to save him. Mary had nursed him unceasingly day and night, but, painfully with Hyrum, bowed to the inevitable. Hyrum's anguish and grief were excruciating; Mary wept with him and shared his heartache.

Earlier, there had been two other deaths which affected the lives of Mary and her loved ones. On August 7, 1841, Don Carlos Smith died of pneumonia. The death of Robert B. Thompson, Mercy's husband, followed quickly on August 27, 1841, of the same cause. These two men had been close in life as they were in death. They had been associated in the publishing business. Their demise left the Smith and Thompson families stunned and bereaved. Both men had promising futures. Each was intelligent and skilled in writing and the use of the English language. They were men of exceptional literary talents, and the Church was deprived of the power of their pen and press by their untimely deaths. Mary thought of Don Carlos' kindness to her in Far West in helping her to get to Liberty jail and out of Missouri. The pathos of his death lingered long with her.

The passing of Mary's two brothers-in-law dampened the joy and expectancy that had been aroused by word that had been received from Joseph Fielding that he would be returning soon from England with his family. They set sail from Liverpool, October 21, 1841, on the *Tyrian* but, in fact, went on

[10]Pictures are in possession of author. They are mounted in frames 10¼" x 15". When Mary Smith fled Nauvoo, the pictures and her mirror were carefully packed to protect the glass and placed in her large chest together with her husband's diary, *Bible, Book of Mormon,* cane, sword, watch, etc. For list of relics see Pearson H. Corbett, *Hyrum Smith—Patriarch* (Salt Lake City 1963), pp. 452-453.

board five days earlier to sleep and get settled. After a good passage, Joseph and his family and a large number of Saints in his charge landed in New Orleans in November. Joseph chartered a river boat to take the company up the Mississippi to St. Louis which they reached in ten days. From St. Louis, they took a boat to Warsaw,[11] the water being too low to admit the boat farther. The rest of the journey to Nauvoo, for Joseph and his family, was made overland by sleigh and team, Lorenzo Young being the driver. At times they were compelled to get out and walk to warm themselves which was very painful for Joseph because of broken ribs and an injured knee which he had suffered in a bad fall of ten feet from a wharf to the ground at New Orleans.

When they came within two miles of Nauvoo, they began to see the effects of the industry for which the Saints were well-known. Fences of rails and pickets, houses and garden lots extended to the edge of the prairie. This, all in so short a time, was a source of wonder to Joseph. They passed the Temple which was under construction. The arches of the vaulted windows were not all finished. The sight of the structure in the light of the moon gave Joseph peculiar feelings—the idea that it was being built at the special command of the Almighty. This thought led to many others—to the promises of God and the establishment of His kingdom on the earth.[12]

When Joseph and his family arrived in Nauvoo, they went to the home of his sister Mercy Thompson, recently widowed. In expectation of Joseph's coming, Robert Thompson had set to work to prepare a house for him, but he died before it was finished. Instead of finding Robert Thompson, a friend, he found his widow who stood in need of a friend. However, Joseph had not recovered sufficiently to be of much help. He

---

[11]Note: "Wednesday, 24.—Elder Joseph Fielding, who sailed from Liverpool on the *Tyrean,* with 204 Saints, arrived at Warsaw with his company; and Elders Willard Richards and John Taylor went to meet them and to give such counsel as their situation required."—Smith, *HC, op. cit.,* IV, 460.

[12]Fielding, Bk 5, pp. 6-7.

was unable to cut the smallest stick because of his injuries. Business was dull, and there was little to do. He found himself in poor circumstances.

Four days after his arrival in Nauvoo, Joseph Fielding met with Joseph Smith and others. Concerning this, the Prophet wrote: "Sunday, 28—I spent the day in the council with the Twelve Apostles at the house of Brigham Young, conversing with them upon a variety of subjects. Brother Joseph Fielding was present, having been absent four years on a mission to England. I told the brethren that the Book of Mormon was the most correct of any book on earth, and the keystone of our religion, and a man would get nearer to God by abiding by its precepts, than by any other book."[13]

There is little doubt that Joseph Fielding's report of his missionary activities and things in general in England was of great interest to the Prophet and the members of the Twelve who listened to him. He could speak with the assurance of a veteran missionary for that was what he was, having served faithfully and longer, perhaps, than any Mormon missionary up to that time. His words carried the prestige of that long service to command the respect and attention of his listeners.

Mary Smith rejoiced to have Joseph back home again and to meet his wife Hannah and their two daughters, Rachel and Ellen, the latter still a baby. Long conversations followed as Joseph brought Mary up-to-date on family news from England. Sadly, he described the obstinacy of their brothers James and Thomas and sister Ann. One heartening spot was the reported warmth and interest of dear Martha Watson. His words had a depressing effect on Mary filling her with sorrow. She had implored the Throne of Heaven so earnestly that her loved ones in England would come into the Church. She took comfort, however, in Joseph's success in taking the Gospel to many others.

Joseph, when he was able, worked some for Hyrum Smith. As stated earlier, Hyrum had acquired a farm; he needed help

[13]Smith, *HC*, *op. cit.*, IV, 461.

with it. He offered to let Joseph have some of the land to farm on shares with Hyrum furnishing the team. As there was nothing better, Joseph accepted the offer. On April 1, 1842, he left his sister Mercy's place and went to live in a small log house near the land he was to work. In exchange for the labor he did, Hyrum furnished him with some flour and pork. Joseph began to plant corn, beans, potatoes, etc. With care and economy, they got along until they had corn and meat of their own.

It was late when Joseph began to plow. He sowed eight acres of oats, but it being so late, the rain came when it was ripening and beat it down, so that Joseph's half did not pay him for the trouble of gathering it. But early in the summer, an important event occurred for Joseph and Hannah. A loan of money in some amount was received from Hannah's brother, George Greenwood, in England, entirely unasked and unlooked for, followed by another sum of the same amount—in all, several hundred dollars. With the money, they purchased twenty acres of land on the prairie in its wild state at eight dollars an acre.[14] They rejoiced exceedingly at this good turn of fortune. They felt that the Lord had led her brother to send the money in view of their straightened circumstances. Without it, they would have been poorly off for money. George Greenwood was among the first to help the Mormon cause in England with monetary contributions to Elder Kimball and others.

---

[14]Fielding, Bk. 5, p. 13.

Chapter XIII

Nauvoo Climate

The domestic tranquility of Mary Smith's life fluctuated as the fortunes of the Church and its leaders shifted between good and bad times. The first two years at Nauvoo were comparatively quiet ones. This permitted what was needed to demonstrate to the world what the Church could accomplish. The strength of the Church increased constantly with the stream of converts into Nauvoo. The spiritual life of the Saints was progressive. New revelations received by the Prophet Joseph Smith kept the Church pointed to new heights and zeal. The fusion of the spiritual and temporal was discernible in all daily activities. People were taught to work and eschew idleness. Secular discipline achieved through good local government brought to the community law and order.

Mary was all too aware that the Church still had enemies. Any hostile gesture from within or without the community caused a tremor of alarm to course through her being. This was the natural reaction of all those who had passed through the ordeal at Far West, the very thought of which made them shudder. When they first settled in Nauvoo, Heber C. Kimball remarked that their stay would be only temporary. Those who heard him were greatly agitated over the remark. But it was prophetic. He undoubtedly had in mind the prophecy in Isaiah 2:2: "And it shall come to pass in the last days, that the mountain of the Lord's house shall be established in the top of the mountains, and shall be exalted above the hills; and all nations shall flow unto it."

Tremors that brought anxiety anew to Mary Smith started to be felt early in 1842. They originated within the Mormon community as a new Korah emerged. This Korah was to eclipse the Korah of Kirtland, the aforementioned William Parrish, who, at the time with other apostates, had caused Mary to fear and tremble. The new Korah was Dr. John C. Bennett who was the mayor of Nauvoo and a general in the Nauvoo Legion. As his immoral life came to light, he resigned his office as mayor. He was cashiered from the Legion and disfellowshipped from the Church. This man's iniquity was the beginning of serious times. He became an implacable enemy and gathered others around him in a conspiracy to destroy Joseph Smith. To this end, he corresponded with the Governor of Missouri and became an intimate of the Governor of Illinois.

The next dangerous tremor that aroused new fears in Mary was the attempted assassination of Lilburn W. Boggs, the former governor of Missouri, May 6, 1842, while he was sitting in his living room. In July, Orrin Porter Rockwell was accused of the crime[1] with Joseph Smith named as accessory before the fact. Boggs asked Governor Thomas Reynolds of Missouri for a requisition on Governor Thomas Carlin of Illinois to deliver Joseph to Missouri to be dealt with by the law. Joseph was also charged with being a fugitive from Missouri, growing out of his escape in 1839 which, in fact, had been aided and abetted by those who had him in custody.

The matter dragged on for nearly six months, punctuated by considerable legal maneuverings. Joseph, free on habeas corpus, went before Judge Pope in Springfield, January 4, 1843.

---

[1]Rockwell went into seclusion to escape being extradicted to Missouri. Later in St. Louis, he was recognized, seized, and carried to Independence, Missouri. After a mock trial and false testimony against him, he was kept in prison for eight months. When he was released, he went to Nauvoo and the home of Joseph Smith. He entered in the midst of a Christmas night party, 1843, and was joyfully received by the Prophet Joseph Smith.

In Preston Nibley, *Joseph Smith the Prophet,* (Salt Lake City, 1946) pp. 488-489, he states: "In September, 1906, I visited Nauvoo in company with my father and President Joseph F. Smith. Standing in the front room of the Prophet's old home, President Joseph F. Smith told us that he was present at this Christmas party in 1843. 'My mother brought me and sat me down on the fiddler's platform in the corner of this very room,' he said. He then related that while the dancing was going on, he noted the confusion caused by a man trying to get in at the door. He saw the Prophet make his way through the crowd and take the man to his heart."

Joseph's attorney (Butterfield) read in evidence affidavits of several persons to the effect that, on the date Boggs was shot and seriously wounded, Joseph Smith attended an officers' drill of the Nauvoo Legion and, the next day, reviewed the Legion in the presence of many thousand people. The judge's decision that followed set Joseph free.

When he returned to Nauvoo, many friends assembled to greet him. To celebrate his freedom, Joseph and his wife Emma invited a large number to attend a dinner party. Seventy-five guests sat down to a sumptuous feast. Because of limited space, four sittings were required to accommodate the guests. Joseph and Emma did the serving. Hyrum was present, but Mary was home sick, as noted by Joseph in his journal.[2] Although not able to attend the festivities, she had much to celebrate in the release of her brother-in-law. After months of apprehension and worry for fear that her husband would be the next to be sought by the Missourians, she could now breath a little easier. In the depth of her heart, she was very grateful, but her anxiety persisted.

Treacherous John C. Bennett saw in Joseph's difficulty, on account of the Boggs affair, a move suitable to his purposes. He stated in a letter to Sidney Rigdon and Orson Pratt, January 10, 1843: "New proceedings have been gotten up on the old charges, and no habeas corpus can save them now. We shall try Smith on the Boggs case, when we get him into Missouri. The war goes bravely on, and although Smith thinks he is now safe, the enemy is near, even at the door."[3] He was right; the enemy remained very near, at the very door, and no one knew this more than the wives of Hyrum and Joseph Smith.

Mary Smith found herself being hemmed in by hostile forces beyond her control or that of anyone in the Mormon community. The eventful year of 1843 was capped by still a greater shock for Mary to cause her new alarm—again because of her husband's position in the leadership of the Church and,

[2]Smith, *HC*, *op. cit.*, V, 252.
[3]*Ibid.*, 251.

after Joseph, the next target of their enemies. The Prophet Joseph was kidnapped while on a visit with his wife to the home of her sister, Mrs. Wasson, living at a place called Inlet Grove, near Dixon, Lee County, Illinois, 212 miles northeast of Nauvoo.[4]

The details of this case indicate how determined the Missourians were to get Joseph Smith in their clutches. They were fanatical and would go to any length to accomplish their diabolical purposes. The story, as will be seen, shows the fiendish planning that went into the move and how persevering the men were in putting it into execution. Missouri wanted the Prophet alive, and this fact helped save his life.

The Prophet Joseph and Emma left on their trip by carriage on June 13, 1843. Two days later a message from Judge Adams of Springfield, Illinois, was received in Nauvoo stating that Governor Thomas Ford was going to issue a writ for Joseph on requisition of the Governor of Missouri, and that it would go forward the next day. Hyrum Smith immediately dispatched William Clayton and Stephen Markham to Inlet Grove to warn Joseph.

When they arrived, the Prophet sent William Clayton to Dixon to try to find out what was going on there. Half way to Dixon, Clayton met Joseph H. Reynolds, the sheriff of Jackson County, Missouri, and constable Harmon T. Wilson of Carthage, Illinois. The two men were not immediately recognized as they were disguised. In Dixon, they had represented themselves as Mormon missionaries who wanted to see the Prophet. They hired a man with a team and wagon to provide transportation, as they had run their horses almost to death on the way to Dixon. The two officers arrived at the Wasson residence, knocked on the door, said they were Mormon Elders, and wanted to see Brother Joseph. This was the beginning of one of the strangest episodes in the life of Joseph Smith and the history of the Church.

---

[4]*Ibid.*, 431.

Wilson spotted Joseph in the back yard of the Wasson home going to the barn. He accosted the Prophet in a very uncouth, ungentlemanly manner. Then Reynolds stepped up to Joseph and collared him. Both of them put cocked pistols to his head. They profaned loudly and threatened to kill him. Finally, the Prophet bared his breast and told them to shoot away, that he was weary of life and not afraid to die and to kill him if they pleased. He also told them that he was a strong man and with his own natural weapons could level them both, but if they had any legal process to serve, he was at all times subject to the law and would offer no resistance.

They put their pistols to his sides and jabbed him repeatedly. Stephen Markham appeared, and they pointed their pistols at him threatening his life if he came any nearer. He paid no attention and advanced. They hurried Joseph away and put him in their wagon without serving any process and without permitting him to say goodbye to his family or even allowing him time to get his hat or clothes. Markham sprang and seized the horses by the bits and held them until Joseph's wife could bring his hat and coat. They again threatened to shoot Markham. The brutes continued to punch Joseph in the sides with their pistols. He called to Markham to go to Dixon and obtain a writ of habeas corpus against his abductors. Reynolds declared: "G— d— you, you shan't have one."[5]

The officers took Joseph to Dixon and held him incommunicado. During the eight mile trip, they kept jabbing him in the sides with the muzzle of their pistols.

The next day, Joseph got word to William Clayton to go to Nauvoo, post haste, with a message to Hyrum telling him what was being done and requesting him to send assistance immediately. Joseph's wife and children, and her nephew, Lorenzo D. Wasson, left for Nauvoo immediately after Joseph was seized.

When Joseph's message reached Hyrum Smith, the lat-

[5]*Ibid.*, 441.

ter called a meeting in the Masonic Hall in twenty minutes. The place was soon packed, with more on the outside, so they adjourned to the green and formed a hollow square. The news Hyrum had for them was electrifying. Joseph had been kidnapped and needed help. Hyrum called for volunteers to leave immediately to go to the assistance of their leader. Upward of 300 volunteered. General Wilson Law and Charles C. Rich left in the evening with 175 men on horseback. Wilford Woodruff donated a barrel of rifle powder. Brigham Young quickly raised $700 to meet their expenses.

It was a tense time for the Saints, as the mounted troopers started. They were the flower of Mormon manhood, grim-visaged and determined. They made an impressive sight as they rode away on spirited mounts — their bedrolls lashed to their saddles. They were well armed and prepared for any contingency. A hard ride lay ahead through the night. They separated into smaller groups and fanned out taking roads over which Joseph might be carried toward the Mississippi. The loyal men rode hard, pressing on despite growing fatigue, in order to rescue their leader. This show of Mormon strength and determination was impressive. Nauvoo was swarming with spies and strangers, and the mobilization of Mormon manpower for action far beyond the environs of Nauvoo did not go unnoticed. It gave the enemy camp something to think about and respect. Future action against the Saints would require the neutralization of this power in order to succeed.

The snatching of the Prophet Joseph by armed men to carry him to Missouri had tremendous impact upon the Mormon community. The deed was reminiscent of his capture by foul play in Far West. In both instances, a sort of evil madness was displayed by his captors. In the name of the law, illegal and brutal methods were employed. Evil scheming lurked in the background bent on the destruction of Joseph Smith and the Church. The full implications of it were apparent to the sober heads and leaders in Nauvoo. The Saints passed through a bad time. Terror seized the hearts of many.

They sorrowed for their leader and implored divine help for his return.

During the crisis, the situation in Hyrum Smith's home was one of severe trial. Memories of the Far West ordeal were revived with sickening force. A cold terror crept over Mary. She thought of what might happen to her husband and their children. Their enemies might attempt to kidnap them next. The hours wore on with little sleep for her and little appetite for food. The waiting for further word drained her of strength. She watched her husband's ordeal. She saw him bowed with worry and torn inside for the safety of his brother. Joseph in the hands of their enemies again, in chains, in prison, before a firing squad — heaven forbid. It must not be Far West all over again. Mary steeled herself and, with Hyrum, waited news of Joseph. Outside and about the city, spies were spotted. Were they part of the conspiracy? With Joseph in the grasp of the enemy, would some of these strangers try to take Hyrum? This was a logical fear. Hyrum was on his guard as were members of the Twelve. Weapons were kept close at hand. The crisis was not lost on the Saints. It was another fear-laden time for them.

Mary Smith sensed that it boded ill for the future — that things beyond their control had been set in motion which would not stop until relentless enemies had her husband and Joseph in their power.

In the meantime, Joseph's situation improved somewhat. The citizens of Dixon came to his defense and expressed themselves in such strong and indignant terms that Reynolds and Wilson finally permitted counsel to have access to him. Mr. Cyrus Walker, the best criminal lawyer in that part of the state, offered to defend Joseph if, in turn, Joseph would promise him his vote in Walker's race for Representative to Congress. This Joseph did.

It was the intention of the officers to run Joseph to Rock River, where a steamboat waited to take him across the Mississippi to Missouri. They were induced to wait until morning, at which time a writ of habeas corpus in Joseph's behalf was served against them. Another writ was served on the two officers for private damages for assault and false imprisonment on the grounds that the writ issued by the Governor of Illinois was a void writ in law. The officers were held to bail in the amount of $10,000 each. They had to send to Missouri for bondsmen. In the meantime, they were taken into custody by Mr. Campbell, the sheriff of Lee County. They were quite subdued by this counter action. Nevertheless, they again mistreated Joseph. At a place called Pawpaw Grove, they abused him so badly with their pistol-jabbing that Mr. Walker asked Sheriff Campbell to stay by Joseph which he did. The sheriff also took away their pistols.

The first of Joseph's friends to reach him were Peter W. Conover and William L. Cutler. The Prophet could not refrain from tears upon seeing them, the first help to arrive. Joseph said to his attorney: " 'I am not going to Missouri this time. These are my boys.' "[6] Later, sixty more mounted friends came up in several little squads.

The writ of habeas corpus that had been obtained for Joseph was returnable before the nearest tribunal in the Fifth Judicial District authorized to hear and determine such writs. Accordingly, it was arranged to go before Judge Stephen A. Douglas at Quincy, a distance of 260 miles. However, Joseph consulted with his lawyers and told them that Nauvoo was the nearest place where writs of habeas corpus could be heard and determined. As this was true, based on the Nauvoo Charter, they headed for Nauvoo. Joseph sent a message ahead to let the Saints know of his coming. His entourage numbered 140 made up mostly of his friends who came to rescue him. The whole setup made for an anomolous situation. Joseph was still a prisoner of Reynolds and Wilson. However, they were both prisoners of Sheriff Campbell who served the writs of habeas corpus on them. In turn, all were guarded by the men of the Nauvoo Legion.

[6]*Ibid.*, 449.

When they approached Nauvoo, they were met by a company from the city. In the lead were Hyrum and Emma, both mounted, Hyrum on Joseph's favorite horse, Old Charley. Joseph got out of the buggy in which he was riding and embraced Emma and Hyrum who wept tears of joy to see him again. A great company surrounded them. The band struck up, "Hail Columbia." Joseph mounted his horse, and he and Emma led a memorable parade into Nauvoo. He was greeted by cheers, the firing of guns and cannons, the playing of the band, and the happy smiles of the faithful.

To celebrate the occasion of his return, Joseph was host to fifty guests who sat down to his table. At the head of the table, as special guests, sat his captors, Reynolds and Wilson. Joseph's gracious treatment of his two enemies was a perfect example of charity and forbearance. His sides, which he showed to his friends, were black and blue from the pistol prodding of the two crass guests at his table. Still, he extended the hospitality of his home and every courtesy to his erstwhile tormentors. Emma was also gracious to them.

The court in Nauvoo discharged the writ against Joseph. Reynolds and Wilson had pretended to act under authority of a writ obtained from the Governor of Illinois given in consequence of a pretended requisition made on him by the Governor of Missouri for the arrest and delivery of Joseph to the authorities of Missouri. Reynolds and Wilson returned to Carthage, threatening to raise the militia and come again and take Joseph out of Nauvoo.[7]

This threat was new cause of alarm for Mary Smith filling her with continued anxiety. She knew the awful temper and sadistic tendencies of a hostile militia and what life would be like if depraved soldiers marched again on the Saints. There was a possibility of another Far West. She lived with impending danger and tension from day to day. It was about as much as a mortal could stand. Yet, she went on in the best tradition of her race — a personification of the rugged British spirit.

[7]*Ibid.*, 473.

Chapter XIV

Before the Storm

While Joseph Smith was having his difficulties with Reynolds and Wilson at Dixon and vicinity, Nauvoo had still another kind of excitement which affected Mary Smith. A delegation of Pottawatamie Indians visited the city. They came out of the West and were ferried across the Mississippi. They desired to see the "great prophet" and talk with him. The dignity of the old chief would not permit him to see a lesser white chief. Although he had much to speak about, he would not communicate his feelings or wishes to anyone else. So he would just wait until Joseph returned.

This made it necessary for him, his braves, and their squaws to wait several days. Hyrum Smith received the Indians hospitably and endeavored to make their stay comfortable. They were poor and hungry, so the squaws appeared at many doors for food. The Saints treated them kindly and shared with them. The redmen, in their buckskins, moccasins, beads, and feathers, were an impressive sight. However, the fact that they were Indians, and had about them a strange, wild appearance, made them awesome and kept the whites at a distance. Mothers kept their children close to home. However, the children were eager to see real, genuine Indians of whom they had heard so much. So they ventured close to get a good look. The children of Mary Smith were no exception. She kept a close eye on them.

At the same time, Mary was kind to them. When a squaw came to her door and held out her hand for bread or something sweet, she usually went away satisfied. Mary looked deep into their eyes and they looked into hers. There was silent appraisal — each mother of the other. As Mary could see, the lives of these Indians were not easy. Thus, she understood and sympathized. She let them linger and have not only food but water from the well. The squaws felt free to sit by her house and relax. Mary's niece, Mary Jane Thompson, carried the memory of a picturesque Indian mother nursing her papoose by Aunt Smith's window during the visit of these Indians.

One day, a proud Indian chief came to Mary's door. He stood there with frightening mien in all his colorful regalia. He did not want food. His gaze had been drawn to little Martha Ann's golden hair. He wanted to make a deal, a pony for her two braids. Mary, sensing difficulty, held the tense child in the folds of her skirt. With a positive shake of her head, she indicated, no deal. He was persistent, but she made him understand that "she would not cut off her daughter's hair for all their ponies."[1] His black eyes, deep set in full-bronzed face, riveted Mary with a displeased look. But he saw that this white squaw could not be moved. He finally turned and went away. Mary took a deep breath.

When Joseph Smith returned to Nauvoo and was free of his captors, he and several of the Twelve and others met with the old chief and his sub-chiefs to hear the purpose of their mission. The Indian spokesman arose and said that they had long been distressed and oppressed. They had been driven from their lands many times. They had wasted away in wars until only a few of them were left. The white men had hated them and shed their blood. They had talked with the Great Spirit to save them and let them live. The Great Spirit had told them he had raised up a great prophet, chief, and friend who would do them good and tell them what to do, and that Joseph (pointing to the Prophet) was the man. They had come a great way. Their horses had become poor in traveling, and they were hungry. They would await the great prophet's words.

[1]Harris, *op. cit.*, p. 12.

Joseph was very much affected by the oration and shed tears. He arose and told them that the words spoken were true; the Great Spirit had told them the truth. He said that he was their friend and brother, and he wished to do them good. The Great Spirit was their friend, but they had left Him and would not hear His words nor keep them. Consequently, He had then left them. They had killed one another, and they had been poor and afflicted ever since. Then Joseph said that the Great Spirit had given him a book and told him they would be blessed again. The book stated what they would have to do. Joseph said: " 'I now want you to begin to pray to the Great Spirit. I want you to make peace with one another and do not kill any more Indians; it is not good; but ask the Great Spirit for what you want, and it will not be long before the Great Spirit will bless you, and you will cultivate the earth and build good houses like white men. We will give you something to eat and to take home with you.' "[2] When he was through, the chief asked how many moons it would be before the Great Spirit would bless them. The Prophet told them, not many. Joseph had an ox killed for them. They were furnished some more horses, and they went home satisfied and contented.

Mary Smith often joined her husband in calling on the sick and making social calls. In August 1843, they called on Brother Cahoon.'[3] While they were there, the Prophet Joseph and his wife Emma also called. Members of the Church considered it an honor to be visited by the Prophet, or his brother. This visit of the two distinguished leaders and their wives was no exception. It gave Brother Cahoon much pleasure. It was customary to ask such visitors to say a prayer, or to administer to anyone who was sick. It goes without saying that this visit was concluded by all kneeling down in prayer in which a blessing was invoked upon the home of Brother Cahoon, his wife, and family.

---

[2]Smith, *HC, op. cit.*, V, 479-481.
[3]*Ibid.*, 525.

Another visit of record also included Mary Smith. On an October afternoon, 1843, Hyrum, Mary, Joseph, and Emma went together and called on Brother John Benbow and his family.[4] This brother was an early convert to the Church in England. His farm there had been the scene of many baptisms by Wilford Woodruff and other missionaries. He was well-to-do and gave liberally of his means before and after coming to Nauvoo which benefitted the Church immensely. Joseph and Hyrum loved and respected him and, on this visit wtih their wives, left their blessings upon him and his family to give them much pleasure.

Mary enjoyed walking with her husband. They made a fine looking couple on the streets of Nauvoo — Mary neatly dressed, holding her husband's arm. She was tall and came nearly to his shoulder. Her dark hair was pretty under a pert little bonnet created in the style of the day. As she moved, there were the rustle of taffeta and the fragrance of lavendar sachet. She enjoyed the prominence of their position and thrilled when people spoke to them respectfully. She was proud of Hyrum and liked being at his side. These were occasions that she would always cherish. She would hold them dear when, as a widow, she would walk alone. Mary and Hyrum often called on Mercy Thompson to see how she was getting along and take her something from the farm.

Life as a widow was a lonely struggle for Mercy. She had her own home and took in boarders to support herself and little daughter. Nearly two years after her husband's death, Mercy was married for time to Hyrum Smith by his brother Joseph in the presence of Mary Smith. Mercy wrote of this event in a letter to her posterity, as follows:

> On the 11th of August 1843, I was called by direct revelation from heaven through Brother Joseph the Prophet to enter into a state of plural marriage with Hyrum Smith the Patriarch. This subject, when communicated to me, tried me to the very core. All my former traditions and every natural feeling of my heart rose in opposition to this principle,

[4] *Ibid.*, VI, 53.

but I was convinced that it was appointed by Him who is too wise to err and too good to be unkind. Soon after marriage I became the inmate with my sister in the house of Hyrum Smith where I remained until his death, sharing with my sister the care of his numerous family. I had from the time I moved to his house acted as scribe recording Patriarchal blessings.[5]

According to Mercy, her husband Robert appeared to Joseph Smith several times telling him that he did not wish her to live such a lonely life, and for Joseph to request his brother Hyrum to have her married to him for time. Hyrum, when he learned of this, communicated it to Mary. She, by request, opened the subject to Mercy. But everything within Mercy rose in opposition to such a step. The Prophet Joseph called her in and explained the subject. She could not refuse to obey his counsel, "Lest peradventure I should be fighting against God," especially when Joseph told her that the last time her husband appeared to him, he came with such power that it made him (Joseph) tremble. Mercy learned further that when this occurred, Joseph inquired of the Lord what he must do. The answer was: " 'Go and do as my servant hath required.' " In regard to this, Hyrum stated that when his brother communicated the request to him that the Holy Spirit rested upon Joseph from the crown of his head to the soles of his feet. The time was appointed with the consent of all parties. The marriage was performed in Mary's room with a covenant entered into by Hyrum to deliver Mercy up in the morning of the resurrection to Robert Blasel Thompson with whatever offspring should result from the union. At the same time, Joseph counseled Hyrum to build a room for Mercy and

[5]Thompson Centennial letter.

The statement of Mercy Fielding Thompson that she entered into plural marriage on the date stated lends support to the existence and practice of the principle well before the martyrdom of Joseph Smith, June 27, 1844. Her attestation adds to existing weight of evidence that the ancient principle was restored through the Prophet Joseph Smith as affirmed in the *Doctrine and Covenants,* Section 132. Without such a restitution, it could hardly be said that the Church was established again on earth as the restoration of all things, as spoken by the mouths of holy prophets (*D&C* 27:6, Acts 3:21), in this the dispensation of the fullness of times (Ephesians 1:10; *D&C* 27:12-13).

move her to his house, which he did. Mercy remained there as a wife the same as Mary until Hyrum's death.[6]

While it was a great trial for Mercy to enter into plural marriage, it was even a greater trial for Mary to consent to it. Truly, it was the most difficult thing both ever had to do. It was equally difficult for Hyrum. The principle of plural marriage was given as early as 1831. Joseph Smith had inquired of God to know and understand wherein He justified His prophets of old as touching upon the principle and doctrine of their having plural wives and concubines. The principle was then revealed by the Lord to Joseph.[7] He was commanded to obey it. He did not immediately comply. Then, according to Apostle George A. Smith, an angel with a flaming sword appeared to the Prophet Joseph and warned him that unless he obeyed it, he would be destroyed.[8]

The sisters of the Church in Nauvoo, who were made acquainted with the revelation, were deeply troubled over it, as were the brethren. Some rebeled and refused to accept it. The truly faithful listened to an explanation of it, prayed about it, and received a witness in their souls that the ancient order of marriage was a commandment of God and divinely instituted as in Biblical times. Hyrum Smith was a patient preceptor and advocate of the principle. He taught Mary the will of the Lord, but it was so contrary to her sensitivities and convictions that she labored greatly on account of it. She passed through a period of hard struggle with her feelings because of this the most soul-testing word revealed by the Lord. She accepted it and came through the struggle strengthened and added upon in her faith. It was a monumental test of faith.

---

[6]Mercy Fielding Thompson's letter, Sept. 5, 1883, Salt Lake City, to Joseph Smith, son of the Prophet Joseph Smith, Lamoni, Ill.—*Deseret Weekly*, Feb. 17, 1886, Vol. 35, p. 79.

[7]*D&C*, Sec. 132.

Note: Polygamy or patriarchal marriage was discontinued by the Church in 1890.

[8]Journal History, L.D.S. Church Historian's Office, Salt Lake City, Oct. 9, 1869, containing copy of letter from Apostle George A. Smith to Joseph Smith, son of the Prophet Joseph Smith.

In August 1843, the Prophet Joseph and his family began moving into the completed Mansion House. The move gave impetus to Hyrum's plans for a new home. It would be built of brick on the same lot where the family was living—across the street from his new brick office building. Mary and Hyrum regarded their old house as only temporary until a more commodious place could be built.

In the meantime, the Nauvoo Temple was nearing completion. Hyrum Smith had been named a member of the Temple Committee upon the death of Judge Elias Higbee. The experience gained on the construction of the Kirtland Temple stood him in good stead. Money raising was a constant problem. An ample labor force had to be maintained. Men were active in the Pinery in Wisconsin getting out logs for the lumber needed. Another crew worked in the quarry to obtain the necessary stone. The workmen had to be fed and paid. These responsibilities weighed heavily upon Hyrum and wrote anxiety in his brow. His family took an active interest in his problems. As the Temple started to take final shape, expenses mounted. When the walls were up and the roof on, considerable money would be needed to buy glass for the windows and nails needed to complete the structure. Mary and Mercy saw Hyrum's increasing concern and sought ways in which they might help. In due course, Mercy got a capital idea:

> At one time after seeking earnestly to know from the Lord if there was anything that I could do for the building up of the Kingdom of God, a most pleasant sensation came over me with the following words. Try to get the Sisters to subscribe one cent per week for the purpose of buying glass and nails for the Temple. I went immediately to Brother Joseph and told him what seemed to be the whispering of the still small voice in me. He told me to go ahead and the Lord would bless me. I then mentioned it to Brother Hyrum who was much pleased and did all in his power to encourage and help by speaking to the Sisters on the subject in private and public, promising them that they should receive their blessings in that Temple. All who subscribed the cent per week should have their names recorded in the Book of the Law of the Lord. I assisted by my sister took down and kept a record of all the names, and not-

withstanding the poverty of the people we had (by the time that the committee were ready for the glass and nails) in the treasury about $500.00 which they gladly received just in time of need. Perhaps I should have mentioned that while the mob were threatening to rob and massacre the inhabitants of Nauvoo we hid up the bag containing that money in a pile of bricks which Hyrum had intended for building had his life been spared.[9]

Mercy and Mary pursued the penny collection project with vigor. They left no stone unturned in contacting all the sisters in the Church at home and abroad. For example, the following letter, written on Christmas day, was dispatched to England:

Nauvoo, Dec. 25, 1843

To the sisters of the Church of Jesus Christ
in England, greetings:

Dear Sisters:—This is to inform you that we have here entered into a small weekly subscription for the benefit of the Temple Funds. One thousand have already joined it, while many more are expected, by which we trust to help forward the great work very much. The amount is only one cent or a halfpenny per week.

As brother Amos Fielding is waiting for this, I cannot enlarge more than say, that myself and sister Thompson are engaged in collecting the same.

We remain,

Your affectionate sisters in Christ
Mary Smith
M. R. Thompson

Hyrum Smith penned the following endorsement to the letter:

Nauvoo, Dec. 25, 1843

The ladies subscription for the Temple, of one cent per week, is fully sanctioned by the First Presidency.

Hyrum Smith[10]

Hyrum was serious about the success of the penny fund. He had considerable time on his hands to develop the idea. He had been home for several days with an injured leg. Concerning this, his brother Joseph made this entry in his day

[9]Thompson Centennial letter.
[10]Smith, *HC, op. cit.*, VI, 143.

book: "I arrived at the assembly room [upper room of Joseph Smith's store] about noon; found all present, except Hyrum and his wife. He had slipped and turned his knee-joint backward, and sprained the large muscle of his leg, and I had been ministering unto him."[11] Mary had her hands full serving as a nurse which entailed massaging and bandaging Hyrum's bad knee to strengthen it and relieve the pain. Gradually the knee improved, and Hyrum hobbled around on it cautiously. He chafed under the inactivity. There was so much to be done and a lot of money to raise to complete the Temple. The penny fund remained close to his heart, and in a conference address, April 6, 1844, he spoke of it to the Saints. The following portion of his remarks shows his concern:

> We want 200,000 shingles, as we shall resume the work on the Temple immediately. All who have not paid their tithing, come on and do it. We want provisions, money, boards, planks, anything that is good; we don't want more old guns or watches. I thought some time ago I would get up a small subscription, so that the sisters might do something. In consequence of some misunderstanding, it has not gone on as at first. It is a matter of my own; I do not ask it as a tithing. I give a privilege to any one to pay a cent a week, or fifty cents a year. I want it by next fall to buy nails and glass. It is difficult to get money. I know that a small subscription will bring more than a large one. The poor can help in this way. I take the responsibility upon myself, and call again upon the sisters. I call again until I get about $1,000. It only requires two thousand subscribers.[12]

The penny fund gradually caught on with the sisters of the Church, and thousands of pennies came in for the noble cause. By December 5, 1844, 50,000 were on hand. They were an amazing sight to behold and no small quantity to lift for they weighed 343 pounds. Having no bank in which to put them, they were kept by Mary and Mercy in a secluded place at home. The treasure of pennies would one day buy glass and nails for the temple, but first, the pennies would protect the credit of the Church.

[11]*Ibid.*, 98.
[12]*Ibid.*, 298.

A special crisis arose for Hyrum and Mary which required very careful handling. A man by the name of Joseph H. Jackson, who had been in the city for several months, desired to marry Lovina Smith. Jackson asked Hyrum if he were willing to receive him as a son-in-law. Hyrum's answer was a definite, no. Jackson then went to Joseph Smith and asked him to use his influence in his favor. Joseph refused the request. Jackson next applied to one of the Laws, who was a secret enemy of the Smiths, for assistance in stealing Lovina from her father. From that time on, Jackson continued to seek out enemies of the Smith family. He succeeded in getting a number to join him in a conspiracy to murder all of the Smiths. They began holding secret meetings, one of which was attended by a man named Eaton who was a friend of the family. He exposed the plot.[13]

The Prophet Joseph told the Saints about it publicly — that the conspiracy was formed by a group of prominent men, including apostates, who had been excommunicated. They were William Law who had been the Second Counselor in the First Presidency, his brother Wilson Law, a Major General in the Legion, and Dr. Robert D. Foster. They allied themselves with the aforementioned Joseph H. Jackson, a non-Mormon, a man known to be a murderer, thief, and perjurer. These men were joined by two others away from the Church: Francis M. and Chauncey L. Higbee.

In May 1844, Hyrum Smith received an anonymous letter — supposed to have been written by Jackson — threatening his life and calling upon him to make his peace with God, for he would soon have to die. This threat against Hyrum posed a new crisis in Mary Smith's life. It hit the household like a thunderbolt and left Mary stunned and alarmed. Why would anyone want to kill her husband? He had done no wrong. In essence, the threat was a true indication that their enemies were out to get Hyrum as well

[13]Lucy Mack Smith, *op. cit,.* pp. 530-531.

as Joseph. Mary's days and nights were again filled with fear. This latest, in a series of dangers, left her drained of strength. But she could not falter nor show the effect of the war of nerves being waged against them. The hour called for calm courage.

The aforementioned apostates had revolted from the Church, saying that Joseph had fallen, as other apostates — Parrish, Cowdery, Harris, Russell, etc — had said. The new conspirators went to Carthage where they joined others, of the same stripe, who were bent on taking the lives of Joseph and Hyrum Smith. On their testimony, Joseph was charged with polygamy, and a writ was issued against him. There was much false swearing. Francis W. Higbee swore so hard that Joseph Smith had received stolen property that his testimony was thrown out. Joseph went to Carthage (not the final trip) with a strong bodyguard which included his brother Hyrum. The Foster brothers, who had aligned themselves with the conspirators, in a prick of conscience, warned the Prophet that there was a plot afoot to take his life, and that there were some persons who were determined that Joseph should not leave Carthage alive. Jackson, one of the plotters, was seen loading his pistols. He was heard to swear that he would have the satisfaction of killing Joseph and Hyrum. However, they returned home safely.

On top of this, another crisis developed that brought new alarm to Mary Smith. The Laws, Higbees, and Fosters set up a printing press in Nauvoo, to publish a newspaper called the "Nauvoo Expositor." It was the design of the instigators to publish all they could find against the Prophet. The city council took counter-action and passed an ordinance declaring the paper a nuisance, issuing an order to abate it. The press was burned, June 10, 1844. As a result, an order came from Governor Ford at Carthage for Joseph, Hyrum, and the rest of the city council to appear at Carthage. Things looked dark and threatening. Joseph and Hyrum decided to leave the city for the West. Mary sorrowfully packed Hyrum's things. To be left behind was almost more than she could bear. He was her security and strength. She needed his presence as did his family.

Chapter XV

Farewell

The mounting politico-religious storm that engulfed the Mormon community of Nauvoo was prelude to a tragic and historic event. Forces of satanic magnitude stood fully arrayed against a modern-day prophet and his brother. These intended victims were not to be allowed the slightest quarter nor a hearing before a fair court. Their evil persecutors lusted for blood. Blood they got — on their hands and garments to stand as a witness against them for their crime throughout time.

In the quiet of the night, the moment for saying farewell arrived for Mary and Hyrum Smith. He was about to take leave of his family for some unknown place to be gone an indeterminable length of time. The hour was very early morning. The children were sound asleep. The older people were awake, but they remained respectfully in the background feeling the impact of the moment. Hyrum's heavy pack was on the floor with his rifle leaning against it. He was dressed in clothing for roughing it — heavy boots and durable trousers and coat. He held Mary gently, comforting her. She could not let him go. She was distraught and tired from anxiety and loss of sleep. She clung to him and cried on his bosom.

Then came a quiet knock on the door. It was Joseph Smith. Cautiously the door was opened and he entered. He beheld Mary in tears. He himself had been through such a scene in his own home before joining Willard Richards and calling for Hyrum. Porter Rockwell would go with them to man the skiff. Joseph comforted Mary as she wept with these words: " 'Sister Mary, don't feel bad, the Lord will take care of you, and he will deliver us, but I do not know how.' "[1]

Their true intentions were to go to the Rocky Mountains to seek out, if possible, a place of peace and safety for the Saints. The two brothers then started across the Mississippi. But later, on account of the feeling expressed by some of the brethren who should have been their truest friends, word was sent to Hyrum and Joseph requesting them to return. They were seen being rowed back across the river. They landed on the bank and walked up to Hyrum's house, where they both entered. Joseph seated himself, while Hyrum changed his clothing. Then they both went to the Mansion House. Although it was not known that they had returned to be taken as "lambs to the slaughter," the feeling in Hyrum's home was indescribable. The very air seemed burdened with sorrowful forebodings. The awful scene at Carthage followed in a few days.[2]

At Carthage, through monstrous perfidy, Joseph and Hyrum were shot down by a cold-blooded and cowardly mob with blackened faces. They were denied life and liberty without due process of law. The impact of the terrible news on the Mormon community was overpowering. The homes of the two victims were plunged into great anguish. The reaction in Hyrum's home was described by his youngest daughter Martha Ann, as she remembered and wrote of it, thus:

> I remember well the night that he was murdered. I had the measles and I had taken cold. It had settled on my lungs and I could not speak above my breath. I begged my dear mother to lie down and rest once. She would read the Bible awhile then walk again until the day began to dawn. Then there was a knock at the door. My mother asked who

---

[1]"Mercy R. Thompson Describes the Parting Prior to the Martyrdom," *Juvenile Instructor,* XXVII (1892), 399-400.

[2]*Idem*

Note: Hyrum Smith returned with his brother Joseph on Sunday, June 23, 1844. It was Hyrum who felt that they had better return and give themselves up, trusting in the Lord and facing whatever was in store for them. Probably another reason for Hyrum wanting to return was that his daughter Lovina and Lorin Walker were being married that day. It would be natural for a father to want to be present at such an important event involving his oldest daughter.

> was there. The answer was George Grant. She opened the door and asked what news. He gave answer that Joseph and Hyrum were both murdered. My mother stepped back calmly exclaiming it cannot be possible can it? He answered yes it is true.
>
> She fell back against the bureau. Brother Grant took her and placed her in a chair. The news flew like wildfire through the house. The crying and agony that went through that house and the anguish and sorrow that were felt can be easier felt than described but that will never be forgotten by those who were called to pass through it.[3]

Earlier, at the time Hyrum and Joseph returned from across the river, Mary rejoiced to see her husband again. However, the decision to go to Carthage brought her new sorrow and apprehension. She hid her feelings and turned to helping her husband get ready to leave again. Crisis upon crisis — sorrow upon sorrow — was the pattern of her life. Hyrum tried to reassure her that everything would be all right. But both of them labored with a persistent heaviness of heart. Each knew that going to Carthage meant a new confrontation with their old enemies and possible death. None could predict the outcome. Discomforting forebodings pervaded their thoughts and feelings. Mary studied the faces of Hyrum and Joseph. She saw deep trouble, and her womanly instinct conveyed to her ominous warnings. Joseph was in a fatalistic mood. After Missouri, he had said that he knew all the time that his life would not be taken. He did not have that confidence this time.

Mary tried to be brave. She would not forget Joseph's words spoken to her as he and Hyrum were about to take leave in flight to the West: " 'Sister Mary, don't feel bad, the Lord will take care of you . . .' " These words would ring in her mind the rest of her life to help her over the rough spots. They would sustain her now in the twilight of disaster.

When Hyrum was ready to leave for Carthage, he prayed with his loved ones and bade everyone goodbye, except his young, five-year-old son Joseph F. who was out playing.

[3]Harris Centennial letter.

Hyrum mounted his horse and was about to ride away when he spotted the boy not far away in the street. He rode up to him, reached down, picked up the lad, and held him in front of him as he had done many times. He kissed the little fellow and told him to be a good boy while papa was away, then put him down. Joseph F. never forgot this incident and visited the site years later.[4]

The rapid march of events, which brought about the death of the two noble Americans at Carthage, was intimately described by Mary's brother Joseph who mourned the tragedy. Into his account, he poured the story as it came to light, as he understood it, and as his sister Mary understood it, capped by his own solemn reflections (which he said helped take the edge off his deep grief) and by his fervent expression of loyalty to the men he loved. His stirring denouement, a resume of which is presented here, beginning June 22, 1844, draws the curtain aside and reveals what transpired and the pathos of the awful deed.[5]

On orders from Governor Ford at Carthage for Joseph and Hyrum and the rest of the city council to appear at Carthage, i.e., upon being informed by letter, two or three of the brethren went there to see him. The prospects now looked very dark and threatening. Joseph and Hyrum were greatly perplexed over the situation. After holding council together most of the night, they, with one or two others, left the city before daybreak. Early in the day after their departure, a company of men arrived with an order from the Governor, but as Joseph and Hyrum could not be found, they returned

[4]Related by Preston Nibley to author in an interview. President Joseph F. Smith visited Nauvoo with his wife, accompanied by Charles W. Nibley and his wife. Preston, in his teens, was with his parents. They walked about seeing the sights. The sun got warm and the two ladies and brother Nibley decided to go to the hotel. However, President Smith desired to look around some more. He invited Preston to accompany him. They reached a certain point in the road near where President Smith had lived as a boy. He looked about and got his bearings then related how his father bade him farewell, indicating the place in the road, saying: "It was about here where my father picked me up," etc.

[5]Fielding, Bk. 5, pp. 36-51.

to Carthage leaving one of their number to try and find the Smiths and see if they would go to Carthage. Joseph and Hyrum were located by messengers, but the two men refused to surrender to the Governor. The prospect, however, was dark and seemed to threaten the safety of the city, the Governor saying that if they refused to go to Carthage, the entire city stood on a keg of powder and a spark would blow it up. Also, the officers said that the town would be put under martial law until Joseph and Hyrum were delivered up if it took three years.

These things, together with the memory of the horrid scenes in Missouri and a firm trust that God would deliver them, induced many of the Saints and Joseph's friends to wish him and his brother to go to Carthage. Yet it was several hours before the two consented to do so. This they finally did on Monday morning. Joseph and Hyrum, with Willard Richards, John Taylor (the only two of the Twelve at home), and several others started for Carthage with solemn feelings. It appeared that Joseph, in particular, anticipated the fatal results in part, but said he wished Hyrum might be spared to stand in his place. He expressed himself to this effect, that he should die for his people and, if so, he would be murdered in cold blood.

Some time before they reached Carthage, they met a company of men with orders from the Governor of the State to take away the public arms, i.e., the arms belonging to the State.[6] The captain of this company was polite and friendly and gave the strongest assurance of the safety of the two Smiths. It was agreed that the brethren would return with the company to Nauvoo.

According to Joseph Fielding, he was in Nauvoo when they arrived and also in Hyrum's company in his home. Hyrum was in better spirits by far than when he left. He

---

[6]With the surrender of the State weapons, the enemies of the Church, with forethought, neutralized to a large degree Mormon armed strength, but the Saints had personal arms of their own and were not left defenseless.

told his brother-in-law that he thought that all things would go well, etc. As soon as the arms were collected, Hyrum and Joseph took leave of their families for the third and last time and went to Carthage, henceforth of cursed memory.

The Governor, it appeared, treated them respectfully and lodged them in his own quarters until, owing to his fear of the people, he desisted. After leaving the Governor's quarters and a trial in part, they were unexpectedly and unlawfully, but for their safety, thrust into Carthage jail.

They went to Carthage on Monday evening the 24th of June 1844. On Thursday, Governor Ford left the city and, with a company of men, went to Nauvoo, having left a guard at the jail. The Carthage Greys were entrusted with the care of the prisoners. They had just before been in a state of mutiny, still, all of them had pledged themselves to abide by the law. At the same time, a party of mobocrats had come to Golden's Point on their way to Nauvoo, but messengers were sent ordering them to disperse. At this their leader, Colonel Williams, ordered all men, not willing to go to Carthage to kill the Smiths, to lay down their arms and the rest to step out together, that now was the time or never. A few laid down their guns. The others disguised themselves by blacking their faces, then proceeded on their way to shed innocent blood. They reached Carthage about 5 o'clock in the evening of the 27th.

A young man named Daniels who had given up his gun went with them to see what they would do. He was an eye witness to what transpired. He heard one Wills say that he had shot Hyrum. This Wills, an Irishman, was one of the company of Saints who, with his wife and two children, had come with Joseph Fielding from England. He was an Elder in the Church. It was understood that he received a wound in the arm from a shot fired by Brother Joseph.[7] It hit his wrist

[7]"When the jail in Carthage was assailed, and the mob was pouring murderous volleys into the room occupied by himself and friends, the Prophet turned from the prostrate form of his murdered brother to face death-dealing guns and bravely returned the fire of his assailants 'bringing his man down every time,' and compell-

and went up the bone, of which wound he later died.[8] A ball passed through the jail door and struck Hyrum on one side of the nose just below the left eye. He exclaimed, "I'm a dead man," and fell. Joseph cried out, "Brother Hyrum!"

As Hyrum lay, another ball entered under his chin. Two other balls hit him. John Taylor attempted to get out a back window, but a ball hit him, throwing him back into the room. It had struck his watch, stopping it and pinpointing the time. He had received four balls before he was taken by Brother Willard Richards and put under a bed. He suffered much but survived. Joseph, too, endeavored to escape by a window, but the mob quickly met him and fired. He fell from the window and was taken by the blood-thirsty wretches and set against the curb of the well. Four men shot him in the upperpart of the body. The leader, Williams, then said, "Take his head off," but at this moment, as Daniels stated, a light shone between Joseph and the mob which so affected them that they had no power to touch him. The four men dropped their arms and had to be carried off by their companions. They all rushed away leaving their victims sweltering in their blood.[9]

Their bodies were washed of blood and put in boxes. The next day they were conveyed in two wagons under guard to

---

ing even John Hay, who but reluctantly accords the Prophet any quality of virtue, to confess that he 'made a handsome fight' in the jail."—Smith, *HC, op. cit.*, VI, Introduction, XLI.

A footnote to this statement adds the following: "This is the late Secretary of State John Hay, in the Atlantic Monthly for December, 1869: 'Joe Smith died bravely, he stood by the jam of the door and fired four shots, bringing his man down every time. He shot an Irishman named Wills, who was in the affair from his congenital love of a brawl, in the arm; Gallagher, a Southerner from the Mississippi bottom, in the face; Vorhees, a halfgrown hobbledehoy from Bear Creek, in the shoulder; and another gentleman, whose name I will not mention, as he is prepared to prove an *alibi*, and besides stands six feet two in his moccasins.' In a later paragraph he refers to "the handsome fight in the jail.' "—*Idem*

[8]Daniels' account of Hyrum's death with respect to the part played by Wills remains unconfirmed.

[9]Daniels' account of Joseph Smith's death is unconfirmed. According to the historian Gregg, Daniels was subsequently subpoened as a witness "but the nature of his testimony threw it out of court." Gregg stated further: "Mr. [Willard] Richards, it seems, saw nothing of the blinding light which so overpowered the mobbers, though standing at the window at the time."—Thomas Gregg, *The Prophet of Palmyra—Mormonism* (New York, 1890), pp. 288-289.

Nauvoo. It was the most solemn sight that the eyes of the faithful had ever beheld. They were aware that two of the greatest men had sealed the truth which they held and now bought with their blood thus becoming martyrs with the martyrs of old. In the mind of Mary's brother, the mourner, were these questions: Was this an indication of what had to take place in this dispensation? Was the blood of the sheep again to be shed like that of the shepherds as in former days? Then he prayed: "Father, if it be possible, let this cup pass from us, but if not, let thy will be done and let us be strengthened to endure to the end."[10]

Joseph and Hyrum were of large stature, well proportioned, and with noble appearance. This appearance was by no means lost in death as they lay side by side, prompting the thought to Mary's brother: ". . . for what can make men more noble than to hold the truth of God against his own interests (temporally) to be at war with the world for the salvation of the upright in heart and finally seal that truth with their blood." [11]

The reflective Mourner, in his account, spoke the mind of many wherein he felt as though he wanted to ask forgiveness of Joseph and Hyrum for not mourning them more deeply. Joseph had been brought before rulers and judges scores of times but was never convicted of any crimes — neither Hyrum — and though the Governor said the burning of the printing press was unlawful, yet, the persecutors said they knew the law would not reach them but powder and lead would.

The chief consolation expressed by the dejected Mourner was that in the midst of the affair Joseph and Hyrum had done all they could have done, and the foundation of the great work of God in the last days was laid so that it would be finished by the Twelve Apostles who had been instructed in all things pertaining to the Kingdom of God in the earth. Some, also,

[10]Fielding, Bk. 5, pp. 52-57.
[11]*Ibid.*, p. 49.

besides the Twelve, had received their endowments with further blessings expected at the completion of the Temple.

The Mourner propounded some of his convictions. He believed that Joseph Smith was the only one who had received the keys of the Priesthood of the Kingdom of God on the earth since the days of Peter and the other apostles. Joseph must not only minister the same on earth but also to the whole world of spirits who departed from this life in the time of the broken covenant, even as Jesus did to those before him to the flood; that those who had died without the Priesthood had to remain without it until it was restored to the earth; that it was necessary that they as well as those who were alive should be made acquainted with the ordinances, signs, and tokens of the Priesthood and the terms of admission into the Kingdom in order that they might come forth with those who received it here, so that Joseph was as much needed there as here and perhaps more.

The Mourner — growing more analytical — approached the end of his lamentation by going to the depths of his heart and revealing some of the innermost feelings of his soul. His grief brought from him a bold appraisal of the martyred men who had touched his life so powerfully. He was sure of his declaration that the earth was once more stained with the blood of the Saints, even the anointed of God. Their blood echoed the cry of the former Saints for vengeance to be taken on the wicked, that the earth might be cleansed from the blood of unrighteousness.

Then, in his dissection, he got down to specifics and went to the bottom of the tragedy. He focussed on what he considered the basic cause of it. To his already-stated reflections, he added others in a cogent commentary on plural marriage. These reflections, in a great measure, took the edge off the grief he might have felt, for he thought that Joseph had fulfilled his own purposes, and he was willing to say amen to it. According to the Mourner, the wives of the two martyrs ". . . had been .... them on account of certain principles that had been revealed through Joseph. This seemed to make their lives a .... to them."[12] It seemed as though the Lord had pushed things forward rather prematurely on account of the shortness of Joseph's time. He alluded in particular to the doctrine of women being sealed to men for eternity. It appeared that several had had women sealed to them, and it appeared, in general, to have given great offense to the wives. In some instances, their anger and resentment had risen to a very high pitch, saying it was abomination, whoredom, etc. This, the Mourner felt to be a strong charge against Joseph, especially, and also Hyrum and, now that they were gone, it was aimed at the Twelve. A passage in the Book of Mormon was quoted by some in opposition to the doctrine of plural marriage, wherein it stated that man should have one wife and no concubines.

Then the Mourner leveled off and pointed a finger at the women of Nauvoo. He deplored their lack of understanding and expressed pity for them for their stand on polygamy, saying that he felt sorry for "our women" for it was plain that if the principle of plural marriage were of God, as he believed it to be, their conduct in the matter was very wrong. But for the sealing power and ordinance by which they were sealed to their husbands many would cut themselves off the Kingdom. His own wife, he said, was opposed to it. As for himself, he desired to obtain all the glory he could. Some said that it was because of the "abomination" of plural marriage that Joseph and Hyrum were "cut off." But the Mourner was of the conviction that a man's dominion would be as God's is, over his own creation and the more numerous, the stronger the dominion; but how true that "straight is the gate and narrow is the way that leadeth unto exaltation and eternal duration of lives and few there be that go in thereat."

[12]*Ibid.*, p. 54.

Chapter XVI

Hour of Sorrow

Perhaps, Mary Smith's finest hour was when she rallied after the martyrdom of her beloved husband. She reached deep into the well of her courage and found strength to go forward. At his bier, despite her profound grief, she maintained a reverent composure which stamped her as a woman fortified with a reserve of physical and spiritual strength.

When the bodies of Hyrum and Joseph were returned to Nauvoo, they were taken to the Mansion and prepared for burial. When this was done, the widows, their children, and other family members were admitted to view the bodies. Emma, who was expecting, on first seeing the corpse of her husband, screamed and fell back but was caught and supported by Dimick B. Huntington. Mary, the Patriarch's wife, maintained a relative calmness and composure during the trying scene which was affecting in the extreme.[1] She showed her grief but held on to herself. It was a heartrending ordeal for both widows.

Before Emma finally reached the corpse of her husband, she was removed six times by her kind attendant. Finally, she fell forward to the Prophet's face and kissed him, calling his name, and begging him to speak to her. Hyrum's wife summoned all her strength and entered with her children, having resolved to brave the scene with her little ones.

> She trembled at every step, and nearly fell, but reached her husband's body, kneeled down by him, clasped her arm around his head, turned his pale face upon her heaving bosom, and then a gushing, plaintive wail burst from her lips! "Oh! Hyrum, Hyrum! Have they shot you,

[1]Smith, *HC*, *op. cit.*, VI, 627.

my dear Hyrum—are you dead? Oh, speak to me, my dear husband. I cannot think you are dead, my dear Hyrum." She drew him closer to her bosom, kissed his pale lips and face, put her hands on his brow and brushed back his hair. Her grief seemed to consume her, and she lost all power of utterance.

Her two daughters,[2] and two young children clung, some around her neck, and some to her body, falling prostrate upon the corpse, and shrieking in the wildness of their wordless grief.[3]

It was an excruciating ordeal for the entire Smith family. The weeping and anguish of mother, brothers, wives, and children were heartbreaking. Emma was carried back to her room almost in a state of insensibility. Pale Mary and her children took a long last look and withdrew from the room. After the funeral, she returned to a silent home that had lost its spark.

After the Saints had viewed the bodies, a mock funeral was held. The boxes, which contained the coffins, were taken to the cemetery in the hearse. However, the bodies had been secretly removed to be buried elsewhere in order to prevent the enemies of the martyrs from gaining possession of them. Then, sometime later, Emma Smith decided to rebury the bodies for greater security and notified Mary of the plan. But in the late afternoon, she sent word that the plan had

---

[2]While only two daughters are mentioned, there were three still at home: Jerusha, Sarah, and Martha. It is written of Martha: "Her most vivid childhood memory, however, was the death of her father when she was but three years old. Hyrum had passed uninjured through many dangers, but this time Mary seemed to know what had happened. Far into the night she walked the floor while little Martha, just recovering from the measles, lay and watched her. . . . Later Martha was wrapped in a blanket and a man carried her a block from their home to the Mansion House and let her look at the bodies of her father and uncle."—Harris, *op. cit.*, p. 12.

[3]This account given by B. W. Richmond appeared in the *Chicago Times* (reprinted in the *Deseret News*, November 27, 1875, Salt Lake City). Richmond, an anti-Mormon and formerly a resident of Palmyra, New York, where he knew the Smith family, was a guest at the Mansion House at the time of the martyrdom of the Smiths. His fortuitous and graphic account movingly depicts the grief of Mary and Emma Smith and their families. Earlier, he had visited each of their homes. In connection with his visit to the Hyrum Smith home, he gave this description: "At the home of Hyrum, a little way off, the scene was not less heartrending. His wife had gathered her family of four children in the sitting-room, and the youngest [Martha] about four years old, sat on her lap. The poor and disabled that fed at the table of her husband, had come in and formed a group of about twenty around the room. They were all sobbing and weeping, each expressing his grief in his own peculiar way. Mrs. Smith seemed stupefied with horror."

been postponed. Mary retired at an early hour with her children. In the night, she awoke with a strange presentiment that something was wrong. Everything, inside and out, was wrapped in the silence and darkness of night. She tossed restlessly, her faculties acutely alert. Her intuition communicated to her a feeling that something strange was either impending or happening.

The hour of midnight found her still sleepless and uneasy. She arose and paced the floor then peered out the window. Things were too quiet to suit her — a good night for ghoulish enemies to execute their diabolical plan to remove the bodies of her husband and his brother. Impelled by a sudden urge, she dressed quickly, threw a shawl around her shoulders, and slipped outside. A cool breeze was coming in from the river. Silently, she stole toward the burial spot, crossing the road to the Nauvoo House. There, she came upon dark forms moving around the graves in the basement which was up to the joists in construction.

Four men worked rapidly in a dim light under the direction of Emma Smith. The men were Dimick B. Huntington, William D. Huntington, Jonathan B. Holmes, and Gilbert Goldsmith.[4] The caskets with the bodies were cautiously removed and taken to the bee house (also called the spring house) and buried side by side. The house was then moved and placed over their graves. After the reburial, all traces of the action were concealed. Mary remained to see that all was done to her satisfaction. The new location was twenty-five paces in a direct line from the southeast corner of the Old Homestead[5] where the Prophet and family had lived. Undoubtedly, Mary had agreed to the removal of her husband's body. However, as an interested party, she was entitled to be informed of the hour and be present when it took place.

---

[4]Smith, *HC, op. cit.*, VI, 628.

[5]Brigham H. Roberts, "Truth Told Regarding Prophet's Burial Place," *Deseret News*, Sec. 2, (Jan. 1928), pp. 1 and 6.

Failure to let her know was disquieting — an unfortunate mistake.

After the death of her husband, Mary Smith had frequent callers who came to express their sympathy and love in her hour of bereavement. The lingering grief of the Saints was genuine and heartfelt. On the occasion when the bodies of the martyrs were returned to Nauvoo, the effect on the community was overwhelming. Each side of the line of march was massed with mourners, reaching past the Temple to the Mansion House. They manifested their grief in spontaneous weeping and lamentation that grew louder through the throng and along the *via dolorosa* as the procession passed. Part of their grief was because they had allowed the tragedy at Carthage to happen. The scene touched deeply, and the very air seemed heavy with sorrow. There followed a period of soul-searching, a period of spiritual rebirth, coupled with a resolve to make amends, to do right by Joseph and Hyrum.

Out of their grief, many came to the door of Mary Smith to pay their respects. Some did so with a loaf, a cake, a jar of fruit or preserves as a manifestation of their sympathy and love. One of the callers was Wilford Woodruff who was preparing to depart to preside over the British Mission. On August 23, 1844, he visited first Emma Smith to whose life he sought to bring consolation in the hour of her great sorrow. She gave him a piece of oak for a cane. It had been taken from Joseph's coffin. In addition, she presented him with a pair of white cotton gloves. To his wife, she gave a handkerchief. The visitors were to cherish these things the rest of their lives.

They next called on Mary Smith to show their love and respect. She was most interested in President Woodruff's mission to her native land. Her ever present desire was that her loved ones in England would one day have a change of heart and affiliate with the Church, although she did not expect an expression of their sympathy upon learning of her husband's death. The visit was highlighted by Mary giving to

Elder Woodruff several locks of hair taken from the heads of Joseph, Hyrum, Samuel, and Don Carlos, the brothers who had passed away while engaged in a noble cause. In connection with this event, Elder Woodruff stated, "'I also obtained some hair of the Quorum of the Twelve Apostles. My purpose in getting it was that I might put a part of each of these collections in the knob of my staff as a relic of those noble men, the master spirits of the nineteenth century.'"[6] He held these relics as something sacred during his life time.

On September 14, 1844, a knock came on Mary Smith's door. The visitors, this time, were President Brigham Young, the new leader, Heber C. Kimball, and George A. Smith.[7] It was, without a doubt, a pleasant surprise for Mary to have these good friends call on her, to inquire about her health, and her situation in general. It would be characteristic for her to reply that she and her family were in good health and getting along as well as could be expected; that with the harvest on the farm, they had sufficient to eat and to make them comfortable. Undoubtedly, another purpose of this visit was to inquire concerning the Temple penny fund over which she had jurisdiction. It was kind of them to call and good for Mary to know of their interest in her welfare.

Like the water in the great river by her house that rolled on toward the Caribbean, life went on for Mary Smith. The old homestead stood not far from the water's edge, allowing the family a sweeping view up and down the river. The sloping, grassy bank was a pleasant place for the children to play. They could watch the boats that passed or tied up at the wharf. The "Maid of Iowa," a river boat which had been purchased by the Church, berthed at the wharf near the Nauvoo House. This allowed the children a chance to watch the passengers leave or board the boat. The children at play could dig their toes into the wet sand on the river's edge and build

---

[6]Matthias F. Cowley, *Wilford Woodruff—History of Life and Labors* (Salt Lake City, 1909), pp. 227-228.

[7]Smith, *HC*, *op. cit.*, VII, 270.

sand castles to their delight. They could pick wild flowers and make garlands and bouquets.

The memory of the locale remained vividly fixed in the minds of the children after their departure from Nauvoo. In particular, Joseph F. and Martha Ann, years later when visiting together, would reminisce about events, places, and people they recalled in Nauvoo. Sometimes their memories would differ a little. Joseph would say, "Martha, you are not quite right about that." Whereupon, Martha would reply, "I remember it distinctly, Joseph." Then she would argue a bit thinking she might stir her brother's memory to agree with hers.

At the time of the martyrdom of the Smith brothers, Nauvoo had a population of approximately 15,000 and 2,500 homes including 500 in the suburbs. Conversions were running high in England and, in addition to the English Saints who had arrived in Nauvoo, nearly 1,000 were waiting to come to America. These English members were mostly tradesmen and craftsmen which made it difficult to absorb them immediately into the economy of the community owing to the lack of industries. The English Saints made a real contribution to Nauvoo with their penchant for creating neat, orderly homes and gardens. For three to four miles up and down the river, Nauvoo presented a city of dwellings ornamented with gardens making it most beautiful. Many of the houses were but shanties built of logs, some of poles covered with plaster, some frame, and some two story brick houses. However, neat fences enclosed most of them and the well-kept vegetable gardens. Flowers were an added attraction about the homes—marigolds, hearts-ease, and lady-slippers grew in profusion. Two mills were in operation, and many other buildings for mechanical labor came into being.[8]

However, the building on the hill was the pride of Nauvoo and a thing of beauty. The House of the Lord was moving along rapidly in construction. Brigram Young said of it:

[8] *Times and Seasons*, (Liverpool, England), Oct. 1, 1842.

There are thirty capitols around the Temple, each one composed of five stones, viz. one base stone, representing the sun rising just above the clouds, the lower part (obscured), the third stone represents two hands each holding a trumpet, and the last two stones form a cap over the trumpet stone, and these all form the capitol, the average cost of which is about four hundred dollars each. These stones are beautifully cut, especially the face and trumpet stones, and are an evidence of great skill in the architect and ingenuity on the part of the stone cutters. They present a very pleasing and noble appearance, and seem very appropriate in their places. The first capitol was set on the 23rd of September last, and out of that time the workman lost about three weeks through bad weather and having to wait for stone.[9]

In the meantime, the leaders were getting a grasp of things and picking up all the details of Church business. They were chiefly concerned with advancing the work on the Temple but had other temporal matters to think about as well. On Thursday, December 5, 1844, an important meeting was held at Nauvoo of which the following are the minutes:

Afternoon, a council was held in the Recorders office, Pres. B. Young and H. C. Kimball of the Twelve, were present, also N. K. Whitney and George Miller, Trustees, and Alpheus Cutler and Reynolds Cahoon, the Temple Committee. The Council was called for the purpose of devising means to raise the sum of $3,100, which is due from the Trustees to several individuals for Church lands, and which will have to be paid within three months or land be forfeited, worth from ten to fifteen thousand dollars. About one thousand of the aforesaid sum must be paid in a few days.

After conversing some time on the prospect of raising funds, Pres. Young said that his feelings were to draw the money lying in the possession of Sister Mary Smith and Mercy R. Thompson and A. Cutler, which money has been donated by the Sisters of the Church, by paying one cent a week for the purpose of purchasing the nails and glass for the Temple and which amounted to five and six hundred dollars, already collected. It is considered wisdom to do this to save the Church property from the hands of our enemies, and the straightened circumstances under which the Trustees labor in consequence of persecution and oppression, are considered sufficient to justify the course. It is also considered certain that the money will be ready by the time the nails and glass are needed

[9]Journal History, Dec. 5, 1844.

for the Temple and that the money will be saving so much interest, whereas at the present it is useless.

The suggestion of Pres. Young seemed to meet the feeling of all the brethren and it was concluded to draw an order for the money on Mrs. Mary Smith and Mercy R. Thompson which was immediately done Friday 6.[10]

According to the wishes of the brethren, the pennies were removed from the pile of brick which Hyrum had intended to use in the construction of a new house, counted out, and put to timely use. The penny fund, conceived in the mind of Mercy Thompson, through the inspiration of the Lord in answer to her prayer, and nurtured and fostered by Mary and Mercy together, played an unexpected role in the affairs of the Church. The available pennies helped the Church to maintain its credit at a time of dire need. The money was replaced and available when it came time to purchase the nails and glass to finish the Temple.

After the martyrdom of Joseph and Hyrum Smith, things were quiet for awhile in Nauvoo, but this did not last long. The mobocrats regained their courage and started abusing outlying families, burning their homes, stealing their cattle, and kidnaping their menfolk.

The death of the Prophet Joseph had left the Saints bewildered and uncertain as to who the new leader should be. There was danger of the Church breaking up completely as small factions developed behind men ambitious to be the new leader. It was a critical time. However, the order of succession was well understood by the Quorum of Twelve and the crisis passed. The Twelve, united under Brigham Young, the president of the Quorum, were sustained as the presiding officers of the Church by the uplifted hands of the Saints in an assembled body. The Quorum, eventually, would appoint a new Church president.

The following year, 1845, a new war of attrition against the Saints blazed into full fury. The scattered families gathered

---

[10] *Idem*

into Nauvoo for safety. The mobs were resolved on driving the Mormons from the State. On September 22, 1845, a mass meeting was held in Quincy, Illinois, by the opposition to take united action against the Church. As a result, a resolution was drawn up asking the Saints to leave the State as speedily as possible.

Brigham Young replied that the Mormon people proposed to leave the country the next spring for some remote place. He asked for time to get ready and for the assistance of the non-Mormon populace in disposing of personal and real property to obtain means sufficient to move the poor, fatherless, and widows. He pleaded for relief from vexatious law suits and for help in procuring dry goods, groceries, good oxen, beef cattle, sheep, wagons, teams, and harnesses in fair exchange for their property. The proposition to leave was accepted by their enemies, but the persecutors were not inclined to render assistance nor buy property that they knew would be abandoned and be theirs for nothing.[11]

During the fall and winter months of 1845 and 1846, hasty preparations were made by the leaders to remove the entire Mormon population in the spring. In the meantime, work on the Temple, which the Lord had commanded them to build, continued with increased diligence, as if there were no thought of moving until that structure was completed. The building was far enough along to hold the General Conference of the Church in it, October 1845. In December, the ordinance work was commenced and continued day and night to afford the Saints an opportunity to receive their endowments.[12] By January 1, 1846, the assembly room was nearing completion. On May 1, 1846, after the majority of the people had departed

---

[11]Smith, *ECH, op. cit.*, p. 397.

[12]The endowment comprises a course of instruction relating to the journey of man from his premortal state of existence, through mortality, and into eternity. Certain covenants, tokens, and signs are made known by which he may attain exaltation in the celestial kingdom.

from the city, the Temple was publicly dedicated in the presence of about three hundred persons.[13]

The exodus from Nauvoo commenced on Wednesday, February 4, 1846, as the first Saints left and crossed the Mississippi River. On the 6th of February, Bishop George Miller and a company with six wagons made the crossing. Commencing a few days later, the work of ferrying the Saints to the Iowa side continued day and night. Elder Parley P. Pratt left Nauvoo on February 14. The following day, President Brigham Young, Willard Richards, and George A. Smith, with a large company, crossed the Mississippi on the ice. They went on about nine miles to Sugar Creek in Lee County where a temporary camp was formed for the exiles fleeing Nauvoo. They tarried on Sugar Creek for some time where a number of council meetings were held and the needs of the people duly considered.[14]

With the coming of warmer weather, the journey was resumed on March 1, 1846. The homeless people endured great suffering and many physical hardships, as they made their sad and weary way across Iowa. The weather was inclement with heavy rain storms. The roads were deep in mud and, with several hundred wagons slogging along, many became bogged down in the mire. Coupled with their physical discomforts, including hunger and cold, were the pain and grief of having to part with their homes, surroundings, graves, and many little things that had become part of their lives, such as a grape arbor, fruit trees and flower gardens. Behind them were their silent dwellings, doors open, gates ajar, furniture that had to be left, and cold hearthstones—all sacrificed to a greater thing in their lives.

As they crossed Iowa, the outcasts passed through several temporary stations which had been set up by an advance company under Colonel Stephen Markham. This vanguard built roads and bridges, sought out suitable locations where

---

[13] *Ibid.*, p. 400.
[14] *Ibid.*, p. 403.

shelter could be provided and where fields could be planted to provide food for those to come later. Some 145 miles west of Nauvoo, on the east fork of the Grand River, the advance company established the temporary settlement of Garden Grove on April 24, 1846. Mount Pisgah was established twenty-seven miles west of Garden Grove.[15]

At last, the Missouri River was reached. Brigham Young, Heber C. Kimball, Parley P. Pratt, and others arrived first, June 14, 1846, at a point above Council Bluffs, and were received well by the friendly Pottawatamie Indians. The leaders decided later to cross the river and move back on the bluffs on land inhabited by the Omaha Indians, where springs of good water were found. This location provided better protection against Indian incursions, although, as a whole, the Indians were friendly, extending to the Saints many favors.[16]

The site selected on the west bank was, in due course, converted from its virgin state to a bustling community. Streets were laid out, a council house constructed, many homes built, dugout-shelters established, together with meeting places, including a school. A blacksmith shop and grist mill were erected on a nearby stream. The place was to be a wintering point and was given the name "Winter Quarters." Today, it is called "Florence" located six miles north of Omaha, Nebraska.

Nauvoo was not entirely evacuated by the Mormons until the fall of 1846. The remnant of the Saints included many who did not have transportation to leave and many who were sick, infirm, and indigent. Some were engaged in temple work to the last. Mary Smith, her sister, and brother, together with their families were among the remnants and the last to leave.

[15] *Ibid.*, p. 406.
[16] *Ibid.*, pp. 407-408.

Chapter XVII

Mary Leaves Nauvoo

The months following the loss of her husband were a time of important decisions for Mary Smith. Having been close to the governing circle of the Church and familiar with the facts, she hardly dared hope for any mercy from the evil machinations and intrigues of their enemies. New pressures and dangers were in prospect. However, the brief lull that followed the outrage at Carthage allowed her time to make some recovery from her great shock and heartache. But never would she bridge the awful void in her life nor the utter loneliness caused by the loss of her dear one. Still, sweet was her satisfaction, sanctified in her soul, for having had him as a companion for a few years and having borne him two children.

Her precious Joseph F. and Martha Ann were now even more important to her. She must look to their future as well as that of Hyrum's other children. Being a sensible woman, she knew that this was no time for self-pity nor bitterness; there was work to do. With determination, she marshalled her forces and brought to bear the full resources of her mind to meet her many problems. Her primary preoccupation was in obtaining sufficient food for her large family. Aside from this, her mind was engaged in planning for the future. In this, she had the benefit of her brother's counsel and the help of her sister Mercy.

The resurgence of mob activity and the agitation of citizen groups for the removal of the Mormons from the State had put tremendous pressure upon the new leaders. Brigham Young, a tough-minded realist, proved equal to the occasion. Like a military commander, he saw the weakness of his tactical situation, hemmed in as he was by hostile forces, and without present capability of sustaining his position. The only practical solution was to work for time and effect a strategic withdrawal through terrain not in possession of enemy forces.

The decision to evacuate Nauvoo was electric to the Saints, particularly to Mary, filling her with an elevation of spirit and mingled emotions. She was not taken completely by surprise by the announcement, as she knew that the Prophet Joseph and her husband had in mind such a move. Yet, the dramatic decision caught her psychologically unprepared for its full implication. She was now faced with a big decision of her own.

She had noticed the significant and instant reaction of the Mormon community upon receiving the evacuation announcement and how it aroused the hearts of the faithful impelling them to great exertion to make ready for the day. This, she saw, was good tonic for a dispirited people so recently cast into deep grief and dismay by the death of their two leaders. A virtual transformation took place before her eyes. A group of up-and-doing men were shouldering responsibility and supplying the impetus and leadership needed.

Faced with her own decision, Mary had many reasons for not leaving Nauvoo. She had a roof over her head, the old loved home, which was dear to her and rich in memories of her husband. She was a widow with many dependents. It took means, wagons, horses, oxen, and supplies of many kinds to support a long journey and begin life in a new place. Everyone was poor; she could not ask for help and expect to get it. In fact, she seemed all but forgotten in the frenzy of preparation to leave. Emma Smith and Mother Smith were offered every assistance and encouragement by the brethren. Assistance was eventually given to Mary and accepted, but it was long in coming, and the brunt was left for her shoulders. Emma declined all inducements, but Mother Smith indicated that she would go if her remains could be brought back to

Nauvoo for burial. This was promised; however, she remained in Nauvoo.

Mary's spirit said, "Go." She knew down deep that was what she must do. Her brother was in a reconciled mood to leave. She recoiled at the thought of being separated from him. His presence gave her comfort. Too, she needed the Church. To remain behind was to be severed from the vine, to wither and die. Also, to stay might mean sinking into oblivion for herself and children. Of further concern to her was what life would be like in Nauvoo after the departure of the Saints. Who would there be to fill the need for social contacts and companionship? There would be Mother Smith and Emma and probably some of the other Smith widows. There was also William Smith who lived at a distance, but they saw little of him. What kind of companions would be available for her children? The prospects, indeed, were pretty dim.

Prior to Carthage, Mary and Emma were often together. Like Mary, Emma was a strong personality, but actually they were not close in common interests after the martyrdom. They came from different cultural and social backgrounds. There was reason for the relationship between them to be strained after the reburial episode. Too, Emma had broken with the new leaders. They would not accept her oldest son ahead of the Twelve, as the successor to his father, with her acting in a regency role until he was old enough to assume his duties. This was not the order of the Priesthood. Authority of leadership resided in the Apostles, as at the death of the Savior, and could not be thus conferred or delegated. So there was little about Emma that could influence Mary to remain in Nauvoo.

A move was afoot to pressure Mary and family to remain in Nauvoo. She was approached by certain members of the Smith family (persons that were out of harmony with the Church), who endeavored to persuade her not to make the journey but to remain behind. It was presented to her that if she refused to follow Brigham Young and the Twelve, she would not be harmed but could remain in peace in Nauvoo.[1]

When the vanguard of refugees from Nauvoo crossed the Mississippi to begin the journey to the distant West, young John Smith, the elder son of Hyrum Smith, quietly went along in the company of Heber C. Kimball. This angered his uncle William Smith, an apostate. Presumptuously, he visited Mary Smith and raised his voice in angry expostulation against her for having permitted John to be "spirited away." He demanded the return of the son of the deceased Patriarch. Mary, quietly and firmly, refused to accede to the angry man's demand.[2] As she faced him, it was a tense moment. Her heart was pounding, but she maintained her composure. She saw William looming large in her path against the realization of her objectives. Without flinching, she looked him in the eye and stood her ground. He finally left the house in a fit of temper.

He had underestimated Mary, thinking he could handle her. He found her difficult to intimidate. His defeat added to his anger. His approach was wrong, a fatal affront, pushing Mary farther from her husband's people. While he was heaping abuse upon her, her young son Joseph F. was listening in an upstairs chamber into which ran the pipe of the living room stove below, thus enabling him to hear distinctly the voice of his uncle. Joseph F. wished that he were bigger to protect his mother and give this man what he deserved for his harsh words.[3]

However, relations were better with other members of the Smith family. Mary had true esteem for Mother Smith and tender regard for the children of the late Samuel H. Smith and his widow Levira. Samuel had died soon after his brothers Joseph and Hyrum from complications brought on by the exertion incident to a desperate ride on a swift horse to escape his pursuers. He was on his way to Carthage in behalf of

---

[1]Smith, *ECH, op. cit.,* p. 138.
[2]Gates, *op. cit.,* p. 13.
[3]*Idem*

his imprisoned brothers when evil men tried to intercept him. Samuel was the fourth son to die in the Mormon cause. His first wife had died in 1841, leaving him with three small children. He had married again—Levira Clark. They had had two children—one died. However, after Samuel's death, his widow—expecting again—was in a delicate condition. Mary Smith had compassion for the family. Her kindness was described by Mary B. Smith Norman (daughter of Samuel H. and Mary Bailey Smith) in her autobiographical sketch, outlined below, in part.

After the death of Samuel, his wife, Levira, went to see her parents who lived some distance from Nauvoo. She gave the older children permission to play on the river bank but admonished them not to venture into the water. She told them that she would be back as quickly as possible. Then taking her little one, Levira, with her, she left them. It was well into the afternoon when she went. The children left at home were happy in the thought of the long play hours afforded them. They made their way to the river and amused themselves playing in the sand and gathering pretty cornealions which, at that time, were very abundant at that point on the banks of the Mississippi. They played until the sinking sun warned them that they had better return home. When they reached the house, they found the door locked. They sat down on the doorstep to await their stepmother's coming and finally fell asleep. But Levira couldn't return; she had taken dangerously ill.

Grandmother Smith sent for little Mary B. and cared for her a few days. The grandmother's old age and ills worked against caring for the child longer. In the meantime, Aunt Mary Smith had been caring for the young brother and sister. She also took charge of Mary B. Every night the children would meet and sit on the steps of the house that had been their home until their Aunt Mary would send for them and have them brought to her home.

Then came a day when, for some reason, they expected

their stepmother home in the evening, but she did not come. When their Aunt Mary's handyman came for them, they objected to going and cried bitterly. A boy had come with him to assist in carrying them. But the handyman sent the boy back to state the condition of affairs. The boy soon returned with a message not to grieve them by trying to bring them against their will but to wait until they were asleep and then bring them. Left to themselves, they huddled together and were soon asleep. The next thing they remembered was being awakened to eat their supper. This act of kindness, "so delicate, so tender, so beautiful," lingered in the mind of Mary B. Norman during her long life, but she felt unable to express in words the gratitude she had always felt. "Aunt Mary Fielding Smith," she stated, "was the second wife of my father's brother Hyrum Smith and the mother of President Joseph F. Smith. I will give a pen picture of her. She had a fine personality, was at that time tall and rather slender, fair in complexion, and a perfect type of English gentlewoman. To complete my story-Aunt Mary took care of us until we were otherwise provided for. . . ."[4]

Young Samuel H. B. Smith and probably the others stayed with Mary Smith during the following winter. Their stepmother did not return for the reason that, while she was at the home of her parent's-just three weeks after her husband's death-she gave birth to another child which lived only a short time.

The above story tells much concerning Mary's love of children. Her home was already crowded, but there was room for a few more. She demonstrated an outgoing nature by the way she cared for Samuel's little ones. She took them under her wing, watched out for them, and mothered them as if they were her own. This provides an indication of her generous feeling and sympathy for the unfortunate. Also, in the above description of her, we see a lady not only tall and fair to look

---

[4]Ruby K. Smith, *Mary Bailey* (Salt Lake City 1954), pp. 92-93; Mary B. Norman, Autobiography, MS.

upon but a person with tact, understanding, and goodness of soul.

During the last days of Nauvoo, as the mantle of darkness descended with its curse upon the stricken city, Mary Smith was occupied in the Temple doing ordinance work, etc. In this, she found satisfaction. She had opened to her in each endowment and sealing, in which she participated, the majesty of the Gospel. She and her sister Mercy had been present in the Temple at 3:45 p.m. on December 10, 1845, with a select group which completed arrangements of the east room preparatory to giving endowments. At 4:25 p.m., Elders Brigham Young and Heber C. Kimball commenced administering the ordinances of endowment. Joseph Fielding was also present. The work went on through the night until 3:30 a.m., during which time thirty persons, including Mary Smith, received their endowments. The next day, Mother Lucy Smith and Mercy R. Thompson received their endowments.[5] Mary became a worker in the Temple. Concerning this, her daughter Martha Ann wrote: "She worked in the Temple for three weeks. I was with her all the time."[6] Mercy was also a Templeworker. Of this, she stated: "I remained with my sister until the Temple was finished so far that the ordinances of the holy priesthood could be administered there, when I was called by

[5]"She [Bathshebh W. Smith] was one of the very few who had their endowments in the Prophet's lifetime, and it is worthy of mention here that her testimony is that the ordinances in our temples today are exactly the same as was that of the first ordinances given under the Prophet's direction. She had her blessings in 1843 in Nauvoo. The services were held in a large room over the [Prophet's] store. Here was given the initial blessings to the Apostles then in Nauvoo, and here began the mighty work which is now of such magnitude. She remembers the names of the first couples who received endowments, and these were: The Prophet and wife, the Patriarch and wife, Brigham Young and wife, Heber C. Kimball and wife, Dr. Willard Richards and wife, Father Smith and wife and Father Joseph Smith and wife, Bishop Whitney and wife and Amassa Lyman and wife."—*Young Woman's Journal*, IV (Apr. 1893), 295. Accordingly, the endowment which Mary Smith received December 10, 1845, was a second endowment.

In further regard thereto, in Fielding, Bk. 5, p. 75, it states: ". . . on Friday, the 12th [Jan. 1846] I and my wife received our endowments, having formerly received it in the days of Joseph and Hyrum, but it is now given in a more perfect manner because of better conveniences. The 12 are very strict in attending to the true and proper form. On Sunday the 21st, 986 had received their endowment."

[6]Harris Centennial letter.

President Young to take up abode there to assist in the female department, which I did laboring night and day, keeping my children with me. My beloved friend mother Granger staying there also. On my return I commenced making preparation for the journey west. I remained in Nauvoo until September, when I with my sister and family, crossed the Mississippi River a day or two before the mob commenced firing on the city."[7]

For Mary Smith, it was no easy thing to get away from Nauvoo. It is difficult fully to appreciate the magnitude of the burden that rested upon her shoulders in undertaking to leave. Probably no other pioneer was placed in such an inextricable position as that in which Mary found herself. She had too many dependents for such an undertaking. She could hardly take them all and provide for their needs. If anything looked hopeless, her situation did. Certainly, it took a powerful desire and will to do to accomplish the seemingly impossible. Her anxiety of mind, assuredly, was tremendous. The sleepless nights definitely were many. To say the least, it was a sad predicament for her to be in, shackeled by a web of circumstances ordinarily beyond the ken of women to solve and of such complexity as to defeat the strongest person. If she wavered, it is understandable for she had every excuse not to budge an inch from Nauvoo. In reading on, the mind begins to grasp what this spunky woman was really up against and what she accomplished.

Her dilemma was apparent in the spring and early summer of 1846. During this time, she either prolonged her decision to leave or else expected to achieve some calculated economic advantage in waiting as long as possible. Her brother Joseph

---

[7]Thompson Centennial letter.

Also, in the *Young Woman's Journal, op. cit.*, 291, it is stated: "She [Mercy Thompson] went to work in the Nauvoo Temple the very first day and worked there constantly until the work was over. . . . She had charge of the washing and ironing of clothes for the workers, a labor that often kept her up nearly all night. She also at one time had charge of the cooking department. . . . As Aunt Mercy says she worked at one time or another in every department of the work in the Nauvoo Temple. She had one child, a daughter, and she was obliged to take her with her. She lived in the temple, the baby sometimes being in there for days without ever seeing outside the temple."

Fielding seemed to have made up his mind that their position was untenable. His journal reflects some of his difficulties:

> But to return to Nauvoo where I spent the summer for want of means to get away. I sold my house and 20 acres of land for 200 dol's in trade, taking 2 horses a waggon [sic], a coat—cloth, and a few ($4\frac{1}{2}$ dol's) in cash. The land was in good cultivation; 120 rods of good rail fence; a frame house 16 feet by 24 filled in with bricks; a pretty garden; a number of apple trees and peach trees just ready to bear fruit; and an excellent well 21 feet deep, not 2 miles from the Temple. I paid for the land in its wild state 160 dol's, built a house, etc., so that the price of the whole would not near pay the cost . . . One of the horses I took for the place I soon found to be baulky [sic], and I only got in trade for her a small yoke of young oxen.[8]

This situation, multiplied many times, is indicative of how the Mormons were victimized in a pitiless, property-sales squeeze. They had to get out but received little help from outsiders. Each sale was on a take-it or leave-it basis. It was strictly a buyers' market. The price index for Mormon property was in terms of the desperate minimum needs of the seller at the time and whatever a buyer would pay. Joseph Fielding loved his little place—the humble house, garden, fence, and fruit trees. To leave all and lose his investment caused him much sorrow. He reluctantly sold and vacated the premises. He recorded further: "Soon after I sold my place I removed my family and goods to the house on my sister's farm called brother Hyrum's where my sister thought of planting grain but we found it to be useless, and I did not so much as plant the smallest garden stuff."[9]

In wanting to plant some grain, Mary's practical mind was thinking right. It would give her breadstuff to take with her if she left, and she might be able to sell the rest. Yet, one might suspect that she was doubtful about being able to leave Nauvoo. Still, Joseph's success in disposing of his farm, even though the buyer drove a hard bargain, must have lent encouragement to Mary that she could do the same. But no doubt the mere

[8]Fielding, Bk. 5, p. 90.
[9]*Ibid.*, p. 91.

pittance Joseph got for his place left Mary apprehensive. She must sell or exchange her property to an advantage or remain in Nauvoo. She wracked her brain, twisted and turned, and thought of many conceivable plans to solve her dilemma.

At his death, Hyrum Smith owned considerable realty in and around Nauvoo. The property consisted of farm land, some of it hills and hollows, amounting to 243 acres,[10] suitable for farming and grazing sheep and cattle; also, fifteen city lots and some fractions of lots and at least two houses. If Mary could sell this property to some fair-minded person, it would enable her to get outfitted to go west. It would also enable her to satisfy the claim of Lovina to her portion of her father's estate. Lovina had married Lorin Walker, June 23, 1844. They were pressing for their share.

To satisfy the interest of Lovina and her husband, Mary, the legal guardian of John, Jerusha, Sarah, Joseph F., and Martha Ann Smith, acting through her attorney, George Edmunds, Jr., petitioned the Circuit Court of Hancock County, State of Illinois, to sell certain specified property in behalf of the Walkers, together with the city lots for the support and education of the children still at home, with due regard for her own dower right. The Circuit Court, May Term, 1846, sitting in Chancery, authorized the petitioner to sell the property after posting notice in five public places for a period of six weeks and publication in the nearest newspaper for six weeks before the day of sale, the sale to proceed at the door of the Post Office in Nauvoo to the highest bidder.[11]

Two bids were received for the property. The Trustees-in-Trust of the Church, Almon W. Babbitt, Joseph L. Heywood, and John S. Fullmer whom Brigham Young had left in Nauvoo to carry on the finishing of the Temple, dispose of Church property, and fit out the Saints to go west, entered a bid of $500 for 103 acres of land and nine city lots.[12] This had the

---

[10]Hancock Circuit Court records, Recorder's Office, Carthage, Hancock County, Illinois, Aug. 9, 1846, p. 229.

[11]*Idem*

[12]Hancock Circuit Court records, *op. cit.*, p. 230.

effect of protecting the property from sale to an unconscionable lower bidder. John Hartwell, a citizen of Nauvoo, bid $600 for the same property and $400 for the Hyrum Smith farm of 127 acres, with improvements, and two city lots.[13] The sale of this latter property to Hartwell was consummated for $400. Apparently, Hartwell withdrew his offer of $600 for the other property. It went to the Trustees for $500.[14] The portion of it made up of city lots was sold by the Trustees at a later time, November 8, 1848, to Phineas Kimball, Orange County, Vermont, for $500.[15]

The Walkers received $200, in hand paid, for their share, leaving $700 for Mary Smith and her children at home. These sales opened up the way for Mary to leave Nauvoo. It gave her a boost in morale as well as the means to procure the things she desperately needed to get away. Whether the Trustees paid her in cash, stock, or equipment made little difference.[16]

She required at least six wagons and teams to accomplish the big move, as she had to transport eighteen people, counting herself, and, in addition, the necessary supplies and equipment plus all their baggage. She undoubtedly had one or more wagons of her own, but would need still more with sufficient teams of good quality. However, having the means to obtain her additional requirements did not necessarily lighten her burden. Wagons and teams were at a premium because of the critical demand for them by the earlier evacuees from Nauvoo. Accordingly, the problem was posed as to where Mary would find the needed transport and teams. She would have to go to the nearest communities that might be disposed to help her. For a certainty, Mary still had her problems.

Toward the end of summer, the mob-militia was begin-

---

[13]Deed, recorded in Deed Book "Q" pp. 302-303 Recorder's Office, Carthage, Hancock County, Illinois, Mary Smith, Grantor, to John Hartwell.

[14]Hancock Circuit Court records, *op. cit.*, pp. 229-231.

[15]Deed, Vol. 4, p. 141, Recorder's Office, Carthage, Hancock County, Illinois.

[16]Mercy Thompson also realized something for her property: $260 for Lot 1 in Block 149 (Book U, page 235, June 30, 1846) and $50 for Lot 2 in Block 11 (Book V, page 126, Aug. 17, 1846). The first sale was to William Cooper, Jr. and the second to Eliza Dollinger. —Recorder's office, Carthage, Illinois.

ning to press in on Nauvoo. Of this, Joseph Fielding journalized:

> Not long after this [his move to the Hyrum Smith farm] the mob began to collect and to threaten us with extinction, first at Golden's point to the number of 200 or 300 from which they dispersed in fear, but soon began to gather again near Carthage where they lay encamped a number of weeks to the number of 900 as far as I can gather until early in September [1846]. They marched into Nauvoo; my two sisters Smith and Thompson and myself with our families had just got over the River Mississippi with all our goods except two boat loads before they came in contact with the citizens. They came and camped on the farm [Smith] that I had just left. They took this course to avoid any ambushment that might be laid for them. From there they sent balls into the city but before they came near the Temple they were met and repulsed but I shall not attempt to record the whole scene of outrage. The poor Saints had to flee, sick as well. They hastened to the river but the citizens judged it not best to let them leave when they were so much needed, but the sick and the women and children got over as far as they could. I went down to the bank of the river and found many of the Saints in distress. Some had left their husbands. In the battle the cannons roared tremendously on both sides for several days.[17]

None too soon, Mary and her sister and brother had commenced making final preparations for their journey west. She had made her big decision and cast her lot with the body of Saints who had crossed the big river. Her efforts in preparing to leave were heroic. It was a stupendous undertaking — a momentous thing in her life. The last days in Nauvoo were chaotic. Around them were scenes of turmoil in the stricken city — people frantically packing, loading, and hastily departing; wagons passing toward the river; neighbors saying farewell—great choices to make, decisions to reach—Mary's feverish activity to prepare for a great adventure. Then there was the last night in the beloved home; the scanty supper; chests and

---

[17]Fielding, Bk. 5, pp. 100-101.

The Hyrum Smith farm was the scene of actual military operations in the Battle of Nauvoo, as disclosed by the following: "The mob made another attempt to flank on the south and succeeded in getting into the orchard on the Smith farm where they were repulsed and retired to the brow of the hill near the west part of Hyrum Smith's field where they encamped and entrenched themselves." —Journal History, Sept. 11, 1846.

baggage crowding the floor ready to be taken to the wharf; Mary working late into the night finishing the packing, trying to decide how to take a few more cherished belongings — her face tense and sober.

The beseiged city lay quiet, awaiting the final thrust of the adversary. Tension filled the air. The firing of muskets on the outskirts by the mob-militia left no doubt of the serious plight of the doomed city. Come morning, exertion and more exertion, then all in readiness; a long last look at a silent abode and a secret grave — henceforth only a memory. Then teams straining, wheels turning, and for the refugees no turning back. They set their faces irrevocably to the west. Heavy wagons moved out toward the Mississippi for loading on the flatboat.

All that transpired left their stamp upon the young people in Mary's group.[18] Never would they forget their fear, anxiety, and sadness in having to leave their dear home. Years later, Martha Ann wrote the following lines:

> We left our home just as it was, our furniture, and the fruit trees hanging full of rosy cheeked peaches. We bid goodbye to the loved home that reminded us of our beloved father everywhere we turned.
>
> I was five years old when we started from Nauvoo. We crossed over the Mississippi in the skiff in the dusk of the evening. We bid goodbye to our dear old feeble grandmother [Lucy Mack Smith]. I can never forget the bitter tears she shed when she bid us goodbye for the last time in this life. She knew it would be the last time she would see her son's family. We did not realize this so much at that time as we have since.[19]

Mary took along all the livestock which had been on the

---

[18]From the outset of the evacuation of Nauvoo, young Joseph F. Smith had watched the crossing of the Mississippi. Soon after Brigham Young's company had crossed over the ice, a traveler rode up mounted on a large bay horse with a fine saddle and bridle. He asked the boy, Joseph, where the Mormons had crossed the river on the ice. Joseph pointed out the place. The man, in a gruff voice, declared: "By G—, if the Mormons can cross on the ice, I can, too." He started over in the gathering darkness. Later, when the ice had melted, the horse with the saddle and bridle still on was found down the river on a sand bar. There was no trace of the man. (Related by Preston Nibley to the author in an interview. President Joseph F. Smith told the story to Nibley during a sightseeing tour of Nauvoo when the latter was a young man.)

[19]Harris Centennial letter.

farm, including horses, cows, and sheep; also, all vehicles. She also took the farm implements. In addition to her own baggage, she took all the baggage and belongings of the various members of her household. The flatboat was crowded during several crossings of the great river during the last day.

Further word concerning Mary's departure from Nauvoo is contained in this description:

> . . . Mary and the children, driven by the mob, barely escaped from the city of Nauvoo before its destruction. The mother had succeeded in getting provisions, bedding, wagons, ox-teams, her husband's big white horse, and a few other necessities, loaded on a flat boat and taken across the Mississippi river to Montrose, Iowa. The children were taken across in a skiff and they and their mother spent the night in their camp on the bank of the river listening to the bombardment of the city of Nauvoo, at that time the largest and most beautiful in Illinois.[20]

It was on September 8, 1846, when Mary and her family and loved ones crossed the river. They remained two or three days within sight of their comfortable home, now deserted, on the opposite bank of the river. For the want of sufficient teams, they were unable to travel. Before the cannonading ceased, they moved a few miles inland from the dreadful sound of it. In the meantime, Mary went twelve miles down the river to Keokuk, Iowa, and completed certain transactions that gave her the rolling equipment and teams needed to move all her household and belongings. She obtained wagons, oxen, cows, calves, and four horses, with which she was able to get her family moved to Winter Quarters.[21]

The distress of the Saints who were the last to leave Nauvoo was very severe. They were marooned on the west bank of the Mississippi without shelter, food or means to move away from the river. The psychological and physical impact of this expulsion and the rude adjustments they were forced to make were indescribable. The shock of being dispossessed, deprived of their homes, personal dignity, and subjected

---

[20]Harris, *op. cit.,* 12.
[21]*Idem*

to extreme want, left many in a state of stupor and despair. Empty stomachs, constant weariness, red eyes, colds, and general lassitude, combined to sear and debilitate their spirits. Wretchedly, the aged huddled about the camp fires, hypnotized into blank, empty staring by the flicking flames. The cruel ordeal, the inhumanity, the crude flight, the exposure day and night, the cold earth, and the elements took their toll in sickness and death. The Lord took mercy on their situation and assuaged their hunger. Large flocks of quail suddenly appeared. They were so tame that the outcasts were able to catch them with their hands in large numbers and use them for food. Their coming was regarded as a miracle.[22]

On September 11, 1846, President Brigham Young was at Cutler's Park on the Missouri. About 10 a.m., he and Elders Heber C. Kimball, Orson Pratt, Wilford Woodruff, George A. Smith, and Amasa M. Lyman walked northward, selected the site for Winter Quarters, then returned to camp. He then directed that twenty-five persons, at Nauvoo and intermediate points, be sent for. Mary Smith's name was among them.[23]

Then President Young learned of the distress of the poor stranded on the bank of the Mississippi opposite Nauvoo and sent Captain O. M. Allen to help them. Allen arrived on October 7, called the refugees together, and informed them that he was sent by the Twelve to give them aid. He inquired into their circumstances. He found that they had lived some time on boiled corn and, for a ten-day stretch, had subsisted on parched corn. He wished them all to exert themselves, yoke up their cows, and move out for the West. He made this interesting report: "Sister Hyrum Smith and Mercy R. Thompson had donated $18 for the company's benefit."[24]

---

[22]Concerning the quail, Joseph Fielding stated: "Here the Lord sent upon them, as it were, a shower of quails. They came in vast flocks. Many came into the houses where the Saints were, settled on the tables and the floor, and even on their laps so that they caught as many as they pleased. Thus the Lord was mindful of his people, and it was truly a matter of astonishment that in all this persecution, etc. only 3 of our Brethren lost their lives." —Fielding, Bk. 5, p. 103.

[23]Journal History, Sept. 11, 1846.

[24]*Ibid.*, Oct. 7, 1846.

Mary Smith finally got organized, everyone in her group accomodated, bade a final farewell to Nauvoo, and headed for the wilderness. No one would ever know her thoughts or heartache, as she put mile after mile between her and the things that were tinged with sentimental attachment — things which were most precious and dear to her — but which were now blanketed with the shroud that lowered, as it were, over Nauvoo and shut out the glory and light of a previous day. She thought of the sad parting with Mother Smith; also, of her husband's people, some of whom censored her for her lack of loyalty to the clan in pulling out and taking Hyrum's family with her. Mary's feelings were masked by a resolute, determined will that registered in her expression. However, there was a special look in her eyes — the light of her great faith. It represented a certain satisfaction, inspired by achievement. She was the leading spirit of her caravan and quite independent of man. She imparted aid to many — men, women, and children. She possessed some means, had the biggest investment, and became the guiding spirit of the undertaking. She was generous and gave freely of her services as well as her substance. Many were deeply grateful.

She could now breathe easier, for she was out of reach of the ruthless mob that had taken possession of Nauvoo. The tension of the last frenetic days, while the mob came closer and closer, had mounted to the breaking point. Knowing what the wretches had done and were capable of doing had filled her with righteous anger. She had again felt their hot breath, as they camped on what had been her farm, then pressed near to her abode. The fiends of hell found the old home deserted.

They had killed her husband; had forced her from her property; had caused her new mental anguish, but she had escaped them. She chose the dangerous way of the wilderness rather than live near and among the unregenerate. She now emerged into the sun. Her gratitude knew no bounds.

Chapter XVIII

Trek Across Iowa

Mary Smith's caravan was composed of nine wagons, six of them belonging to her, one to Mercy Thompson, and two to Joseph Fielding. In her group were eight menfolk, five womenfolk, and a sister in the Church (perhaps Mother Conklin, a widow) who came with her four children, making a total of eighteen. In Mercy's group besides herself, was her little daughter Mary Jane. Joseph's family consisted of two men, two women, and five children.[1] They had in common, in addition to their teams, twenty-one loose cattle (cows, etc.), and forty-three sheep. But the sheep soon began to diminish. At first, the road was through woods with thick underbrush making it difficult to drive the stock. When the sheep got lost in such terrain, it was sometimes necessary to seek them for two or three days which hindered the party in traveling. Some of the other travelers lost some of their stock. However, with great care, Mary's party lost only a young calf or two.

At Bonapart, Iowa, they bought flour thinking it was the last market. However, about forty miles farther, they found some more to buy. It was prudent of Mary to lay in all the supplies possible, as so many hungry people with her imposed a drain on their provisions. To see her precious supplies dwindle and empty space appear in the commissary wagon was a matter of grave concern to her. There must be enough food to last until they reached Winter Quarters and to sustain them for a period after arrival. Food was extremely essential to their morale.

---

[1]Fielding, Bk. 5, p. 104.

One day a shot was heard in camp which caused considerable excitement. A member of the group happened to press the trigger of his gun at the wrong time which did him irreparable damage. It happened forty miles west of Bonapart. Joseph Fielding made this note of it: ". . . Brother E. Clifford and one of Sister Smith's men accidently shot off his right thumb and we had to send for a doctor to take it off."[2] This unfortunate event marred the journey and added to Mary's concern as the hand had to be carefully nursed, dressed, and protected against infection.

Something of Mary Smith's super-burden and what she had to contend with on account of certain uncooperative menfolk in her party is revealed by her brother's journal: "Sister Smith labored hard, and her men were slothful. She might cook for and serve them, and then gather together the cattle while they stood by the fire, but J. Lawson was a blessing to her; he was very diligent. But we got on our way as well as could be expected, sister Smith and sister Thompson often walked several miles a day, driving the cattle. My women had each a young child, and they in general managed the team of horses they rode with."[3]

The reference to the men standing by the fire suggests the beginning of chilly fall weather for the travelers. Joseph mentioned it specially, thus: "Before we got to journeys end the weather became cold and the nights frosty so that the grass was killed, and as our corn was spent our horses began to fail. One of mine became lame in her shoulder so as to disable (her) for work and it was so much the harder on the cattle and other horse."[4]

Mary's caravan passed through Garden Grove, one of the stop-over points established by Brigham Young as a place to rest and recuperate and where crops were planted to be harvested by those who would come later. A similar place by the

---

[2] *Idem*
[3] *Ibid.*, p. 105.
[4] *Ibid.*, p. 106.

name of Pisgah was reached. According to her brother, the latter was by no means a handsome or healthy place. Many of the Saints had died there, and the people looked sick and pale. "Much of the corn planted there was too late to ripen. We tried to buy some corn but no one had any to sell but brother Charles C. Rich gave Sister Smith a bushel of green corn and some pumpkins. Of these we all shared. Sister Thompson was very liberal."[5]

When Mary Smith and her family were within 150 miles of Winter Quarters, they got a happy surprise that lifted their spirits. While journeying along, they met some travelers headed east, one of whom was John Smith. Upon receiving word that his family was westward bound, he set out to meet them in company with Almon W. Babbitt. It was a happy reunion for all. The children were tickled to see their brother. They all rejoiced to have him back after an absence of several months. He had left Nauvoo with Heber C. Kimball in February 1846. The Kimball party had reached the Missouri River and crossed it at a point near the present site of Omaha, called at that time Sarpee's Trading Post, among the Pottawatamie Indians. Their next move was north about six miles to the Little Papillon River where they remained briefly. About August, they moved to the vicinity of Winter Quarters.[6]

To allow John to go west had been no mistake. As heir to the patriarchship of the Church, he belonged with the body of the Saints. Although only fourteen years old, he was robust, mature, and large of stature. He brought back with him an air of western sophistication. For a boy, he had had a great adventure. He imparted to Mary and her party a feeling of security and comfort through intelligence of the trail ahead and conditions at Winter Quarters. John piloted the company the rest of the way and brought the wagon-train safely to the camp of the Saints.

---

[5]*Idem*

[6]John Smith (obituary), "Patriarch Smith Summoned Home," *Deseret News* Nov. 9, 1911, p. 2.

As they came within twenty miles of their destination, they found brethren who had settled in choice spots for water, food, and feed for cattle. These individuals, generally, tried to discourage them from going on to the main camp. They said that there was no wood but what was fetched several miles; also, that the Indians were killing the cattle—some said two and others said seven, and the last report, fifteen head a day. The truth was that many of these men had some property and did not wish to go to the camp and, of course, were willing to believe or raise an evil report to justify themselves for not doing so. An entry by Mary's brother stated: "Some thought we had better go and find out the truth about it before we took our stuff over, but we felt no desire to stop short of camp. We had seen such things before. We crossed the river and came to the camp. This was not long after the Saints removed to the river."[7]

It was after dark when they pulled into Winter Quarters, October 21, 1846. This led Mary's brother to comment: "The lights of the camp of the Saints as we saw the lights at a distance were interesting. It reminded us of Israel of old in the wilderness. . . . there were few houses; nearly all were in their tents upon about a square half mile."[8] The weary travelers were conducted to the house of Heber C. Kimball. He sent a young man to drive in the cattle and put them into his yard. The newcomers stopped by brother Kimball's house for the night. Arriving with them were the Benbows.[9]

For Mary and the others it had been an exhausting final day's drive. They had pushed their animals hard to make it in by nightfall. Although she was tired to the bone, it was a memorable day for Mary. She had achieved her first big goal. By sheer determination and superb effort, she had caught up with the body of the Church and taken her place among

[7]Fielding, Bk. 5, p. 108.

[8]*Idem.*

[9]Journal History, Oct. 21, 1846: "John Benbow and his wife, Joseph Fielding and Sister Hyrum Smith arrived in camp. Sister Benbow was very sick." She died later in Winter Quarters due to the exposure she suffered in being driven from their home in Nauvoo.

the Saints to become a part of what lay ahead. She slept well, knowing the sweet satisfaction of a splendid achievement.

The next day, Brother Kimball took the family to the place reserved for them, where they pitched their tents. The next thing was to obtain feed for their stock. Their horses, in particular, had become "feeble" and run down for lack of corn and hay to feed them. The worst part of it, it was far too late to cut any grass for hay. The grass, what there was of it, had been killed by the frost. Accordingly, Mary was advised by Brother Kimball to send the horses to an island some eight miles from the camp. They were all taken there except one which strayed off a short distance and was later found dead in a creek where she had mired. Later when they went to see the others, they found two more in the same situation, one belonging to Mary and the other to Joseph. The rest were brought home, and hay was bought for them. The main part of the oxen and cows was sent about twenty miles to feed on rushes.[10]

Heeding counsel, two yokes of cattle were kept at home to to be used in obtaining logs to build their houses. The sheep were put into the general flock, the Twelve agreeing to furnish half the number over the mountains. But as soon as winter came on, it was no longer any use to take them onto the prairie. They now had to live on hay and some corn.[11] Joseph wrote: "The flock [general] which numbered 1400 began to die and it was found that they would not be sustained and we were advised to take them [family sheep] home having lost 5 of them. But they still kept dying so that before winter was over, we had 18 left of the 43 that we started with."[12]

Besides the sheep which were lost, Mary's brother recorded other losses. He had on leaving Nauvoo one pair of horses and two yokes of oxen but long ere the end of winter one horse and two odd oxen had died leaving him an odd horse and two

---

[10]Fielding, Bk. 5, pp. 109-110.
[11]*Ibid.*, p. 110.
[12]*Ibid.*, p. 111.

oxen. Mary lost two good mares, one young colt, and one or more oxen. Several of Mercy Thompson's cows and oxen also died.

The first important task was to get houses constructed before the onset of winter. In this, they all labored with their might. Mary's brother wrote:

> I labored hard to get Sister Smith a house built. First, we drew the logs about 1½ miles, built a double house each and being 16 feet by 16, put on clap boards and then laid sods over them to keep out both cold and rain. We also built Thompson a room by setting up poles in a slanting form and then covered them with earth and my own house of logs 14 feet by 16 with clap boards and sods on the roof. The fall of the year was very fine and pleasant and it was a blessing for the Saints as it was late before we got our houses up. I was much troubled with diahre [sic] which made me very weak and my work was a burden to me and as my sisters men were not the most active we seemed to move slowly. I suppose [I] earned something of my sister Smith but she as well as sister Thompson assisted me far more than what I had any claim on her for. She had a little money and she let it go for corn and hay for the cattle and flour, etc., the Lord reward her for her kindness.[13]

John Smith literally filled the role of the man of Mary's family. He worked hard at the countless chores that had to be done. He had a hand in building the house. It is written of him: "John went to work with hired help, built a log house for winter. . . ."[14] During the summer of 1847, he tilled the soil and filled a man's place in the hay and harvest fields as the only male member of the immediate family able to do heavy work.

The whole camp was divided into twenty-two wards, one of which was across the river. The Smiths, Fieldings, and Thompsons were in the 13th Ward presided over by a Bishop and two counselors. "The Saints are tithed," stated Mary's brother, "and the tithing is applied to the relief of the poor, by this means the poor have been furnished with financing, etc., and I suppose the Bishops generally have been faithful in

---

[13] *Ibid.*, p. 112.
[14] John Smith (obituary), *op. cit.*

taking care of the poor. I myself, was made a counselor to Bro. Rolf of the 13th Ward, who judged that with my family and my 2 widowed sisters with whom also were 3 other widows, if we provided for ourselves, we should be free from another tithing."[15] Their hard times were pointed up by Joseph recording that his children had worn out their clothes and the prospect of getting more was bad.

Gradually the Smith family conditioned itself to the new environment and a primitive way of life on the slope west of the Missouri River. There was plenty of work to do, and everyone worked hard to sustain body and soul. The big focus and over-riding thought was to prepare for the day when they would hitch their teams to the wagons and start the big journey to a new home in the midst of the Rocky Mountains. Their present abodes were only temporary places to be endured until the day arrived to venture forth upon the long, long trail to a place far in the West.

Mary made every effort to make a home of the crude log house. A thorough chinking job with clay fortified it against the wind and storm of winter. Despite its rough interior and dirt floor, she made it habitable. It was a haven of peace and rest. It was a place of good cheer enhanced by the play and laughter of children, the whetting of appetites by newly baked bread or the savory aroma of a stew cooking in the iron kettle at the fireplace. Despite the rusticity of the cabin, it had sanctity of atmosphere engendered by a pilgrim humility and refreshment of spirit rooted in the reading of scripture, verse, and the pursual of learning in a few precious books. There were hymns, also, Mormon and Methodist.

Mary presided with calmness, all home activities centering in and revolving about her. The prayer of faith, uttered in gratitude and love, was a ritual night and morning. At bedtime she tucked the children in and gave them a goodnight caress. They arose in the morning to a breakfast she had waiting for

---

[15]Fielding, Bk. 5, p. 113.

them. They looked for her when they returned from work or play. If she were absent, they were crestfallen. They would look about and call: "Mama! Mama! Where are you?" She was mother in all that the word meant—long-suffering, hard-working, God-loving, and dutiful. She made the crude cabin a home. It became hallowed—the prototype of a house she would build out of adobes one day when she reached the mountains.

During the next winter, the Saints at Winter Quarters suffered greatly from their primitive mode of living. Their diet was sorely deficient and out of balance—their resistance at low ebb. As a result, an epidemic of scurvy ravaged the camp taking the lives of hundreds. The scurvy (also called "black-leg" and "black-canker") was relieved by potatoes brought from Missouri and horseradish found growing at an unused army fort nearby.[16]

Their trials and suffering, grief and sorrow, dejection and heartache were pointed up and reflected in the 600 graves that were dug during the terrible sojourn at Winter Quarters. Today in the hill-top cemetery a magnificient monument by Avard Fairbanks enshrines the grief and sorrow of those Mormon refugees. The bronze figures of a pioneer father and mother, looking down into the grave of their little child wrapped in a blanket, tell the story. A bronze plaque in front of the monument bears the names of 385 known dead ranging in age from one day to ninety years. The names of whole families are listed. One cannot stand before this monument without being deeply touched and moved to solemn reverence. Forcefully, there is conveyed to the mind some understanding of what those noble exiles endured. So stirred is the heart that the visitor departs with an ache in his throat, made more acute with the knowledge that loved ones passed through that trying period.

---

[16]George Q. Cannon, "History of the Church," *Juvenile Instructor*, XVIII, (Aug. 1883), 237.

Those soul-testing days of poverty and misery were passed through by the outcasts with the help of a powerful faith and a splendid courage, plus the spiritual uplift that came to them when assembled together in worship, or during festive moments, enlivened by singing, orchestral music, and dancing. Their support and stay was a divine pronouncement: "If thou art merry, praise the Lord with singing, with music, with dancing, and with a prayer of praise and thanksgiving. If thou art sorrowful, call on the Lord thy God with supplication that your souls may be joyful."[17]

The suffering of the faithful, the body of the Church, who departed from their homes in and around Nauvoo, brought to the Church depth of soul, the *sine qua non* of greatness. When a people undergo hardships, suffer and die for a cause, a new soul-quality is born. This intangible something that comes from great sacrifice, struggle, and suffering cannot be acquired in any other way. It is the thing that binds people together, gives them internal strength, tradition, pride in accomplishment, and spiritual force. A nation which is born of struggle, bloodshed, and sacrifice of patriots has something of the same soul-quality. It is the element that gives strength, stirs the patriotism of a nation and promotes a deep sense of fervor and loyalty. This feeling, which is essential to true democracy, cannot be thrust upon a people or a nation but must be awakened by a crisis, a titanic effort, or struggle. So it was with the exiled Saints. Their years of persecution, misery, heartache, exertion, and affliction gave the Church great solidarity, character, and nobility of soul. Pioneer members, who passed through Winter Quarters and endured to the end, acquired these characteristics. From them have been transmitted a heart and a heritage.

[17] *D&C* 136:28-29.

Chapter XIX

Journey to St. Joseph

Various places in Missouri became supply points for the Saints at Winter Quarters. During good weather, Mormon wagons and teams shuttled over primitive, back-country roads to distant towns along the Missouri River to bring back food and clothing. In the late fall of 1847, Mary Smith decided on such a trip with her son Joseph F., daughter Martha Ann, and her brother Joseph Fielding. Their goal was St. Joseph, Missouri, 160 miles away. If there existed some trepidations in Mary's mind about undertaking the trip, she had a right to them, for it meant going back into enemy country of cursed memories where she, her husband, and family had suffered intensely—she nigh unto death. When in St. Joseph, she would be forty-five miles directly west of Far West which fact certainly would bring back stabbing memories.

But their necessities were the compelling factors in making the trip. Many others had been to St. Joseph and returned with precious stores of supplies without encountering old foes nor being subjected to any untoward incidents. If others could make the trip, surely she could, too. So Mary and her brother worked out all the details and proceeded on the journey. They took two wagons with two yokes of oxen on each. Joseph F. was about nine years of age at the time but large enough to serve as teamster for his mother.

Mary was fortunate to have the means to buy the things she needed. She and the children needed clothing as well as food for what lay ahead. Upon her arrival in St. Joseph, she shopped carefully, stretching each dollar all she could. The proprietor of each business establishment where she went found her to be calculating and shrewd in every detail. They noted her sober face and the sure way she handled her money. She bargained to get the best prices and was all business. Her son Joseph F. remembered the trip well and recounted it later in life, the substance of which follows.[1]

The weather was stormy and the roads bad, for it rained a good deal during the journey making the trip very hard, trying, and unpleasant. At St. Joseph, Mary shopped for groceries and dry goods to do the family through the coming winter and the trek across the plains in the spring. She purchased corn at St. Joseph and had some of it ground at Savannah, ten miles to the north, on the return trip, where she laid in a store of flour, meal, bacon, etc. Everything went well, and they started for home with the precious supplies in the two wagons. The rains and the heavy loads made travel miserably difficult and taxed the oxen to the limit. Consequently, the journey, which required one week in going down, took much longer coming back.

During the return trip, they camped one evening on an open prairie on the Missouri River bottom by the side of a small spring creek which emptied into the river about three quarters of a mile from them. Where they were camped, they were in plain sight of the river and could apparently see over every foot of the little open prairie in the direction of the river to the southwest, the bluffs on the northwest, and the timber which skirted the prairie on the right and left.

Camping nearby on the other side of the creek were some men with a herd of beef cattle which they were driving to Savannah and St. Joseph for market. Joseph F. and his uncle usually unyoked their oxen and turned them loose to feed during their encampment at night, but this time, on account of the proximity of the herd of cattle, and fearing that they might get mixed up and be driven off, they turned the oxen out to feed in their yokes. The next morning when they came to look

---

[1]Smith, *Life of JFS, op. cit.*, pp. 131-133.

for them, to their great astonishment, their best yoke of oxen was not to be found.

Joseph F. and his uncle Fielding spent all the morning and well nigh until noon hunting for them but to no avail. The grass was tall and in the morning wet with heavy dew. Tramping through this grass, through the woods, and over the bluff, made them wet to the skin, fatigued, disheartened, and almost exhausted.

In this pitiable plight, Joseph F. was the first to return to camp. As he approached, he saw his mother kneeling serenely in prayer. He halted a moment then drew gently near enough to hear her pleading with the Lord not to suffer them to be left in this helpless condition but to lead them to recover their lost team that they might continue their travel in safety.

When she arose from her knees, Joseph F. was standing nearby. The first expression that he caught upon her face was a lovely smile which gave him renewed hope and an assurance that he had not felt before.

A few moments later, Uncle Fielding returned to camp soaked with dew, faint, fatigued, and thoroughly disheartened. His first words were: "Well Mary, the cattle are gone!"

Mary replied in a voice which fairly rang with cheerfulness: "Never mind. Your breakfast has been waiting for hours and, now, while you and Joseph F. are eating, I will just take a walk out and see if I can find the cattle."

"Why Mary," he exclaimed, "what do you mean? We have been all over this country, all through the timber and through the herd of cattle, and our oxen are gone; they are not to be found. I believe they have been driven off, and it is useless for you to attempt to do such a thing as to hunt for them."

"Never mind me," replied Mary, "get your breakfast and I will see."

She started toward the river, following down the spring creek. Before she was out of speaking distance, the man in charge of the herd of cattle rode up from the opposite side of the creek and called out: "Madam, I saw your oxen over in that direction this morning about daybreak," pointing in the opposite direction from that in which Mary was going.

Joseph Fielding and Joseph F. heard plainly what the man said, but Mary went right on and did not even turn her head to look at him. A moment later, the man rode off rapidly toward his herd which had been gathered in the opening near the edge of the woods. They were soon under full drive for the road leading toward Savannah, and quickly disappeared from view.

Mary continued straight down the little stream of water until she stood almost on the bank of the river, and then she beckoned toward the wagon. Joseph F. was watching his mother's every movement and was determined that she should not get out of his sight. Instantly, he and his uncle arose from the mess-chest, on which their breakfast had been spread, and started toward her. Joseph, like John who outran the other disciples to the sepulchre, outran his uncle and came first to the spot where his mother stood. There, he saw their oxen fastened to a clump of willows growing in the bottom by the little spring creek, perfectly concealed from view. They were not long in releasing them from bondage and getting them back to the camp, where all the other cattle had been tied to the wagon wheels all the morning. They were soon on their way rejoicing. The worthy herdsman had suddenly departed when he saw that Mary would not heed him.

This story of the lost oxen gives a deep insight into the makeup of Mary Smith. She was confronted with an awkward crisis in her life—a difficult situation which happened far from anywhere with no human to call upon for help. She did not panic but put perfect trust in the Lord to come to her rescue and help find the oxen. In the moment of alarm, she went to her knees and talked with Him and asked for assistance. She arose smiling and serene as if the spirit of the Lord had given her an immediate answer. Her instinct resisted the false and beguiling direction of the herdsman, knowing for certain that he could not be trusted. Then with resolute will, she walked unerringly to where her oxen were concealed. This was a clue, as the cowman quickly found out, to the kind of a women she was. She revealed the kind of mind and faith that would triumph and take her to the mountains.

They hitched the oxen to their wagons and went on their way. The supplies that Mary brought back with her on two such trips were highly precious, the best kind of insurance against the dread "blackleg" scourge that visited the Mormon community. However, not only must the supplies provide for their current needs but also last for their journey across the plains which she planned on undertaking at the first sign of spring. She must husband them well; there would be many mouths to feed for many months. Wheat and corn also would be needed for planting over the mountains.

Chapter XX

Indian Scare

Winter Quarters was on the border of Pottawatamie Indian country. At the time of the advent of the Mormon people into the area, there were 2,000 Indian men, women, and children on the east side of the Missouri River. It was thirty-four miles from Pottawatamie town to Council Bluffs, Iowa. In July 1843, Elder Johnathan Dunham was sent by Joseph Smith on an exploratory trip through Indian lands. He went up the Des Moines River and came into contact with the Sac Indians. Sioux and Winnebago Indians were also encountered. He went on and arrived at the Pottawatamie village about sunset. Four Indian bucks and a squaw brought him and his guide, Neotanah, some jerked venison and some half boiled corn. On the second day after his arrival, Elder Dunham recorded:

> Saturday, 30th July. We were sent for to the Chief's house. We went. The Indians, squaws and children came from every quarter to see the man that had come with Neotanah. Breakfast was ready for us as soon as we came in. This was the first time that I ever ate at a wigwam amongst little and great, when the vituals relished as it did at this time; but this is easily accounted for; hunger will make anything that is eatable taste good. Stayed all day at the chief's house. My rifle seemed to be the great wonder amongst all Indians and squaws; it went the rounds, from one to another, as if it had been one of the seven wonders of the world. This Indian town stands on the creek called Pottawatamie Tour-se-pas.[1]

These Indians were very good to Elder Dunham. He was entertained with dances, songs, and speeches. They learned

---

[1]Smith, *HC op. cit.*, V, 543.

that Neotanah had not been a very good guide. The whole nation was much displeased on account of it, and the council gave him a severe flogging. They expressed much regret and feeling of sorrow to their white visitor that he had received such treatment from one who pretended to be a friend and an honorable man of the Pottawatamies, for they considered themselves honorable.

Elder Dunham visited with the old chief and gained an insight into the heart of the venerable Indian patriarch:

> While I now write, I have seven of the most honorable in the tribe around me—the head chief and his counselors. One of them is aged, his head is silvered o'er with age; while in his prime none could endure more fatigue, none whose constitution was stronger than his: but now he says, he is soon to go and shake hands with the great Shaminyto (that is, God) that had made him, and had given him strength to hunt, and in war to fight his enemies. Here the old man would show the wounds received in battle, in fighting for his nation, his wife and little ones. He said he had never fought but on the defensive. Ninety-eight years, as near as he can remember, he has seen; and now, he says, he wants to know how the Mormons worship the great Shaminyto different from what he did; if the best way, he wanted to get into it before he went on his journey to see the great Shaminyto.[2]

Four years later, Brigham Young led the Mormon outcasts from Nauvoo into the environs of the Pottawatamie Indians. They received better treatment from the redmen than they had at the hands of the whites in their former places of abode. Their red neighbors had a peaceful and spiritual quality about them. Except for their proclivity to steal, there was little to be feared from the Pottawatamies.

However, in the summer of 1847, a real crisis arose for Mary Smith involving some mischievous Indians and her son Joseph F. A herd-boy by the name of Thomas Burdick, who had been with Joseph F., came running exhausted into Winter Quarters with the alarming news that Indians had made off with Joseph F. and the cattle they were herding. This produced a great excitement in the community. His mother and

---

[2] *Ibid.*, 547.

family were stunned by the news, supposing he might have been killed or captured by Indians. Poor Mary, it was one of the most agonizing moments of her life. The new crisis left her weak and overcome with grief. Her immediate recourse was prayer; she knew the power of it. What had happened was high drama which made an exciting and enduring story.[3]

On a bright morning sometime in the fall of 1847, Joseph F. Smith started out with his cattle, as usual, for the herd grounds some two miles from Winter Quarters. With him were his herd-boy companions whose names were Alden Burdick (almost a young man, and very sober and steady), Thomas Burdick, cousin to Alden, about Joseph's size but somewhat older, and Isaac Blocksome who was younger. They had two horses, both belonging to the Burdicks, and a pet jack "Jackie" belonging to Joseph. Their herd that day consisted of not only the cows and young stock, but also the work oxen which, for some cause, were unemployed.

Alden proposed to take a trip on foot through the hazel trees and gather nuts for the party and, by the lower road, meet the boys at the spring on the herd grounds. The boys went on with the herd by the upper road which was free of brush. Their arrangements just suited Joseph and Thomas, for they were very fond of a little sport, and Alden's absence would afford them full scope, for his presence put a damper on their exuberance. Joseph rode Alden's bay mare, a very fine animal. Thomas rode his father's black pony; and Isaac, the pet jack.

This jack had crooked forelegs and was very knowing in his way. So Isaac and the jack were the subjects chosen by Joseph and Thomas for their sport. They would tickle and plague the animal until he would kick up, stick his head down, hump up his back, and run, while Isaac struggled in vain to guide or hold him by the bridle reins. No harm nor offense was meant to Isaac, but the tormentors carried their fun too

[3]J[oseph] F. S[mith], "A Noble Woman's Experience," *The Heroines of Mormondom, Noble Women's Lives Series*, Bk. 2 (Salt Lake City, 1884), pp. 16-23.

far. Isaac was offended and returned home on foot turning loose the jack with the bridle on. The two tormentors were sorry when they found that they had given such sore offense.

When Joseph and Thomas arrived at the spring, they set their dinner pails down by it. They mounted their horses again and began to amuse themselves by running short races, jumping ditches, and riding about. While they were doing this, and the cattle were feeding down the little spring creek toward a point of the hill that jutted out into the little valley about a half mile distant, a party of Indians suddenly appeared from behind the hill. They were on horseback, stripped to the skin, their faces painted, and their hair daubed with white clay. They came whooping and charging at full speed. In an instant, Thomas put his pony to a fast run for home crying at the top of his voice, "Indians! Indians!" At the same time, Joseph set out at full speed for the head of the herd in an attempt to save the stock if possible.

He thought of his mother, brother, and sisters and their dependence on their cattle for transportation to the Valley in the spring. This nerved him to meet the Indians half-way and risk his life to save the cattle from being driven off by them. At the moment that he reached the head of the herd, the Indians, with terrific yells, reached the same spot. The yelling and pounding of hoofs frightened the cattle so that it required a super-human effort on the part of Joseph to head them in the right direction and at the same time elude the grasp of the Indians. In an instant, they were all on a stampede toward home. The Indians divided, the foremost passing by Joseph in hot pursuit of Thomas who, by this time, had reached the brow of the hill on the upper road leading to town. He was on foot, as he had left his pony, knowing the Indians could outrun it. He thought perhaps they might be satisfied with the horse allowing him to make good his escape.

Joseph's horse was fleet of foot; therefore, he determined to sell what he had at the dearest possible price. The rest of the Indians tried to capture him, but, in a miraculous manner, he eluded them managing to keep the cattle headed in the direction of the lower road toward home until he reached the head of the spring. Here, the Indians, who pursued Thomas, met Joseph. One had possession of Thomas' horse. The Indians turned Joseph's horse around the spring and down the course of the stream, the whole party in full pursuit. He could outrun them and, now being detached from the herd and in the direction of home, he could have made his escape. But as he reached a point opposite the hill from whence the Indians had come, he was met by another party that had crossed the stream to intercept him, again turning his horse. Making a circuit, he once more started toward home, but his faithful horse began to lose breath and flag. Joseph was still able to keep out of reach of his pursuers until the hindmost of the Indians in the down race began to file in before him by forming a platoon and veering to the right and left in front. As Joseph endeavored to pass, they obstructed his course so that those behind overtook him just as he once more reached the spring.

One Indian fiercely took him by the right arm, another by the left leg, while a third was prepared to close in and secure his horse. Having forced his reins from his grasp, they raised him from his saddle, slackened speed until his horse ran from under him, then dashed him to the ground among the horses' hoofs while the animals were running at great speed. Joseph was considerably stunned by the fall but fortunately suffered no injuries despite a dozen or more horses passing over him. As he arose to his feet, several men with pitchforks in their hands came in sight on top of the hill. Upon seeing them, the Indians fled in the direction from which they had come. The men on the hill, while on the way to the hay fields, had been alerted by Thomas' cry. They reached the hill in time to see Joseph's horse captured.

The jack, still with the bridle on, did not stampede with the cattle but strayed off alone toward the point of the hill. An old Indian with some corn in a buckskin sack was trying to catch him. But Jackie did not fancy Mr. Indian and appeared not to fear him. He would wheel away as the Indian attempted to take hold of the bridle. As the men appeared, the Indian made a desperate lunge to catch the jack but was kicked over, his corn spilling on the ground. The Indian jumped up and took to his heels. The jack deliberately ate up his corn.

By this time, the cattle were scattered off in the brush lining the lower road, still heading toward town. The men with the pitchforks soon disappeared from the hill and continued on to the hayfields. Joseph found himself alone. This afforded him an opportunity to reflect on his escape and situation. His own thoughts made him more afraid than the Indians. What if they should return to complete their task which he had been instrumental in defeating? They would evidently show him little mercy. They had tried to trample him with their horses and, now what would he do on foot and alone? It would take him some time to gather up the cattle from among the brush. However, the Indians might return any moment as there was nothing to prevent them from doing so. Therefore, he concluded that time was precious and the best thing he could do would be to follow Thomas' tracks and head for home.

When he arrived, the people had gathered in the bowery and were organizing two search companies, one on foot and the other on horseback to pursue the Indians. Thomas had told the whole story as far as he knew it. The dire supposition of many was written in their faces. Therefore, when Joseph put in an appearance, his mother and sisters were happily surprised on seeing him not only alive but uninjured. Their tears of joy were even more copious than those of intense grief a moment before.

However, Joseph's sorrow had not yet begun. He and Thomas returned with the armed men on foot to hunt for and recover the cattle if possible, while the horsemen went in pursuit of the horses. When Joseph arrived again at the spring, there was no sign of the cattle. Even the dinner pails were gone. The saddle blanket from the horse Joseph had ridden was found nearby. This was evidence that the Indians had returned, as Joseph had suspected, and had driven off the cattle. All that day, they hunted in vain for the lost stock. They failed to find any trace of them. They finally gave up the search and turned their weary steps homeward, all hope of success gone. Joseph could no longer suppress the heavy grief that filled his heart. He wept bitter tears and wished he were a man.

But when Joseph and Thomas reached home, to their surprise and joy, they found the cattle safely corraled in their yards where they had been all afternoon. Alden had reached the herd ground just after Joseph had left. He found the cattle straying off in the wrong direction unherded but could find no trace of the boys, although he discovered the dinner pails at the spring as usual. Becoming aware that something had happened, he took the pails, gathered up the cattle, and left by the lower road for home, arriving there after the search parties had departed by the upper road. A messenger was sent to notify them of the safety of the cattle, but he failed to overtake them. Alden learned the particulars of the whole affair, feeling thankful he had escaped.

Chapter XXI

Preparing to go West

At the time of the martyrdom of her husband, twenty people comprised Mary Smith's household.[1] Eighteen of these reached Winter Quarters and were sustained for many months after arriving there. In the spring of 1847, George Mills, the old soldier and member of the family, went with Brigham Young's company on the initial trek to the Salt Lake Valley.[2] In June of the same year, Mercy Thompson and Mary Jane, in the care of James Lawson, started for the Valley with a company of the Saints led by Parley P. Pratt.

By the spring of 1848, Mary's household had been reduced to nine people. This number had to be considered in any plans to go farther west. It meant assemblying sufficient provisions, wagons, and teams, in accordance with the basic requirements for each family for the journey across the plains. As it turned out, Mary's major task was in obtaining sufficient oxen to pull the wagons. She had lost some of her trained and mature oxen and nearly all of her horses the two previous severe winters. Conditions were such that there did not seem to be the slightest hope of getting away to the Valley that year.

Mercy Thompson's departure with her daughter caused Mary and her brother considerable worry, for the company was large, the loads heavy, and the country full of Indians. It had been creditably reported that the Indians had robbed an Oregon company causing them much trouble and loss. So great was Joseph Fielding's anxiety that he could scarcely eat

---

[1]Thompson Centennial letter.

[2]George Mills was in the Twelfth Ten, Norton Jacobs, Captain, of Brigham Young's company, 1847.—Roberts, *Comprehensive History of the Church, op. cit.*, III, 187.

or sleep. However, their great concern was relieved as word came back that all was well with the travelers westward bound on the dangerous wilderness highway. Then, as Mary's brother recorded, some Mormon Battalion soldiers arrived in Winter Quarters and reported many hardships—that they had a hard time of it—had to eat their mules, raw-hide and even grass to keep alive. Joseph said: "They have come from the Valley in less than two months. They have brought us (me and my sister) word that my sister Thompson has got married to Bro James Lawson. This has been done without my counsel or consent and is against my mind, but I shall be sorry if she should be a loser by it to any amount."[3] But this report proved to be false.

During the summer of 1847, the people of Winter Quarters were diligent in cultivating the ground, raising corn, potatoes, and buckwheat. It was late in the season before they got started, but their labors were blessed. In further regard to this, Mary's brother stated: ". . . we have I suppose plenty of produce and hay for man and beast for the winter and some to take us to the mountains."[4] Everyone worked hard. Plowing up the sod, fencing it in, having to fetch food from Missouri, herding the cattle, and guarding the camp from bad Indians, kept the camp active and strong.

In the fall of 1847, two deaths occurred in the family of Joseph Fielding. His journal received the sad entry that one male infant, Hyrum T., died on August 4, and an infant boy, John, on September 16.[5] These deaths brought deep sorrow to them all. However, they were fortunate in being spared further tragedies in view of the high mortality rate in the camp, in that many hundreds of the Saints had died of the black-leg or scurvy. Mary's family was fortunate to have escaped it, but her brother was a sufferer. He noted: "At one time also while there I was nearly crippled with the scurvy, a complaint which prevailed much among the Saints there. It appeared in small

[3]Fielding, Bk. 5, p. 129.
[4]*Ibid.*, p. 124.
[5]*Ibid.*, p. 129.

dark specks on the lower parts of the body, and contracting the sinews of the legs, so that they could not be straightened."[6]

Mary and Joseph, in the months of waiting, had felt the isolation of their situation, being so far removed from civilization. The Christmas of 1847 was austere, marked by Spartan simplicity. Their thoughts turned to their loved ones in England. A nostalgic note came from Joseph's pen as he wrote: "I have not heard from my relations this long time. It seems of no use for me to write to them and I suppose they think the same on the otherhand."[7]

At the close of winter, 1848, Mary's brother set about to repair her equipment to prepare for her journey to the Valley. But as he saw no possibility of going himself, he bought the improvements of five acres of land, some of it in wheat. However, he still felt the desire to go west if the way should open. He was advised by President Heber C. Kimball to try to make a start. "I sold my claim, borrowed some corn, and did my best for starting," stated Joseph, "but both my sister and myself found it very difficult to get off."[8]

Mary and Joseph and their families were to travel with Kimball's company, the last big company to leave that year. This company was assembling on the east bank of the Elkhorn River, twenty-seven miles west of Winter Quarters. This river flowed from the north and ran into the North Platte southwest of Winter Quarters. The Elkhorn was nine rods wide and three feet deep, the current swift and not easy to ferry. There was plenty of timber on its banks. However, before reaching the Elkhorn, it was necessary to cross the Pappea, a stream ten feet wide with high banks. It was eighteen miles to this stream. It was a midway camping point on the way to the Elkhorn.

On June 2, 1848, Kimball's company started to cross the Elkhorn, and by 2:00 p.m. all were safely landed. "On their arrival at the Elkhorn, Howard Eagan was dispatched

[6]*Ibid.*, p. 134.
[7]*Ibid.*, p. 131.
[8]*Ibid.*, p. 134.

[by Heber C. Kimball] back to Winter Quarters to urge Mary Smith, widow of the late Patriarch Hyrum Smith to come on as speedily as possible, and to attend to some other items of business."[9]

Meantime, Mary was frantically trying to get ready to leave. "A great part of our teams," stated Mary's brother, "were made up of cows and young oxen that had not been broke, and we were obliged to fix two wagons together for lack of leaders and drivers. Bro. Terry, who had been engaged to drive a team to the Valley and to bring one back to take his own family, was quite discouraged, and said it was great folly to attempt to go as we were not fixed."[10]

This provides some idea of Mary's desperate situation. Words are inadequate to describe her super-effort in preparing to leave. "Every nerve was strained and every available object was brought into requisition. 'Jackie' was traded off for provisions."[11] The little grey donkey had been a favorite pet of the children, especially of Joseph F. To part with him was like leaving behind a member of the family. Joseph F. would never forget Jackie's part in the fiasco the day the Indians picked him off his horse and routed the cattle. Jackie would not bring much, but the few provisions received in exchange for him would help and, maybe, enable Mary to check off one more item that was on the needs list. Being very conscientious, Mary endeavored to have everything that was required before leaving, including food to last them for many months, clothing, firearms, powder, lead.

Mary Smith was assigned to travel in the Third Ten (Second Division) of the Fourth Company. Cornelius P. Lott was the captain of the Third Ten; John Park, of Fifty; and Henry Harriman, of Hundred.[12] In Mary's own group were nine

[9]Journal History, June 2, 1848.

[10]Fielding, Bk. 5, p. 135.

[11]Gates, *op. cit.*, pp. 133-134.

[12]Journal History Dec. 31, 1848; Fielding, Bk. 5, p. 136. Caleb Baldwin was Captain of First Ten; Wm. Burton of the Second Ten and clerk of the camp; Peter Conover of the Fourth Ten; Francis McFerson, Captain of the Guard; William McCallin, Captain of the Herd; and Howard Egan, Captain of the Mississippi Company.

people.[13] Captain Lott was a venerable man who had enjoyed the esteem of the Prophet Joseph Smith. The Prophet had dined in his home and had visited him on another occasion. The Captain could not move and join the main company on the Elkhorn without Mary Smith. He chafed at her delay in getting ready, having little patience for her many difficulties.

In view of all the impedimenta that had stood in her way, it was a moment of great fulfillment when she was set to leave. Mary's wagon-train finally got rolling. "We left Winter Quarters on Sunday, the 4th of June, being about the last," penned her brother.[14] The train assuredly drew the quizzical stare of everyone as she moved out and headed for the rendezvous point where Captain Lott was waiting for her. She had done her best, but it was not enough. The way looked mighty dark for her unless she found more teams. Yet, there was a certain uplift of her spirit even to be on the move. The proverbial start was half the battle. As the young oxen strained to keep the wagons moving, it signalled a great victory for Mary in that she had made the all-important start. Probably no outfit looked as queer as hers did. During the severe winters while at Winter Quarters, eleven of thirteen horses belonging to Mary had died,[15] leaving her destitute of teams and making it necessary to use wild steers, cows, and half grown oxen. They had not been broken and steadied to work together in tandem.

The first half of the journey to the Elk Horn proved to be a nightmare. It was something the family would never forget. When they had gone two miles, grief hit them forcing them to camp for the night—"after a series of most amazing and trying circumstances, such as sticking in the mud, doubling up on all the little hills, and crashing at ungovernable speed down the opposite sides, breaking wagon tongues and reaches,

[13]Journal History, Dec. 31, 1848, lists the following people in the second Division: Mary Fielding Smith, John Smith, Jerusha Smith, Sarah Smith, Joseph F. Smith, and Martha Ann Smith. There were also Hannah Grinnels, Margaret Brysen, and Jane Wilson.

[14]Fielding, Bk. 5, p. 135.

[15]Gates, *op. cit.*, p. 133.

upsetting, and vainly endeavoring to control wild steers, and unbroken cows. . . ."[16]

Ingredients of discouragement were in the making for Mary Smith as she camped the night of June 4. The poor soul was acutely aware of her predicament. If she slept, it wasn't much, for she had too much on her mind. Should she go on or go back? She would go on—things had been so bad that day that they could not get much worse. In fact, they should get better as Mary had had her little talk with her Heavenly Father before sleep overtook her. The will was there plus a large element of positive thinking. In view of these things, there would be a way. There was no room for thought of surrender.

When they reached camp, Captain Lott showed dissatisfaction with Mary's efforts. He asked her how many wagons she had. She told him, seven, which probably included the two wagons of her brother. Lott then wanted to know how many yokes of oxen she had. Her answer was, four, plus a number of cows and calves. Then the Captain "lowered the boom." He told the widow that it was folly for her to start under such conditions. She would never make it and, if she started, she would be a burden upon the company the whole way. He advised her to go back to Winter Quarters and wait until she could get help.[17]

Mary's son Joseph F. heard the Captain's remarks and resented them. He knew how Lott's words hurt his mother after her exhausting struggle to get ready. Had he been a bit older he would have spoken his mind to the Captain. The boy only bit his lip and walked away. After the Captain had had his say, Mary was silent for a moment—an all important moment—then she calmly told the Captain that she would beat him to the Valley and would ask no help from him.[18]

---

[16]*Ibid.*, p. 134.
[17]J.F.S., *op. cit.*, p. 25.
[18]*Idem*

Chapter XXII

Westward Bound

Most individuals in Mary Smith's situation, facing the crisis that she did after being told to remain in Winter Quarters, would have succumbed to discouragement, feeling the futility of the venture, since such a trek could not be undertaken without good, strong oxen. However, as Joseph Smith had told her—that the Lord would take care of her—kind friends, who had seen her efforts, came forward to help, chief of whom was Heber C. Kimball. Perhaps he recalled his own predicament the day he was to leave for his mission to England, and Mary had stepped forward and put five dollars in his hand. Brother Kimball did not forget.

Howard Egan, who had been sent back to Winter Quarters by Kimball to urge Mary to come on as speedily as possible, procured oxen to help her. He proved to be the immediate "angel" in her severe extremity. Mary's brother made this note: "When we got about half the distance [to the Elk Horn] there were received from Bro. Egan 2 yoke of oxen through the influence of Brother Kimball, and we joined the company on Tuesday evening [June 6], and in the morning the company started."[1] The four oxen that Howard Egan located and delivered to Mary upgraded her situation and gave her the team strength to reach the Elk Horn. It would appear that Brother Egan, having left the Elk Horn at the instance of Brother Kimball about June 2, scouted around and hired or borrowed the two yokes of oxen at Winter Quarters or vicinity and got them to Mary at a critical time.

---

[1]Fielding, Bk. 5, p. 135.

Another known benefactor was one Brother Rogers who was not able to go to the Valley that year. He made available some of his oxen for the use of Mary Smith. They were perhaps among the ones Brother Egan delivered to Mary at her camp midway to the Elk Horn. Brother Rogers was held in grateful remembrance by Mary and her family for his timely assistance.[2]

Mary had further cause to be apprehensive during her trying trip from Winter Quarters to the Pappea and farther to the Elk Horn. It was dangerous territory to traverse because of the presence of Indians much different from the Pottawatamies. This was borne out by an incident that happened to Howard Egan, June 6, after he had delivered the oxen to Mary Smith. While he and his companions were camped on the Elk Horn, thieving Indians slipped into his camp and made off with the cattle. Egan and others went in pursuit and came upon the raiders. A skirmish ensued. Egan spotted an Indian taking aim at William H. Kimball. Quick as a flash, he pulled his pistol and fired, saving Kimball's life. This drew Indian fire to him. A bullet hit his horse and turned it. Another ripped through Egan's right arm above the wrist. Thomas E. Ricks was then hit, three heavy buck shot entering the small of his back. Fortunately, Dr. John M. Bernhisel was available to attend the wounded men. They were made as comfortable as possible, but Ricks started to sink. President Brigham Young, who was at the Elk Horn camp, and one or two others, administered to him. It is recorded that the wounded man revived immediately.[3] It is not known whether the stolen cattle were recovered. Certainly, the unfortunate happening caused Mary Smith much distress when she learned of it, especially after Egan's kindness to her.

After the incident with the Indians, a council was held by the Mormon leaders to consider the clear and present danger that the hositle Indians posed and the possibility of

[2]J.F.S., *op. cit.*, p. 26.
[3]*Journal History*, June 6, 1848.

Indian involvement in larger numbers. It was decided to move back away from the wooded area along the Elk Horn.

About 3 o'clock the camp commenced moving off the river, as it was considered wisdom to leave the timber as soon as possible, and all wagons being over, which had arrived, so that the people should not be in so much danger from attacks of Indians, who it is pretty certainly ascertained were the Omaha and Ottoe tribes, and from every circumstance were undoubtedly in the neighborhood for the purpose of plundering the traveling Saints of cattle, etc. Brother Cornelius P. Lott, Joseph Fielding, sister Mary Smith and families had been expected at the "Horn" soon after dinner, and as it was known that they were not far distant some anxiety was felt for their safety, after the camp had moved 2 miles and the encampment had been formed. President Kimball sent back 10 footmen, well armed to meet Brother Lott and company, and about 5 o'clock they arrived all safe, with the exception of having a broken axle tree, and being very short on teams. The wagons were soon ferried across, the chains attached to the raft taken up, the raft made fast, and the last of the wagons composing this company on their way to camp, and before dark the brethren had the satisfaction of seeing about 110 wagons formed in one corral, preparatory to their proceeding on their long journey west. Those who were wounded felt as well as could be expected after the short journey.[4]

Thus we see how Mary Smith joined the main camp on the Elk Horn, the circumstances under which it was done, and the danger that arose prompting an armed escort of the Lott company into camp. It is quite likely that the broken axletree was on one of Mary's wagons, the damage happening the first day in a down-hill crash. Also, there was a shortage of teams. But, she had made it to the main camp. She was in the safety of numbers. It was a significant event for her and also for the Church leaders for again in their midst were the wife and children of the deceased Patriarch, Hyrum Smith. This was no little thing to President Young. In fact, it was a matter of great magnitude and satisfaction to him. Mary Smith's presence in the ranks of her people bolstered the confidence and the morale of the company, for she was a reflection of her beloved husband. She kept his image alive

[4]*Idem*

in the hearts of the Saints by her presence. Indeed, the leaders were thankful to have her with them. Her family would be a support and strength. They were a part of the Smith family tree. Through her efforts, valuable shoots, as it were, would be transplanted into new soil in the mountains—Hyrum's seed—to produce a numerous and righteous posterity for him in the Church. Mary was an important instrument in bringing this about.

When Mary took her place in the light wagon which she chose for her own conveyance in crossing the plains, she was ready for the adventure of a life-time. Ahead lay the deep, deep prairie. Forward the cattle plodded. Onward rolled her wagons. Steadily, the oxen learned to push against the yokes. Steadily, the rhythmic cadence of their hoof-beats continued, mile after mile. The drivers learned how to sound out with, gee! and haw! The oxen, veterans and recruits, in due course, came to respond to those commands, the older ones helping to discipline the younger ones.

After the shake-down period was over, Mary grew confident that she would make it through and nothing would stop her. The deep emotions that engulfed her during the first few days slacked off in a badly needed respite freeing her mind and elevating her spirit. It was good to be moving, to be where she belonged, and heading for a new home, a sanctuary in the mountains where her children would have fulfillment of their birthright. She derived satisfaction in realizing that she was finally fairly well equipped. "For their trip they had four wagons (two of their own and two hired) and a big 'ambulance' [light wagon] each drawn by two yokes of oxen, except one wagon, which was drawn by two yokes of cows. They also had two more cows and some sheep which had to be driven along in the rear. Martha [the youngest] would do her share of the work, small as she was by gathering fuel and taking her turn at driving the loose cattle."[5]

---

[5]Harris, *op. cit.*, p. 12.

Further insight into the journey is gained from these details by Mary's brother:

> We seemed to improve in our traveling and our cattle improved in their condition until we crossed the Platte River. We overtook Bro. B. Young's company at Loup Fork and it was an interesting sight when to behold in the morning a string of oxen reaching from one side of the river to the other about a mile from Brigham's company coming to assist us in crossing for the wagons sunk into the sand and it was hard drawing for the cattle, so we put our cattle to the wagons and put on extra teams to each and got through well. It was indeed an interesting sight. You might have taken us for two armies encamped on either side of the river waiting for the signal for conflict but how different was the case when we saw the whole strength of the one, wading through the river from one to 3 feet in depth to help their friends. Here we stayed over Sunday.[6]

According to family tradition, when Mary Smith forded the Loup Fork, Joseph F. and Martha Ann were tied to the back of her husband's big white horse, "Old Sam." They all crossed safely; however, clothing, bedding, and provisions got wet making it necessary to camp and dry out the wet things.

We can appreciate Mary's feelings as she penetrated the plains area where lay many dangers and a vastness so large as to be terrifying. It could be expected that her vital being registered a certain amount of tension born of natural fear of the unknown. This adventure had been her underlying concern for many months and, concurrently within her, a store of apprehension had mounted, stemming from many causes including reported Indian hostilities. But once under way, her nervousness subsided. She breathed deeply of the exhilarating, clean air of the open country. She experienced a new freedom—no longer any tension from fear of mobs.

There was excitement—not from Indian forays but from the startling newness of things—things never before seen nor experienced by the uninitiated. Some of the travelers were oblivious to God's handiwork and saw nothing to appreciate in the great outdoor wonderland of Western America. Others

---

[6]Fielding, Bk. 5, p. 136.

noticed the shifting colors as the play of light each hour of the day glorified the terrain and brought intriguing contrasts. At eventide, Mary's eyes turned westward toward the setting sun. She experienced the gorgeous sight and thrill of a flamboyant western sunset many times on the plains and when they reached the mountains. She saw the glory of the great ball of blazing gold—that seemed to pause a moment before taking a final curtain call—flashing its resplendent colors in a spray to paint the sky with a galaxy of orange, amber, and yellow—forming an effulgent canopy in the firmament—and at the same time redoing the landscape, round about, in a soft tone of purple that moved outward with amazing speed. This enchanting, breath-taking spectacle was worth coming far west to behold. It was daily recompense for the hardships of the journey.

In the meantime, frosty relations existed between Mary Smith and Captain Lott. Moreover, it was the start of a unique race across plains, hills, and mountains to the Valley of the Saints. The Captain's initial abrupt manner and defeatist attitude had offended Mary and her family. Contrary to his advice not to undertake the journey but to stay in Winter Quarters, she came on despite the lack of reserve oxen. Had she listened to Lott, she certainly would have remained behind. She had brushed aside his advice and pricked him besides by declaring that she would beat him to the Valley. In other words, Mary had thrown down a challenge to a man who had his pride. He definitely couldn't allow her to get away with it. This was a man's world. Crossing 1,000 miles of wilderness where danger and death lurked was no child's play. It was a hazardous undertaking even for a man responsible for an outfit and human lives. A lone woman in charge did not belong. She should know her place.

All this happened in mid-eighteen hundred before woman suffrage. Women had not yet been emancipated. It would be years before they could vote. They were expected to devote themselves to purely domestic matters. To sum it up, Mary was simply *persona non grata* to the Captain. Perhaps, her accent bothered him. She seemed too independent and headstrong to suit him. However, undaunted, Mary entered the world of men. She was traveling "thin." If an animal went down, it would be difficult to replace. The same held for the Captain. Both were gambling. Or were they? Mary walked by a supreme faith, confident that the Almighty would help her. This combination was hard to defeat. Also, had she not traveled eight hundred miles from Kirtland to Far West with her husband; from Far West to Nauvoo; and from Nauvoo to Winter Quarters, etc.? She was no novice to travel by wagon-train. As for the Captain, he underestimated Mary's courage, inner strength, and powerful resolve to accomplish the thing she had set out to do. Never-the-less, unbeknown to his superior officers who were traveling in front, he harrassed the widow of the martyred Patriarch with petty annoyances all along the course of march. She kept her poise and stayed strong in the race.

One reason for the Captain's testiness enroute was the fact that Mary would not let young Joseph F. stand guard duty at night. She did not mind him performing many duties of a man, but in his interest, she would not consent to him standing guard. One night when the Captain was on guard duty, he raised a false alarm of "Indians!" coming directly to the big carriage where Mary, her daughter Martha Ann, and Joseph F. slept. He shook it terrifically and in a loud, hoarse whisper, said, " 'Indians! Indians! Get up quick, Widow Smith! We're beset by Indians!' "

Mary replied, " 'Why don't you arouse the men, I don't see what I can do.' "[7]

At this point, he went to the next wagon where some of Mary's family were sleeping, shook it rather mildly, and then slinked off, not wishing to carry his alarm further.

Another incident involved Mary's charge, Jane Wilson,

---

[7]Smith, *Life of JFS, op. cit.*, pp. 151-152.

who was fond of snuff. Her mother was traveling in Bishop Newel K. Whitney's company. All went well until the company reached the fork of the Platte River. At this point, they came within sight of the company ahead. Jane, being out of snuff, started out ahead to overtake her mother and obtain some, expecting her own train of wagons in the evening. The companies were so near that Jane thought they would camp together that night. However, the Captain, knowing that Jane had gone ahead, concluded to camp in the middle of the day. The result was that the advance company pulled farther away. Late in the afternoon, the Captain came into the center of the circle of the camp and called everyone together.

When all had assembled, he inquired in a very excited manner if all was "right" in camp, repeating it to each group. All answered in the affirmative. He then repeated the question to Widow Smith. Her answer was also, yes. Then he exclaimed in these words: " 'All is right, is it, and a poor woman lost!' "

Mary calmly replied, " 'Father Lott, Jane is not lost, she has gone to see her mother and is quite safe.' ".

Then the Captain exploded: " 'I rebuke you Widow Smith, in the name of the Lord! She is lost and must be sent for.' "[8]

Mary sent young John Smith on foot to overtake the company ahead. The lad traveled in growing darkness through droves of ravenous wolves, fierce for the flesh of dead cattle along the road, howling and even snapping at him on every side, their eyes gleaming in the dark. When he reached the camp that had made a good half-day's travel, he found Jane all snug and comfortable with her mother.

Things went along quite smoothly until they reached a point midway between the Platte and the Sweetwater rivers, when one of Mary's best oxen lay down in the yoke as if poisoned and all supposed he would die. All the teams in the rear stopped, and many gathered around to see what had hap-

[8]*Ibid.*, p. 150.

pened. In a short time, the Captain perceived that something was wrong and came to the spot. The ox stiffened in the throes of death. The Captain blustered about and exclaimed: " 'He is dead, there is no use working with him, we'll have to fix up some way to take the Widow along. I told her she would be a burden on the company.' "[9] But in this, he was greatly mistaken.

Mary said nothing but went to her wagon and returned with a bottle of consecrated oil. She asked her brother Joseph and James Lawson to administer to her fallen ox, believing that the Lord would raise him. It was a solemn moment there under the open sky. A hush fell over the scene. The men removed their hats. All bowed their heads as Joseph Fielding, who had been promised by Heber C. Kimball that he would have power to raise the dead, knelt, laid his hands on the head of the prostrate ox, and prayed over it. The great beast lay stretched out and very still. Its glassy eyes looked nowhere. A moment after the administration the animal stirred. Its huge, hind legs commenced to gather under it. Its haunches started to rise. The forelegs strengthened. The ox stood and, without urging, started off as if nothing had happened. This amazing thing greatly astonished the onlookers.

They hadn't gone very far when another ox "Old Bully," lay down under exactly the same circumstances. This time it was one of her best oxen, the loss of which would have been very serious. Again, the holy ordinance was administered, with the same results.[10]

How the family loved those dumb beasts of burden. So much depended on them. They had heroic association with the family. Sixty-nine years later, Joseph F. Smith at a 24th of July celebration affectionately mentioned the oxen that brought his mother and family to the Valley.

> . . . My team consisted of two pairs, or yokes, of oxen. My leaders' names were Thom and Joe—we raised them from calves, and they were

[9] J.F.S., *op cit.*, p. 31.
[10] Smith, *Life of JFS, op. cit.*, p. 151.

both white. My wheel team was named Broad and Berry. Broad was light brindle with a few white spots on his body, and he had long, broad, pointed horns, from which he got his name. Berry was red and bony and short horned. Thom was trim built, active, young, and more intelligent than many a man. Many times while traveling sandy or rough roads, long thirsty drives, my oxen, lowing with the heat and fatigue, I would put my arms around Thom's neck, and cry bitter tears. That was all I could do. Thom was my favorite and best and most willing and obedient servant and friend. He was choice![11]

On the plains, Mary's naturally pallid skin took on a reddish glow. Her sunbonnet couldn't keep out the dry wind. The dust showed her no mercy. The powdery stuff, stirred up by the wagon train, plagued them all. It coated their hands and faces, settled in their hair, and blocked their nostrils. It seeped into their food and penetrated into their bedding and baggage. Insidiously, it lined their throats, irritated their eyes, and fouled their ears. The smell of it was ever present.

In the heat of the day, dust and sweat joined forces to give the travelers a veneer of sticky grime. Only water cured the situation. Water! How precious to the tongue, the throat, the hands, the face, the feet—cooling water at the end of a hard march under a beating sun—refreshing water before meal time, whether from the barrel on the side of the wagon or from a stream or spring to revive and cheer them—elements as essential as bread and air. How very grateful they were for water for man and animal.

Mary was the moving spirit of the fatherless family. She was flawless in her surveillance and a stickler in caring for details. There could be no miscalculating nor anything left to chance. Wheels were watched for the need of axle-grease. The shoulders of her oxen received special care and attention to ward off soreness; also, their feet to avoid dropping of shoes and to replace one when necessary. She looked out for her children's comfort stops. Each had his assigned tasks. John and Joseph F. became expert bull-whackers. All the children

[11] *Ibid.*, pp. 155-156.

walked barefooted most of the way, Jerusha, Sarah, and Martha helping with the loose stock. The women cooperated in the preparation of the food and putting things away after everyone had finished. It was a poignant scene at supper time. Brave, fatherless family, but they were doing well.

The strains of a new hymn were frequently sung which stirred a responsive chord and buoyed the spirits of the weary travelers. The words "All is well! All is well!" gave them courage to go on.

Chapter XXIII

In the Rockies

After crossing the Elk Horn and the Loup Fork, Mary Smith's caravan continued up the north side of the Platte River—the Mormon Trail. Waterways determined the land route into the heart of the Rocky Mountains. When the travelers reached Fort Laramie, they crossed the North Platte—about a mile wide across the Laramie Fork—then the Platte again where it was quite narrow—then went on to the Sweetwater River. They followed this water course to the Big Sandy and on to the Green, Bear, and Weber Rivers—all of which they forded, as well as many creeks, large and small.

For several hundred miles, the ground showed evidence of buffaloes and thousands of them were to be seen. They were a fascination for the emigrants and a thrill for the hunters who brought down many of them.[1] Mary found herself deluged with fresh, choice meat which she had to prepare and cure. The big shaggy beasts were an awesome sight—a brooding menace. The most terrifying experience for the family during the journey was a buffalo stampede. "At one time a band of buffaloes, which seemed miles in extent, came bellowing and running along side of the emigrant train and frightened the travelers very much, but it passed by on one side and no harm was done."[2]

At night the company drew their wagons into a circle,

---

[1]"We crossed the Platte river [1½] miles below Fort Laramie from which time we had but little good feed and the road was much worse. It is wonderful to see the buffalo and the marks of them for several hundred miles. The prairie is covered with their dung from which one is sure there must be thousands of them. Our company shot many of them and ate freely of the flesh and also dried great quantities and brought on to the valley."—Fielding, Bk. 5, pp. 137-138.

[2]Harris, *op. cit.*, pp. 12-13.

unhitched, and turned the oxen and other cattle out to graze, under guard. Small camp fires provided heat to cook supper. After eating, the tired travelers went about preparing for the night. If they slept on the ground and grass were available, some gathered it and spread it to ease the hardness of the ground before putting down their blankets. As night descended and the glow of camp fires died down, each weary soul settled deeper into his bed and consigned himself to the watch-care of his Maker. Sleep finally shut out the events of the day and, more immediate, the sounds of the great wild prairie emanating from the indigenous life out there in the dark, such as howling wolves and coyotes, the nervous bellow of bull buffaloes not too far distant, the hoot of night owls, the sad cry of killdeers near a water-course, and still other bird calls which could have been Indian imitations.

Pawnee Indians were the most to be feared in the line of march. But Mary's party saw few of them, and they were friendly. They did not molest the travelers nor take any of their stock. A few handouts easily satisfied them.

The travelers crossed many small creeks that ran into the Platte. On the banks of some were patches of wild gooseberry bushes with small green berries on them. There were also some strawberry vines, with blossoms, and white clover in flower. Many beautiful flowers of various colors—chiefly blue and yellow—graced the prairie. Some had a rich appearance and would serve to adorn and beautify an eastern flower garden.

After crossing the North Platte at Fort Laramie, Mary found little good grass for the animals, and the road became worse. Some of the route was partly covered with saleratus or saltpeter which was injurious to the cattle, as they ate it freely. Consequently, many fine oxen died, the carcasses and bones of which could be seen along the road. At one place, they came to a large bed of saleratus. Many families gathered as much as they could carry for whatever subsequent use might be made of it.[3] Through the Black Hills, the road was sandy in places, making it hard for the oxen, especially in warm, dry weather. Their feet sank deep in the loose footing, as they struggled to pull the heavy wagons. Leather shields fastened to the axles and covering the inner hub prevented the sand from reaching the axle bearing. The weakened condition of the animals, due to the lack of feed, made it necessary to lay over to allow them to rest and regain their strength.[4] Travel was slow in the mountain country. The tall sentinel peaks of the West rising in the distance were a thrill for Mary. They relieved the montony experienced earlier while crossing the flat lands of the plains. Chimney Rock standing high in the air was an intriguing sight.

While the company was camped on the Sweetwater under the "graveley bluffs," 306 miles from the Valley, Captain Allen Taylor, enroute to Winter Quarters, visited the travelers. He reported back to Brigham Young that a number of cattle had strayed off at this stopping place. The Captain had gone to help look for them and spotted nineteen head among a very large herd of buffaloes six miles east of Independence Rock. They were recovered, but nine head were still missing. He also reported that ". . . three oxen had died, being too free to work, belonging as follows: 2 head to Sister Smith, 1 head to Sister Rogers."[5] The two that Mary Smith lost were undoubtedly the two that had revived earlier after being administered to. However, the loss was not a serious one for Mary.

---

[3]"A great part of the road the ground is partly covered with saleratus or Salt-Petre which is very injurious to the oxen as they eat it freely. Owing to this many fine oxen died. In fact you cannot go far on the road but you see carcasses or bones of cattle. At one place we came to large beds of saleratus where almost every family gathered as much as they wished to carry and my family got from one to two bushels. In some places the road is sandy and is hard upon the cattle especially when the weather is hot and dry. We sometimes had to ascend mountains of sand several times."—Fielding, Bk. 5, pp. 138-139.

[4]". . . when the feed began to fail we were separated into fifties and finally into tens, as the feed for cattle was very short and each 10 had to do the best they could, and we could travel but short journeys per day, and sometimes it was judged necessary to rest our cattle for several days."—Fielding, Bk. 5, p. 137.

[5]Journal History, Sept. 6, 1848.

At the first crossing of the Sweetwater, deep in present Wyoming, Mary had been met by James Lawson from the Valley bringing a span of horses and a wagon. This was by pre-arrangement. This enabled Mary to unload one wagon and send it with the best team back to Winter Quarters to the owner who had been kind enough to help her when she needed it. Her teamster, Joel Terry, returned with the team and wagon. James Lawson accompanied Mary's party to the Valley and was a big help to her.

At the aforementioned crossing of the Sweetwater, Captain Lott had the misfortune of losing several of his best cattle and a valuable mule. It was supposed that death was caused by eating poisonous weeds. All felt to sympathize with him since he took it so to heart. He needed help in his predicament and Mary was the first to offer him assistance. He refused to accept it from her. Instead, he repulsed the proffered sympathy and help with an insinuation, in the presence of her boy Joseph F., that Mary had poisoned his stock, saying: " 'Why should my cattle and nobody's else die in this manner? There is more than a chance about this. It is well planned.' "[6] Young Joseph F. resolved to demand satisfaction someday, not only for this, but for every other indignity that the Captain had heaped upon his mother.

Day after day, the wagon-train moved slowly ahead over hill and dale. The Continental Divide was crossed through South Pass at an elevation of 7,550 feet. They were now 232 miles from the Valley. They noted that from there on the streams and rivers had a westward course. The journey extended into September and seemed endless. They found some frost in the mornings in the high country, but, as they came nearer to the Valley, the weather became warmer, although some snow could be seen on distant mountain-tops. Finally, the wagons rumbled down Echo Canyon, turned off, and traveled up East Canyon. The primitive road criss-crossed

---

[6]J.F.S., *op. cit.*, p. 33.

the creek several times. This was a severely tortuous part of the trip.[7]

When the wagon train reached the final barriers that stood between them and the Salt Lake Valley, the contest between Mary and the Captain, as to who would reach the Valley first, built up to a climax. On September 22, 1848, the company approached Big Mountain. Things had been routine to this point, but the race between them was still uppermost in the mind of each.

When the company gained the crest of Big Mountain, there was a pause—an unforgettable pause—for the weary travelers. There below them beyond Little Mountain lay the Valley, their future home. The hearts of all exulted at the view of the "promised land," their long-sought goal. Mary was filled with joy, elation of spirit, and thanksgiving. She stood poised and quiet, gazing long and earnestly at the Valley, distant mountains, and the water of the great, "dead sea." Could she have been thinking, ". . . he leadeth me beside the still waters?" (Psalms 23:2)

This was a grand moment—a great moment of triumph for Mary Smith and her family. Many reflections flashed through her mind. She had done what Hyrum would have wanted her to do and, possibly, he was close in spirit. She had come a long way for this moment, and the scene below was worth it. If she wiped away a tear from her tired face, it was understandable. If only Hyrum could have been there to take her hand and gaze with her upon the distant picture, the moment would have been supreme. Also, if only her family in England could have seen her standing there on top of that mountain, happy and triumphant. If only they could have sensed her powerful faith and strength that had made the event possible. If they could have known what their sister, their own Mary, had engineered and achieved, surely their

---

[7]"The last 40 or 50 miles the road is shocking bad. In short, I wonder that so little damage was sustained. It seems a wonder that any wagon can stand it. One creek we had to cross 17 times. . . ."—Fielding, Bk. 5, p. 141.

hearts would have swelled with pride at her great accomplishment. But in their small world, they could not have conceived what a tremendous adventure Mary had been through and how truly big her world and name had become. She—as a bright jewel par excellence—had brought eternal luster to the family name.

Mary had brought Hyrum's family to the place of the new Zion. Her children, tanned and healthy, stood about her enjoying the rapture of the moment. John, the eldest, turned sixteen that day. It was a birthday that he would never forget. What could be a better birthday present than a sight of his future home?

The descent from Big Mountain to the west was quite abrupt. Care had to be taken to avoid disaster, such as a heavily-laden wagon getting away and rolling down the mountain. The rear wheels of the wagons were "rough-locked," thus providing maximum braking action while the wheeler yoke of oxen dragged each heavy wagon down the steep mountain road. The other animals, not being needed, were turned loose to be driven to the foot of the mountain. It is written of John: "On September 22, 1848, his sixteenth birthday, he drove five wagons down the 'Big Mountain,' east of Salt Lake City; it was dark long before he got into camp with the last wagon. On the way, one wheel of his wagon ran into a tree which was about 15 inches through. He had to lie on his back and chop the tree with a dull axe before he could go any further."[8]

A bone-tired and excited family bedded down that last night of the journey. John had been magnificent and merited the highest praise for bringing the wagons off Big Mountain without a crash. Mary went to sleep anticipating the dawn and the order that would start the last day's journey. She had to beat the Captain into the Valley, but she did not know how it would be accomplished. Little Mountain was the last

[8]John Smith (obituary), *op. cit.*

obstacle to be surmounted before reaching the Valley. She was anxious to hurry on and see her sister Mercy and many friends.

However, when morning came, there was consternation in Mary's camp. The Captain, smarting from Mary's prediction that she would beat him to the Valley, had apparently taken steps in the night to make sure this did not happen. She had risen early expecting to get a good start, but when she went to look for her oxen, some of them were missing. Her mind reeled with acute pain and frustration. Agonizing disappointment prevailed in her camp.

Naturally, as was her wont, she went on her knees and spoke with her Friend about it. She talked with Him and asked His aid, as she did when her yoke of oxen was lost on the Missouri River bottom. She told Him of her situation, that her oxen were lost, and to please help her find them. She prayed confidently, with abiding faith, with powerful faith that He would assist her. There was no doubt in her mind about it.

Her Friend above heard her prayer. Suddenly, a storm cloud appeared. It was black and angry looking. It emitted rolls of thunder which grew louder and louder as it approached. Jagged bolts of lightning pierced the cloud mass as if hurled by the hand of a giant. No one would associate that storm cloud with Mary's situation, but it had an important connection. This was a dramatic manifestation of the Lord's answer to her prayerful appeal for help.

As the cloud reached the final mountain barrier over which the wagon-train was about to cross, it broke in all its fury. In great anger, the swishing, driving rain stopped Captain Lott's wagon-train in its tracks. Mary caught up with it, passed out around, and went on into the Valley. She beat the Captain there by many hours. The following account of it as told by Joseph F. Smith reveals how this was brought about—how his mother, who had asked no help from any man on the trip, received help from on high to make her prediction to the Captain of the company come true:

Early next morning, the captain gave notice to the company to arise, hitch up and roll over the mountain into the Valley.

To our consternation when we gathered up our cattle, the essential part of our means of transportation, for some reason had strayed away, and were not to be found with the herd. A brother of mine (John) who was also a boy scout at that time, then obtained a horse and rode back over the road in search of the lost cattle. The captain ordered the march to begin, and, regardless of our predicament, the company started out, up the mountain. The morning sun was then shining brightly, without a cloud appearing anywhere in the sky. I had happened to hear the promise of my dear mother that we would beat the captain into the valley, and would not ask any help from him either.

I sat in the front of the wagon with the team we had in hand hitched to the wheels, while my brother was absent hunting the others. I saw the company wending its slow way up the hill, the animals struggling to pull their heavy loads. The forward teams now had almost reached the summit of the hill, and I said to myself, "True enough, we have come thus far, and we have been blessed, and not the slightest help from anyone has been asked by us." But the last promise seemed to be now impossible; the last hope of getting into the valley before the rest of our company was vanishing in my opinion.

You have doubtless heard description of the terrible thunder storms that sometimes visit the mountains. The pure, crystal streams a few moments before flow gently down their channels; but after one of these rains, in a few minutes they become raging torrents, muddy and sometimes bringing down fallen trees and roots and rocks. All of a sudden, and in less time than I am taking to tell you, a big, dark, heavy cloud rose from the northwest, going directly southeast. In a few minutes it burst in such terrific fury that the cattle could not face the storm, and the captain seemed forced to direct the company to unhitch the teams, turn them loose, and block the wheels to keep the wagons from running down the hill. The cattle fled before the storm down into the entrance into Parley's canyon, from the Park, into and through the brush.

Luckily, the storm lasted only a short time. As it ceased to rain, and the wind ceased to blow, my brother, John, drove up with our cattle. We then hitched them to the wagon, and the question was asked by my uncle of mother: "Mary, what shall we do? Go on, or wait for the company to gather up their teams?" She said: "Joseph (that was her brother's name), they have not waited for us, and I see no necessity for us to wait for them."

So we hitched up and rolled up the mountain, leaving the company behind, and this was on the 23rd day of September, 1848, We reached the old Fort about 10 o'clock that night. The next morning, in the Old Bowery, we had the privilege of listening to President Brigham Young and President Kimball, Erastus Snow, and some others, give some very excellent instructions. Then, on the afternoon of that Sunday, we went out and met our friends coming in, very dusty, and very foot-sore and very tired.[9]

Basically, the race with the Captain was a very human drama which became a faith-promoting incident that would linger in tradition forever. However, the story can never take away from nor overshadow the true success which Mary Smith had achieved. The real victory was in accomplishing what she had set out to do, namely, move her family to the heart of the Rocky Mountains to be with the body of the Saints. In this, she was signally successful. She overcame countless obstacles to achieve her goal. In doing what she did, she made a most important contribution to her people. She had set an example of faith and courage that would become legendary—for others to hear about and be benefitted by. She planted the feet of her children well. Each child would grow and find a destiny. She gave to each a heritage in a new land, where he could develop his maximum potential and become a significant personality in his own right. Mary in her triumph made all these things possible and fulfilled the role that destiny had appointed for her.

[9]Smith, *Life of JFS, op. cit.*, pp. 154-155.

Chapter XXIV

Home in the Valley

An early platting of Salt Lake City shows a lot bearing the name of Mary Smith located in the block at 2nd West and 2nd North Streets. Other lots in the same block bear the names of Joseph Fielding, Mercy Thompson, and James Lawson. The whole block across the street to the north was to become known as "Union Square." It was nice to be assigned a city lot as an inheritance, but Mary Smith was not to be contained by the dimensions of a city lot. She wanted a farm and got a good one. A farm was a necessity considering the number of mouths in her family to be fed.

One day after her arrival in the Valley, she saddled up Old Sam and rode out to Mill Creek, about six miles southeast of the settlement, on a scouting trip. She was looking for a likely place for a homesite. The Mill Creek area was a wilderness, impenetrable in places adjacent to the creek and branching streams. These were bordered with a heavy thicket of brush and willows. Her reconnaissance brought her to a delightful crystal streamlet. Following it along, she came to a number of natural springs gushing forth to form a pool at the base of a hill rising gently to the east. The spot was lovely—the crystal, cool water, pouring up through the clean sand, a delight. This was it—the place for her. She would have those springs and the surrounding land. She got both—good, pure drinking water in sufficient quantity for household needs and for irrigation and, in addition, forty acres of land.

Mary Smith undoubtedly lived in the fort the first winter. "She caused a small cabin to be built in which to do the cooking, but she and most of the family slept in the wagons during the winter of 1848. How they survived through the winter they hardly knew; they were thinly clad and, without needed shelter, suffered intensely from the cold. Her sad experience of the past had trained her to be resourceful and with the watchcare of the Lord over them they managed to endure their lot until springtime."[1]

The weather during the fall of 1848 was favorable to the pioneers. Up to the middle of October, there had been no frost. This allowed Mary time to get somewhat prepared before real, cold weather came. Winter finally arrived and stopped all construction in the Valley. The ground was covered with snow for about twelve weeks. The length of the winter caught everyone by surprise. They were not prepared for it and much suffering ensued. For example, as Mary's brother recorded: "Our children have gone barefoot almost entirely through a long and severe winter, and many times have I been grieved to see their naked feet in the snow, and many a cry have they had."[2]

Food became very scarce. In January 1849, the leaders of the Church took an inventory of all breadstuff. It was found that there was nearly one pound per head available until July. For the rest of the winter, the Saints seemed to live on faith. Wrote Joseph Fielding: "I have taken my breadstuff in corn chiefly on my shoulder 2 miles to the mill, and in the latter part of winter I have had corn of my sister Mary Smith by the bushel, but at this time it is likely I can have no more. We have also had a few bushels of wheat the same way, which I intend to return to her with interest."[3] It would seem that Mary had sufficient food for her family, having brought an adequate supply with her and enough to share with others.

That drab, long winter was terribly hard on families without warm quarters and Mary's family was no exception. It was also hard on the animals. "It is now the 11th of May,"

[1]Smith, *Life of JFS, op. cit.*, pp. 147-158.
[2]Fielding, Bk. 5,. p. 147.
[3]*Ibid.*, p. 148.

wrote Mary's brother, "and the ground is covered with snow, and snow is falling. There is no sign of Spring. The cows and the cattle are poor, and many of the Saints find it very difficult to draw their fuel with their oxen. The wolves have killed some few, but not so many as last year."[4]

The winter was also hard on the Indians, causing them to steal the stock of the settlers. "The Indians have killed from 12 to 20 cows and oxen. Near 2 weeks ago a company of 25 of our brethren were sent by the President of the Church to get back, if possible, some horses and cattle taken by the Indians. . . . They had killed 17 of our cattle last year, making in all 30 head."[5]

That first year in the Valley was a powerful test of the fortitude and faith of Mary Smith. Faith was her strongest ally. Without it, she would have been prey to panic and alarm, situated as she was in a new and untried land without any assurance that she could survive there.

Picture, if you will, that large valley in the dead of winter, blanketed with snow, and magnified by its emptiness and forbidding appearance. Let the mind's eye wander across its floor and note its barrenness. A lone cedar tree is conspicuous to the east, a prominent landmark, a solitary sentinel in the wasteland. A few cottonwood trees on the banks of a few streams from yonder canyons catch the vision. They give a glimmer of hope that other trees might grow, with water and care, where sagebrush and greasewood thrive. Westward from the cedar tree, the newly constructed fort can be seen. Pale smoke from wood burning in fireplaces spirals upward from many chimneys and disappears into the clear air. Still westward can be seen the river named "Jordan" connecting the fresh-water lake in the south with the salt-water lake northwest of the settlement.

With all the bleakness found in the Valley by Mary that first winter, there was a certain majesty about it, especially

[4]*Ibid.*, pp. 148-149.
[5]*Ibid.*, p. 149.

when the sun tipped the mountain-tops and cast its rays downward making the snow dazzling white and the still water of the saline lake a sky-tinted blue. The view from the foothills in the morning or at eventide was exhilarating and inspiring. Even in the cold, silent moonlight, the Valley had enchantment.

While coming into the Valley, Mary had passed through delightful canyons with splashing streams of water. There were mountain pastures and groves of pine and aspen that would provide excellent grazing areas, building material and fuel, and fine places for outings. She would soon learn to love those rugged mountains whose benign peaks looked down upon them protectively—mountains capped with snow and graced with timber—giving forth crystal-clear water to bring life to the deep, rich soil of the Valley. Surely to cast her lot here was no mistake. There would be a future for her and her children. The desert would blossom. This was the right place, their heritage.

The cold, cheerless winter of 1848-49 finally passed, the ground warmed, and the birds returned. The sego lilies bloomed again on the foothills, as did the small, pink filaree. These things signalled renewed activity on the part of Mary and her boys. They cleared a site for a home not far from the springs. This meant removing a thick growth of brush and willows. It was hard work for them all, but, little by little, they succeeded in carving out a building place. Next, adobes had to be made. With water from the springs and compact soil underfoot, the adobes were produced near the building site. Lumber was also necessary. This was provided by going to the canyons, getting out logs, and having them sawed at the mill.[6]

[6]"During the fall [1848] many were busily employed in making adobies [sic] and in getting timber to build on their city lots, and some few got their houses built, but fewer of them got the roofs on, for the winter came on and caught them in all stages of building. I could not make adobies on account of a sore finger which troubled me a long time, but I got up the walls of my house, but could not get boards sawed for the roof, so I spread the tent over the house, and so passed the winter. The tent I borrowed for a week or two, but we were compelled to keep it at least

During the succeeding months, they started construction of a two-room, adobe house. It was completed in 1850. The front of the house faced southward toward the springs,[7] one of which was curbed as a well. Immediately to the north and a short distance to the east of the house was a low hill or eminence. In the side of it, a warm dugout barn was built of rocks for the animals.

The conversion of the wild area that Mary chose for a farm called for much exertion and family teamwork. Her keen eye kept all activities under observation. She assisted with the slacking of lime, mixing the mortar, and handling the bricks. She had a say in the construction of the house which was 14′ x 28′ on the outside. A center partition made two good size rooms. A ladder went up the center wall to the attic where the boys slept. A fireplace was built in the north wall of the living room. Mary kept on the go and was quick to lend a helping hand. All this taxed her strength inordinately and gave her face careworn lines. Her graceful hands became increasingly roughened by the heavy toil. But when the little house was up and the roof on, she was deeply grateful, for it had been a long time since she had a permanent roof over her head. The crude roof and rough walls closed out the elements and brought warmth, peace of mind, and security. It was sanctuary, and her spirit rejoiced.

The early years in the Valley were difficult, but Mary prospered. Her stock increased, and the few cleared acres produced abundantly well. The best tenth of her increase was taken personally by her to the tithing office, where she

---

4 months, the ground being covered with snow about 12 weeks. This length of winter was very unexpected, and took us by surprise and unprepared, and in fact it has been a time of much suffering to the Saints in the Valley."—Fielding, Bk. 5, pp. 144-145.

[7]The Mary Fielding Smith home, with a later addition on the north side, is still standing. What was considered as the back of the house, in its original form, is now the front facing 27th South Street off Highland Drive. A few years later John Smith built himself a house on higher ground to the southeast not far from Mary Fielding Smith's house. His house consisted of a large room on the ground floor and a full room upstairs. A quaint little stairway led steeply upward from the northeast corner of the living room and over the fireplace to room above.

was well-known. She was diligent in paying her tithes and offerings and earned the reputation of being honest with the Lord.

Referring to this in a talk, her son, Joseph F. Smith, related:

> I recollect very vividly a circumstance that occurred in the days of my childhood. My mother was a widow, with a large family to provide for. One spring when we opened our potato pits she had her boys get a load of the best potatoes, and she took them to the tithing office; potatoes were scarce that season. I was a little boy at the time, and drove the team. When we drove up to the steps of the tithing office ready to unload the potatoes, one of the clerks came out and said to my mother: "Widow Smith, it's a shame that you should have to pay tithing." He said a number of other things that I remember well, but they are not so necessary for me to repeat here . . . he chided my mother for paying her tithing, called her anything but wise and prudent; and said there were others able to work that were supported from the tithing office. My mother turned upon him and said: "William [Thompson], you ought to be ashamed of yourself. Would you deny me a blessing? If I did not pay my tithing I should expect the Lord to withhold his blessings from me; I pay my tithing, not only because it is a law of God but because I expect a blessing by doing it. By keeping this and other laws, I expect to prosper and to be able to provide for my family."
>
> Though she was a widow, you may turn to the records of the Church from the beginning unto the day of her death, and you will find that she never received a farthing from the Church to help her support herself and her family; but she paid in thousands of dollars in wheat, potatoes, corn, vegetables, meat, etc. The tithes of her sheep and cattle, the tenth pound of her butter, her tenth chicken, the tenth of her eggs, the tenth pig, the tenth colt—a tenth of everything she raised was paid. Here sits my brother, who can bear testimony to the truth of what I say, as can others who know her. She prospered because she obeyed the laws of God. She had abundance to sustain her family.
>
> We never lacked so much as many others did; for while we found nettle greens most acceptable when we first came to the valley and while we enjoyed thistle roots, segoes and all that kind of thing, we were no worse off than thousands of others, and not so bad off as many, for we were never without corn-meal and milk and butter, to my knowledge.[8]

---

[8]Smith, *Life of JFS, op. cit.,* p. 159.

The months that followed were wearing on Mary. The heavy responsibility of rearing several childen, being the mind and directing force in all farm activities, and seeing to the educational and spiritual needs of them all, taxed her physical reserves. However, she still had the invaluable assistance of Hannah Grinnels who was verily a member of the family. The gruelling hardships of frontier life were hard on both of them. Together, they toiled to make a livelihood and provide the necessities for the family.

Mary believed work to be the best disciplining and training for young folk. She taught her children to be industrious at an early age. She laid out the work for them and expected them to complete a certain amount before stopping. She taught them how to sit and be quiet and how to work. She would measure off so many yards of yarn for the girls which had to be knitted by a certain time. The children knew that when their mother assigned them a task they had to complete it. There was little time for idleness. As for their education, under her supervision, the children learned each lesson well.

Mary's home was a place of industry. In the living room was a spinning wheel, a carding rack, and a weaving frame. Her sheep provided the raw wool which was carefully washed, combed to remove burrs and sticks, and then, hour upon hour, refined into yarn by the whirring spinning wheel. Martha Ann, along with her sisters, worked long hours in preparing the basic fabrics for the needs of the family. It is written of Martha Ann who learned from her mother:

> When very young, at eleven years, she learned to spin. The first work she did was one quarter roll of wool. At thirteen she could spin four skeins per day. She spent ten years spinning yarn. She also spun yarn and used indigo blue and peach leaves, also red madder, a powder for coloring red, to make pretty plaids and stripes and cloth for dresses. When coloring the yarn from the liquid, she would shake it to have it dry evenly. She wove many a yard of lindsey with black warp, and gray yarn for wool sheets for beds, also clothes called jeans for men's clothing.[9]

[9]Mary E. Corbett, (sketch), MS, "Martha Ann Smith Harris."

The home was a practical training ground for the girls which prepared them well for the day they would become wives and mothers. The skills they learned from their mother stood them well in hand in rearing their own families.

Anxiously and wearily rested the burden of directing the energies of a family of fast-growing children. Any departure from established standards of conduct caused Mary Smith pain and distress of spirit. Not intentionally would any of the children add to the burdens and trials of their mother by disobedience or a thoughtless act. Yet, there were occasions when such acts did occur which can be ascribed to the exuberance of youth. Clearly the incident with the air-gun was such an occasion.

One day, young Joseph F., at the age of nine, was out with his air-gun. His sister Martha, wearing many petticoats and a dress to her ankles as they did in those days, saw Joseph. Greeting her brother, she provokingly said, "I dare you to shoot me Joseph, I dare ya! I dare ya!" Whereupon, she turned her back to him, stooped over and held her dress and petticoats around her ankles. Young Joseph, being a remarkably fond brother, took her at her word and her double dare. He pointed the gun at her and shot her in the lower back, at which she let out a terrific howl and went running to her mother.

When her mother removed Martha's clothing, the pellet dropped out from the folds of her petticoats. Then Mother Smith directed her attention to Joseph.

"You weren't trying to shoot your sister were you?" she asked.

"I knew it wouldn't hurt her," replied Joseph. "She doubled dared me, and because of her quaint position—well I knew it wouldn't hurt her anyway," explained the lad.

When it was found that the pellet had made only a small pink dent in her daughter's skin, Mary breathed a sigh of relief. It taught Martha Ann the lesson: never jest unless you want to take the consequences.[10]

Son John was a great tease. He teased the hired man so unmercifully one day that the latter took after him with the pitchfork. Around and through the barn they ran, John laughing and the hired man seething with rage. Joseph F., who was large and strong for his age, became alarmed fearing that John might get hurt. As the two came running by, Joseph swung at the man. The blow dropped him and ended the race. However, the impact of the blow to the man's head fractured a bone in the back of Joseph's right hand. It was not properly set, and he had a lump there the rest of his life.[11]

Mary Smith remembered her own youth and knew that with growing, robust children such incidents were bound to happen. She found that frontier life was not such as to produce perfect gentility in her children all the time. But she did so want them to grow up to be courteous, well-mannered, and decorous in their conduct.

Mary had her pride and was very independent. She applied herself with all her might and mind to keep things going and to compete in a business way. She had horses, oxen, cows, sheep, pigs, and chickens to look after. With so many animals and fowls, feed had to be gathered to last through the winter. She had land to prepare for seeding in the spring which meant plowing, harrowing, leveling, and furrowing. After the crops were up, they had to be irrigated. The garden-plot, potato-patch, and corn-field had to be kept free of weeds. In the fall, the wheat had to be cut and winnowed. After their harvest, potatoes required proper protection which was done by placing them in a pit with a deep dirt covering and an air vent of straw at each end.

There was a large family to think about. Clothing and shoes became too small or wore out too soon and had to be replenished too often. Meat had to be cured and laid away

---

[10]Courtesy of Martha Smith Jenson.

[11]Related by the late Alvin Smith to the author in an interview.

properly for winter. The cellar had to be stocked with vegetables having keeping qualities, such as carrots, beets, and parsnips. The brown, earthen crocks were filled with preserves made from available wild berries and plums. Hundreds of pounds of ground-cherries were gathered and dried by the children. Soap making could not be neglected. It had to be made in the summer—from fatty rinds—and cured in the heat of the day. The daily milk production required attention, the cream allowed to rise, then skimmed, allowed to sour, and then churned to butter which had to be kept cool. Bread-making was a frequent chore requiring the prepartion of potato yeast and leaving the jar containing it by the fireplace so the yeast would "work." A multitude of miscellaneous matters required the attention of Mary Smith. She was well-qualified to run a farm as she had been born and reared on one. However, in the arid West, different methods had to be used to coax a living out of the parched, lazy earth that had lain unproductive for ages. Irrigation was required. It was tricky—water had to flow from a high to a low point on the land in furrows. Long ditches had to be dug. It was a constant preoccupation of the boys and hired hands. Dig ditches—was the order of the day. No ditches—no water. No water—no crops.

The life of a widow called upon to rear a growing family is never an easy one in any age or society. It was no less so for Mary in the raw surroundings of the Salt Lake Valley. She had to manage without the benefit of any monetary income. Consequently, she had to figure and improvise to make ends meet. What items could not be manufactured in the home were obtained elsewhere by barter. Farm products were exchanged for other farm products and sometimes for an imported item. A few dozen eggs might be exchanged for a felt hat, molasses, a pair of shoes.

The life of a widow was sometimes made difficult because friends ceased to be friends and melted away with the passing of a husband. Instead of being helpful, old friends sometimes became too well-meaning or critical of how the widow managed her affairs. Often this critical attitude turned to open derision and snide remarks directed at the widow and her family. If the cows did not get milked on time every morning and off to the pasture, or if her animals strayed and got into a neighbor's field, she became the object of unkind comments. Mary Smith had experienced this situation early as a widow, an example of which was the treatment meted out to her by the Captain of the company enroute to the mountains. Fortunately, Mary was able to hold her own and match wits with him. However, in a male-dominated, frontier environment, this was not always easy. A cure for such a situation was remarriage. And Mary did marry—in plural marriage—taking the name of her old friend, Heber C. Kimball, First Counselor in the First Presidency of the Church. She thus ceased to be a widow—had new status, respect, and the protection of his name. Moreover, she had the benefit of his counsel and advice in temporal and spiritual matters. He was considerate of the family, and the children looked up to him. The youngest, Martha Ann, later wrote: "I was baptized in 1849 by Heber C. Kimball, who was my stepfather."[12] The family knew him to be a friend of long-standing. It was he who welcomed them to Winter Quarters. It was he who helped supply her with oxen and waited for her on the Elk Horn.

One day in 1851 or 1852, Mary had a visitor, a Mr. Harlow Redfield, an old acquaintance of Far West days. He was present in her home when Captain Bogart and his mob invaded the place, broke open her husband's trunk, ransacked the house, and carried away papers and valuable belongings of Hyrum. Redfield had assisted the mob in picking or breaking the lock on the trunk. Apparently, through the years, his conscience had bothered him. Upon his arrival in Salt Lake City, he called on Mary to explain his part in the affair. He said he endeavored to pick the lock so that the mob would not break it. However satisfactory this explanation was to

[12]Harris Centennial letter.

him, Mary would not swallow it. Contemptuously, she told him so. She measured him with a withering look while he talked. Redfield, it seems, was in Mary's home when the mob came and, knowing that opposition was perilous and would be inadequate to deter the mob from its purpose, he quietly joined them, concluding that a seeming willingness for the mob to search the house was the best policy. Although Redfield was a member of the Church, and no matter how pure his motives might have been, Mary would never acknowledge the unfortunate man's explanation of his deed.[13] He had made himself an accessory before the fact, culpable, and subject to scorn and contempt, if not the law.

Mary Smith had little time for recreation. It is not known whether she held any church positions after reaching the Valley. However, she attended meetings and mingled with her sisters. Her quiet manner, alert mind, and cultivated speech were well-known to her peers.

At conference time, she was an early arrival with her family to listen to the general authorities of the Church. Wearing her Sunday, go-to-meeting clothes, she set out early in her light wagon with her family. Neighbors noticed her perched on the front seat with one of her boys who handled the lines and did the driving. They spoke and nodded to her in greeting and recognition. Under the seat of the wagon was a basket of lunch to be enjoyed by the family between the morning and afternoon sessions of conference. The brethren made it a point to greet her and shake hands.

During her four years in the Valley, she became a part of the local scene—a well-known citizen of the thriving, western metropolis. She witnessed the wilderness take on cultivation and beauty. She saw the '49rs stream through on their way to California gold fields. She beheld an industrious people establish a frontier city in a mountain fastness. She watched the miracle of fulfillment—but her presence was to be only for a little while.

[13]Smith, *Life of JFS, op. cit.*, p. 124.

The hard life of pioneering was telling on her. Her hair began to show streaks of grey. Lines appeared in her forehead and around the corners of her mouth. Her shoulders rested wearily forward. Her eyes had a squint as from long gazing across sagebrush flats. Her hands—hands of toil—hands of character—were now showing thickened joints. The strong thumbs appeared flat and shortened. Her whole person bore a suggestion of great fatigue and the need of rest or getting away from all her labors for awhile—a relaxed vacation—a trip to England to which her thoughts often turned.

Chapter XXV

Demise of a Saint

The strenuous labors of Mary Smith finally took their toll. While attending a public function, she caught cold. Not feeling well, she came to the home of Heber C. Kimball. For two months, she suffered from complications which weakened her. She exercised great faith and recovered briefly, but her complete recovery was not to be. She lingered in much distress and finally breathed her last on September 21, 1852, surrounded by her loving friends. Her reported last expressed wish was that her life might be spared to rear her family. Her mighty spirit took its flight, but her name and memory were to endure for all time. It is said of her that she died of a tired, broken heart—she never got over the death of Hyrum.

The grief of her large family at her passing was overwhelming. "Martha's sorrow was so intense that she went out away from the house and prayed to the Lord that she might die. The shock to Joseph was so great that he turned deathly pale and fainted and some of the others had to work with him for hours to keep him alive."[1]

The Mormon community took note of her death and paid their last respects in genuine sorrow. She was esteemed for her fine character and many accomplishments. President Heber C. Kimball delivered the funeral sermon over her bier. His remarks included these words:

> As regards Sister Mary Smith's situation and circumstances, I have no trouble at all, for if any person has lived the life of a Saint, she has. If any person has acted the part of a mother, she has. I may say she has acted the part of a mother, and a father, and a bishop. She has had a large family and several old people to take care of, and which she has maintained for years by her economy and industry.

---

[1]Harris, *op. cit.*, p. 14.

One thing I am glad of, and I feel to rejoice in the providence of God that things have been as they have. She came here sick on the Sabbath, eight weeks ago last Sunday, for me to lay hands upon her. She was laid prostrate upon her bed, and was not able to recover afterwards. I felt as though it was a providential circumstance that it so happened. She always expressed that she knew the thing was directed by the Lord that she should be placed in my house, though accidently. She probably would not have lived so long had she been where she could not have had the same care. On Tuesday evening, eight weeks and two days since, she came here sick; from that time until her death she was prayerful and humble. I have never seen a person in my life that had a greater desire to live than she had, and there was only one thing she desired to live for, and that was to see her family; it distressed her to think that she could not see to them; she wept about it. She experienced this anxiety for a month previous to her death. . . . I am glad I did right to Sister Mary, and took care of her, and that my family had the pleasure of nourishing her; the satisfaction that this gives me is worth more to me than a hundred thousand dollars. Do I believe they know it in heaven? Yes, as much as you do. I want to live all the time in righteousness, as I know that God sees me and all the works of His hands.[2]

Despite the words of praise, eulogies, and tributes from speakers and press, it was not possible then fully to equate Mary Smith nor her accomplishments. Only time would disclose the magnitude of her achievements. The results would require years to unfold. Little did anyone dream that the name of this kindly woman with her English accent and comely face would become the object of respect and pride of many. All that was generally known of her at her death were the few essentials of her life as set forth in the newspaper. The obituary notice in the *Deseret News* of December 11, 1852, contained the following:

Died, in this City, the 21st of September last. Mary relict of the martyred Patriarch HYRUM SMITH, aged 51 years and 2 months.[3]

---

[2]Whitney, *op. cit.*, pp. 467-468.

[3]Mary Fielding Smith was buried in the Salt Lake City Cemetery. On her headstone are these words: "Sacred to the Memory of Mary, Relict of Patriarch Hyrum Smith who died September 21, 1852 in the 52nd Year of Her Age. She Died as She Had Lived Near 17 Years, Firm in the Faith of the Gospel. 'Beloved are the Dead Which Die in the Lord. Rev. 14c 17v.' "

The deceased was truly a "mother in Israel," and her name and deeds will be had in everlasting remembrance, associated as they are, with the persecution of the Saints, and those tragic scenes that can never be forgotten. Possessed, in a superlative degree, of those peculiar qualifications that support and invigorate the mind in adversity, she endured afflictions and overcame difficulties with a degree of patience and perseverance worthy of imitation.

By the massacre of Carthage, June 27, 1844, she was left the sole guardian of a large family of children and descendants, for whom, by her indefatigable exertion, she provided the means of support, and removal from Nauvoo to this peaceful valley of the mountains. And after providing for their future wants here, she has been called to leave them and a numerous circle of kindred and friends, to enjoy the society of her martyred husband, and of the Prophets and Saints that have gone before, in another state of existence.

Her last illness of about two months' continuance, she bore with her usual fortitude and patience, and only wished to live to do good to her family and those around her. She has entered into rest, and may the example she set, during her sojourn on earth, not be forgotten by those she has left behind to follow her.[4]

No one could forsee that Mary Smith, the lady from England, would become an enduring personality nor the mother of a son who would become a great spiritual leader and a daughter who would be the mother of many. No one would discern that many of her descendants would hold high positions of authority and trust in the Church, community, and nation. No one, as they saw her hard at work day after day about the house or in the field, had noted anything that would suggest that she would receive special acclaim someday.

However, down through the years since her death, Mary Smith's name has grown and become significant in Mormon history—a saintly memory—associated with pioneer times. Eloquent speakers have been moved to extoll her tremendous faith in ringing words. Her heroic stature has inspired the teacher, painter, and historian. This one pioneer, perhaps more than all others, seems to epitomize all the magnificent

---

[4]Smith, *Life of JFS*, *op cit.*, p. 161.

Mormon women who crossed the plains to Utah and helped build the new Zion. Hers is an image rooted in outstanding deeds and accomplishments.

Her worthy achievements stemmed from her power of right decision making. This can be seen in her decision to come to America, a hazardous and calculated undertaking; her decision to join the Church; her acceptance of the proposal of marriage of Hyrum Smith; and her decision to leave Nauvoo with the body of the Church. But through the fabric of her life is the recurring theme of nobility of virtue. Yet, the laurel that fits her best is that of one of God's noblewomen.

While she lived, Mary's whole being and soul centered in her children. They were her supreme pride and joy. Her dedication to them was unstinting. Their welfare and future were her constant, protective concern. She endeavored to mold them in the fineness and goodness of her tradition. Her whole seemingly inexhaustable supply of energy was geared to their proper development. Her desire for them and the family, as she said in her letter, was "to train them up in the way they should go, so that they may be a blessing to us and the world." Through each long day, every thought and fiber of her mind were operative to provide for their health and happiness.

As her image has steadily enlarged in word, print, and picture, more and more have come to know about her. Her descendants, who cherish her memory and the heritage she bequeathed to them, number into the thousands. A stirring tribute came from the heart of her son Joseph F. Smith, in these words: "O my God, how I love and cherish true motherhood! Nothing beneath the celestial kingdom can surpass my deathless love for the sweet true, noble, soul who gave me birth—my own, own mother! She was good! She was pure! She was indeed a Saint! A royal daughter of God. To her I owe my very existence as also my success in life, coupled with the favor and mercy of God!"[5]

[5]*Ibid.*, p. 542.

Pioneer home of Mary Fielding Smith, Salt Lake City, Utah—from work of unknown German artist. Courtesy of Melvina Jensen Sheets.

Joseph F. Smith Martha Ann Smith Harris Mercy Fielding Thompson Mary Jane Thompson Taylor

Her life inspired the following words from a member of the L.D.S. Relief Society: "When the roll of the greatest women of modern times is called, we make no doubt that the name of Lucy Mack Smith will head that roll. The second name on that list will be that of Mary Fielding Smith. Her greatness, her power, her beauty and her charm have laid hidden in the modest silence and reserve with which she covered all her own acts. But the pages of history will yet record what she was, what she did and why she is entitled to this exalted rank."[6]

The Mary Fielding Smith story is an inimitable pioneer saga filled with paeans of praise. She was a success, and success sings its own praise. There is little need to say more except to mention the ingredients of her success, which were: self-confidence, hard work, and trust in God. Also, she set an example of faithful adherence to these principles. She followed the voice of the True Shepherd into the wilderness. She chose to be near the seat and repository of the sacred temple ordinances for the living and the dead—the mark of the priesthood, authenticity, and divinity of the restored Kingdom of the Redeemer—the soul of the Church and the way to salvation and eternal life.

The big void left in the family of Mary Smith at her passing was acutely felt for some time.[7] She had been the coordinator of all activities. Her word, suggestion, or expressed wish had been the order of the day. A multitude of little things

---

[6]Gates, *op. cit.*, p. 123.

[7]Martha Ann Harris' grief after the passing of her mother is expressed in the following: "Oh how I loved my mother. I feared to displease her. I would rather burn my hand than vex my mother. I can see the sorrowful look my mother wore to this very day in my mind's eye. God bless her memory. * * * To lose my dear mother at the tender age of eleven was a severe trial in my life. I felt I did not care to live longer. My heart seemed crushed. I was not old enough at my father's death to fully realize it as I did the loss of my mother. I felt that the world was a blank. It was a sore bereavement which I felt I could never wear out with time. . . . When I was a child how sad and sorrowful I have often felt when I have seen children have parents to love and care for them. My path was not a smooth one. After my mother died many times I felt the keen want of a mother to comfort me in trials that I have passed through. I have passed through many trying scenes and privations but through it all I have tried to be true to my integrity." —Harris Centennial letter.

that she had taken care of were to suffer, as it could not be expected that anyone would be mindful of everything as she had been. No longer would she be seen about the farm yard feeding the chickens from a pail on her arm. The cows and horses would no longer receive her friendly caress or pat. Nor would she be seen watering her flowers and trees which she had carefully tended and encouraged to grow. Her mark, her identification, her stamp remained visible no matter where her children looked. Each detail, feature, or project about the house and farm bore the turn of her mind and the touch of her hand. They would not rub off nor deteriorate but would remain fixed to remind the future visitor of her efforts. Her little home would be devoid of her presence but not the evidence of her pioneer spirit.

In the presence of her memory, many are humbled and made aware of how diminutive their own accomplishments are in comparison with her achievements. Her light shines through the years to guide the way for those oppressed with heavy burdens, for the struggling widow with a family, for the poverty laden, for the sorrowing heart, to encourage them to hold fast and not be defeated. Seeing her life in full review is like witnessing a moving pageant and seeing emerge a queenly person in whose presence the spectator is muted and beatified. Then, as if she were speaking, the words from her letter are heard: ". . . blessed be the God and Rock of my salvation, here I am, and am perfectly satisfied and happy, having not the smallest desire to go one step backward."

All may have the same desire—not to go one step backward but only forward—always forward—to stand on a mountain, as Mary did, happy and triumphant.

Chapter XXVI

Epilogue

Upon her death, Mary Smith's mantle of guardianship fell upon John Smith, twenty years of age. He assumed the responsibility of providing for eight people. Three of them—one man and two women—were older persons, including Hannah Grinnels and George Mills. Hannah filled the role of mother to the orphaned children. This imposed a heavy burden upon her which taxed her health. She died two years after Mary Smith at the age of fifty-eight.

The name and accomplishments of Mary remained in obscurity for more than thirty years after her death. In 1884, a faith promoting story by her son appeared giving some basic facts about her at Winter Quarters and later while crossing the plains.[1] In 1911, the Utah Genealogical Magazine mentioned her.[2] Later, 1915, in an independent publication of an album of pioneer women, appeared a brief biographical sketch of Mary.[3] With it was a picture of her, easel mounted, with appropriate vignettes consisting of a covered wagon, a man pulling a handcart, and a pioneer cabin. Following this, 1916, appeared an intimate sketch of her in the Relief Society Magazine by Gates, *supra*.

Further attention was directed to her in the dedication of the beautiful, polished shaft in the Salt Lake City Cemetery in honor of Hyrum Smith, June 27, 1918. Mary's name appeared carved deep in the grey Vermont marble along with

---

[1]J.F.S., *op. cit.*, pp. 16-22.

[2]Osborne J. P. Widtsoe, "Hyrum Smith Patriarch," *The Utah Genealogical and Historical Magazine,* II (1911), 50 and 57.

[3]James T. Jakeman, *Daughters of Utah Pioneers and Their Mothers* (Salt Lake City, 1915), pp. 147-149.

that of Jerusha Barden Smith and the names of all Hyrum's children. Representatives of more than 600 descendants at that time, including Joseph F. Smith and Martha Smith Harris, assembled to witness the event. The occasion focused attention to faithful Mary who brought Hyrum's children west and established them in the mountain heartland of Utah.

Attention was directed anew to Mary Smith upon the occasion of the dedication of a monument with a bronze plaque and stone inscription at the site of her little home in Sugar House. Primary children, with money raised by them, erected the monument to Mary. On one side, a plaque depicted a covered wagon with Mary walking by her oxen. On the other, appropriate lines paid tribute to her. President Heber J. Grant of the Church of Jesus Christ of Latter-Day Saints offered the dedicatory prayer before a large assemblage on June 5, 1927.

The legend of Mary caught on with the public, stirring admiration and sentiment in many hearts. One instance, in particular, stands out and deserves mentioning. Minerva Kolhepp Teichert offered her services in helping to decorate the old First Ward meeting house in Pocatello, Idaho. Bishop William A. Hyde wrote to artist Teichert giving her his original conception of a mural for the Ward house. Hyde informed her that, at intervals, there had been haunting him for several years a subject that was "worthy of the greatest genius." In his mind, he had composed the subject again and again. It became more beautiful each time he looked at it. And if there were some sympathetic soul who could understand it and had the technical knowledge and artistic feeling to treat it sacredly as it should be treated, it would make for that artist's fame and satisfy in him the hunger of his heart.

The picture would show at one glance the heroism and the faith of Mormon women and, at the same time, the Mormon faith and spirit. It would deal with an historic, well attested fact. Then Hyde touched upon the time when Mary Smith was delayed when her ox went down; how, by a courage that was more than human, she helped bring him back to life;

Depiction of Mary Fielding Smith and son Joseph F. Smith—reproduced from work entitled "Not Alone" by Minerva Kolhepp Teichert.

Photographed by Ashton Henderson

MARY FIELDING SMITH HALL

and how she finally overtook the advance wagons, passed them and entered the Valley in the lead. He went on to state:

> The central theme of the picture I get from Mrs. Butler's "Roll Call," and the title of it, unless some better were thought of, would be "Not Alone."
>
> You may have seen the original or a copy of the "Roll Call." If not, then this is the idea. It is after the battle. The victorious remnant of the army is mustered for roll call. They stand in their ranks as they did before the battle, except that the dead stand there in spirit—their shadowed forms intermingled—the majority in this devoted band. It is at the same time spiritual and uncanny. . . .
>
> Having these elements in mind, now let us see coming across the plains a prairie schooner drawn by a yoke of lumbering oxen. Can you idealize these oxen; can you give them the touch of heroism that Sister Smith gave to them by her association? Well then, next will be seen the form of this brave woman with her face set to the horizon, with the look that does not see the intervening things—hers is the eye of faith. The wind had detached a wisp of her hair from the confines of her bonnet, and it swells her dress giving life and motion and dignity to her. Perhaps one hand rests upon the shoulder of the ox . . . and the other may lead the lad who trudges by her side—little Joseph, then less than 10, I think. These would make a picture themselves, but they are "not alone." Who is this shadowy form, mounted on this classical charger that stands so distinct in character apart from these oxen, and is caparisoned for war? This is the captain of the Lord's host. Can you picture him? To this misty form can you give power and dignity? There can be no luster of eye nor no great detail. You see his sword, the pose of the head, the attitude of the confidence as he rides unseen by the side of this Mormon saint. Then those other men—sometimes I see them mounted and sometimes unmounted. . . . I only know that they are the same men that the servant of Elijah saw round about the camp of the Israelites. In the shadows there may be the skulking form of a wolf, or of an Indian. . . .[4]

With the benefit of this description, artist Teichert painted the impressive scene "Not Alone." This recital conveys some idea of the spiritual impact which the story of Mary Smith has had on many who have heard it. The heroic and romantic elements continue to stir the imagination.

---

[4]Kay Webb, "Not Alone," *The Instructor,* (July 1960), p. 215.

Another honor bestowed upon Mary Smith occurred in 1954 with the dedication and naming of a new dormitory for her on the campus of the Brigham Young University. The dedicatory treatment of her life carried these words:

> In few women, either inside the Church or out, have the Mormon ideals of motherhood, courage, faith, integrity and whole-souled devotion to a cause been so conspicuously combined as they were in Mary Fielding Smith, wife of the patriarch of the Church, mother of one of its greatest presidents, and grandmother of the present president of the Quorum of Twelve Apostles. Hers is one of the great stories of devotion, suffering, and final achievement that characterized her people.[5]

The story of Mary Smith has had appeal for children, and many teachers in Primary and Sunday School classes have devoted a class period to her. In May 1955, there appeared in "The Instructor"[6] the flannelboard story of Mary Smith for Sunday School children. This story, in seven scenes, by the use of small figures of people on a flannelboard, presented graphically the story of Mary who, as a widow, with her small children, made it to the Salt Lake Valley in 1848.

The little home of Mary Smith in Sugar House, more than any other thing, projects the memory and life of Mary into the present. In it is the spirit of pioneer times—the image of a hardy people—the simplicity and austerity of the Saints of Deseret. It is quite priceless because of its historic association with the person who built and lived in it; also, because it depicts the spirit of the times in early Utah when people built on faith. The little house perpetuates Mary Smith's memory. It is a constant reminder, in this day of affluent circumstances, of the struggles and sacrifices of the brave band of Mormon homeseekers who laid the foundation of a new commonwealth in the mountains. The pioneer home is a

---

[5]Dedication brochure, Brigham Young University (1954), pp. 30-31.

[6]Marie F. Felt, "With Oxcart and Courage to Salt Lake Valley," *The Instructor*, (May 1959), pp. 155-156.

charming, hallowed, and lasting monument to the noble person who put her personality in it.[7]

Mary Smith left her influence on her children to sustain and help them in life. They partook of her faith coupled with her singleness of mind. The strength of her example, which she imparted to them, rebounded and gave her name added distinction.

For Mary there was little personal glory in life. Her lot, after joining the Church, was one of continual hardship and poverty. She was never the recipient of jewelry bearing precious stones. Many might say that she made a mistake; that her life would have been different had she chosen another course. Others would say that she gambled and lost. Be that as it may, the fact remains that virtue has a way of being rewarded—the inevitable operation of the law of compensation—as ye sow, so shall ye reap.

Mary did sow, and the harvest ripened years later. It was a golden harvest which continues without end. Her great reward came through the children. They married and had large families. Each has been blessed with a numerous posterity—each child a pearl on an eternal strand—gems each for Jerusha and Mary. The two boys, John and Joseph F., became men of affairs in the Church and State.

John Smith married Hellen Marie Fisher on December 25, 1853. He was ordained to the office of Presiding Patriarch of the Church on February 19, 1856. In April 1862, he left to serve a two-year mission in Scandinavia. Upon his return,

---

[7]Jens Hansen bought the Smith farm in 1863. Mrs. Hansen, according to tradition, stuck three willows in the ground and they grew into the three large cottonwood trees to be seen in front of the old home. They are some of the oldest trees in the Valley. Bodell Christine Hansen, who was born in the old home, married Hyrum Jensen. He acquired the property in 1926. He started construction of the "Jensen Mansion" in 1928. This structure stands near the old pioneer home of Mary Fielding Smith. When Jens Hansen acquired the Smith property, only a few acres had been cleared. He built a small reservoir to impound the water from the springs for irrigation purposes. It was also used as a place for baptisms. The reservoir became two decorative garden ponds connected in the center by an artistic footbridge. The ponds are now earth filled. After the sewer line was put through on Highland Drive, the flow of water in the springs stopped.—Courtesy of Melvina Jensen Sheets and A. J. James.

he continued with his patriarchship. He served faithfully in his calling for fifty-five years, giving thousands of patriarchal blessings. Under the inspiration of the Holy Spirit, he had the power of discernment which led him to make many prophetic utterances upon the heads of those he blessed, which in due course were fulfilled. His grandson Hyrum G. Smith succeeded him as patriarch. His great-grandson Eldred G. Smith subsequently became patriarch and presides at the present time. John Smith's descendants form a goodly portion of the faithful posterity of Hyrum and Jerusha Smith in the Church today.

Lovina Smith, who married Lorin Walker in Nauvoo, reached Utah in 1860. Her brother John went east in 1859 with a four-mule team and wagon and brought the family back with him. After reaching Utah, the Walkers settled in Farmington. Lovina was the mother of thirteen children, six daughters and seven sons.[8]

Jerusha Smith married William Peirce, December 28, 1854. They went to Brigham City, Utah, and settled on sixty-four acres of sage brush land which they worked with oxen. They knew well the hardship of pioneer life. They were blessed with nine children. six daughters and three sons.[9]

Sarah Smith married Charles Emerson Griffin on January 16, 1854. They lived in Salt Lake City (Sugar House Ward), where he was employed on the Church farm. Then they moved to the pioneer settlement of Coalville and later to Ogden, where Sarah died. She bore eleven children but lost seven of them. Her husband declared that he had lost a good wife and his children one of the best mothers.[10]

The finest honors which came to Mary Smith were through her son Joseph. It is a pity that she did not live long enough to see his climb up the ladder of success. His achievements would have brought her supreme joy and hap-

---

[8]Courtesy of Edith S. Heaps.
[9]Courtesy of Clarence Fielding Peirce.
[10]Charles Emerson Griffin, *op. cit.*, p. 53.

PRESIDENT JOSEPH F. SMITH
Son of Hyrum and Mary Fielding Smith

MARTHA ANN SMITH HARRIS
Daughter of Hyrum and Mary Fielding Smith.

piness. But her sister Mercy Thompson lived on many years to witness with unstinted pride the accomplishments of her nephew whom she had nursed when he was a baby as his mother lay desperately ill.

At the age of sixteen, he was called to go on a mission to the Sandwich Islands (Hawaii), April 1854. There, under soul-testing hardships, he matured into a man and grew in spirituality.

In 1860, he was called to fill a mission to England, where he remained until 1863. He visited his mother's people. They treated him kindly but would have nothing to do with his religion.[11]

In 1864, he was called on a short mission to Hawaii to help regulate affairs there in the Church. His knowledge of the native tongue enabled him to be highly effective on this mission.

In 1866, when he was twenty-eight years old, he was ordained an Apostle by President Brigham Young and, at the same time, an assistant counselor to President Young.

In civil life, he served as a member of the Territorial House of Representatives for seven consecutive terms—1865-1874. He was chosen as a member and acted as president of the Constitutional Convention which was called to frame a constitution for Utah, 1882, to gain statehood. He was also employed during certain periods in the Church Historian's office.

In February 1874, he started on his second mission to Europe—to preside over the European Mission. In 1877, he was called again to take charge of the European Mission with headquarters in Liverpool.

When President John Taylor succeeded President Young, Joseph F. Smith was sustained as second counselor on October 10, 1880, at the age of forty-one. He held this office successively under Presidents Taylor, Wilford Woodruff, and Lorenzo Snow. Following the death of the latter, the Quorum of the

[11]Smith, *Life of JFS, op. cit.*, pp. 201-202.

Twelve, on October 17,1901, reorganized the First Presidency. Joseph F. Smith was chosen as President of the Church of Jesus Christ of Latter-day Saints.

This action was sustained at a special, General Conference of the Church, November 10, 1901.

During his administration, the Church made substantial spiritual and temporal progress. He cleared the Church of debt, a position it has maintained since. He was an effective expounder of his faith. He gave sound advice to members of the Church urging them to live their religion, pay their tithing, and keep out of debt—virtues he practiced during his notable life.

His first marriage was to Levira Annett Clark, April 1859. No children came of this union. Subsequently, he entered into plural marriage. With Levira's consent, he married Julina Lambson, March 5, 1866. Thirteen children were born to them. On May 1, 1868, he married Sarah Ellen Richards. Eleven children blessed this union. Edna Lambson became his wife on January 1, 1871, and was the mother of ten children. On December 6, 1883, he married Alice Ann Kimball who bore him seven children. Mary Taylor Schwartz became his wife on January 13, 1884, and seven children blessed this home.

His numerous children were comfortably reared and educated. The feeling between Joseph F. Smith and his children was beautiful to see. Whenever any of his sons or daughters came to see him during their early or adult life, he greeted them with a kiss. He was loved and honored by them.

Many of his sons rose to high position in the Church. Hyrum M. Smith became an Apostle on October 24, 1901. Another son, Joseph Fielding Smith, was ordained an Apostle on April 7, 1910. He is, today a counselor in the First Presidency, President of the Quorum of Twelve Apostles, and Church Historian. He is also a theologian and prolific writer on ecclesiastical subjects on which he is a recognized authority. Another son, David A. Smith, served as counselor in the Presiding Bishopric of the Church for many years. Other members of the family have been active and continue so in important positions in the Church and community. President Smith's daughters were endowed with the grace of their illustrious grandmother Mary Fielding Smith.

President Joseph F. Smith reached great heights and brought many honors to his parents. Despite his many accomplishments and affluent circumstances, he remembered his humble start in life and the hardships of his mother.[12] He manifested compassion for the poor and sympathy for the sick and afflicted. He once gave his overcoat to a man who did not have one.

In his personal life, by his thrift, business acumen, wise investments, connections with banks, industry, etc., he became well-to-do. However, he stated publicly that he owed all his success, coupled with the favors of the Lord, to his mother, Mary Fielding Smith. He died on November 19, 1918, at the age of eighty. The Church and community mourned his passing. Today, his influence is still felt.

Martha Ann, the baby in the family of Mary Smith, matured into a faithful young woman. When she was not quite sixteen years of age, she married William J. Harris, twenty, April 21, 1857. Two days later, he left for England on a mission. While he was away (fourteen months), Martha lived with his mother, Mrs. A. O. Smoot, wife of the mayor of Salt Lake City, where she worked for her room and board. In 1869, Martha and William moved to Provo, Utah. Her husband's mining activities took him away from home a great deal. During his absence, Martha presided with quiet dignity over her family of eleven children—five sons and six daughters. The girls were cast in their mother's image and the likeness of their grandmother Smith.

---

[12]In later years, Joseph F. Smith was asked by his son-in-law, Harold Jenson, why he did not go out to the old home. The answer was: "It makes me shed too many tears. My mother wore herself out at that place and, yet, gave her best to the Church."—Courtesy of Harold H. Jenson.

Martha was a widow for fourteen years. She occupied herself with needle and thread making temple clothing. She remained in the old family home which became a mecca for her loved ones and friends. She was a distinguished person. The high and low in life came to call on her. Some would kneel and kiss her hand in recognition of her character and the fact she was the daughter of noble parents. A numerous posterity continues to add to her crown as well as that of Mary Fielding Smith.

This finale would not be complete without a few last words regarding Joseph Fielding and Mercy Thompson. They remained true to the faith and were buried in Utah soil.

Joseph, after arriving in the Valley of the Great Salt Lake, located on a farm at Mill Creek, not far from his sister Mary's place. His house was most pioneer and humble. He and his family, during the early years, lived through severe privation and want, existing on "greens" for months. When he cut the first wheat with a "cradle," he threshed it with a flail on a wagon cover laid on the ground. He took a sack of the new wheat on his shoulder to the mill. When he returned with some flour, the family gathered around while griddle cakes were hastily made. Nothing ever tasted so delicious.

He was made a member of the Legislative Council which met almost every week in the Council House. He often walked the seven miles from his home to be in attendance. At times the roads were bad, and he returned home at night quite weary. While the civil officers were all "gentiles," the legislators were Mormons, but the governor seemed to work well with them.

Joseph, having married Hannah Greenwood in England, took a second wife, Mary Ann Peak, in Nauvoo. Hannah bore him four daughters and three sons; Mary Ann, two daughters and one son. Today, a numerous posterity honors his name; however, none bear the name Fielding, as death took all of his sons too soon in life.

JOHN SMITH
Son of Hyrum and Jerusha Barden Smith.

JOSEPH FIELDING SMITH
Grandson of Hyrum and Mary Fielding Smith.

Joseph went to his reward on December 19, 1863, at the age of sixty-six. "As his life had been virtuous and useful, so his death was peaceful and happy."[13]

* * *

After the death of her sister Mary and brother Joseph, Mercy Thompson lived on for many years extending into the nineties. She took a matriarchal interest in the families and fortunes of her kinsmen. She kept up a correspondence with them.

Mercy, who arrived in Utah in Daniel Spencer's hundred (also known as Parley P. Pratt's company), spent the winter of 1847-48 in the Old Fort. In the spring of 1849, she located on Lot 8, Block 97, Plat A, Salt Lake City Survey (Sixteenth Ward) where she resided until the day of her death.

When the Perpetual Emigration Fund was instituted, she was a generous contributor of funds for emigrating the poor, giving at one time $800 toward assisting needy Saints to reach Zion. She also donated liberally to the building of Temples, assisting missionaries, and many other charitable purposes.

In 1871, she visited her relatives in Upper Canada. On October 15, 1872, she left for England,[14] traveling part of the way in company with President George A. Smith who was on his way to Palestine. On her return trip, Mercy crossed the Atlantic on the steamship *Nevada* which sailed from Liverpool, June 4, 1873. On this occasion, she assisted a number of people to emigrate from England to America.

While in England, Mercy visited her brothers James[15] and Thomas Fielding; also, her sister Ann Matthews, a widow.[16]

---

[13]Andrew Jenson, *L.D.S. Biographical Encyclopedia* (Salt Lake City, 1914), II, 762-763.

[14]*Ibid.*, 725-726.

[15]Sarah M. (Lillie) Wright's letter, Feb. 8, 1915, from Leek, Staffordshire, England, to Pearl Vilate Burton, Ogden, Utah, made mention of Mercy Thompson's visit to England by a quotation from the journal of her father, Rev. James Fielding, as follows: "'Nov. 21, 1872, my sister Mercy from America paid us a visit. I had not seen her for 40 years.'"—Courtesy of Josephine Burton Bagley.

[16]Rev. Timothy R. Matthews died in 1845.

Regretably, Mercy was too late to see her sister Martha Watson, as she had died, June 17, 1872. Accompanied by her brother Thomas, she visited the old home in Honidon. She started out afoot alone on the country road to get there. While she was resting by the side of the road and writing, Thomas caught up with her. They called at a Mrs. Smith's and rested, then walked up the old lane leading to their old home—walked through the meadow, then to the old house which looked quite neat. Mrs. Eat, who lived in the house, was washing but invited them in. Mercy sat down in the chimney corner where her mother had nursed her nearly sixty-six years before—by the little cupboard in the wall just where her mother had always kept her stockings for mending, the sight of which made Mercy's eyes run some, as she said. She then went and sat down in the corner by the cellar door where her father used to sit in summer to read the Bible and meditate on the deep things written therein. They were shown the parlor where their mother's eyes were closed in death. Mrs. Eat said she wanted to make the "chambers" (bedrooms) tidy so that Mercy could see them when she got back from Colmworth.

They proceeded to Colmworth, a mile away, walking through the fields. They found the graves of their father and mother, sister Sarah, and brother Matthews under a grove of evergreen trees which had been planted by Reverend Robert Geary as a token of respect; but the trees had grown too thick which had a tendency to efface the letters on the markers, some of which were scarcely discernible, particularly on their mother's tombstone. Leaving here, they inquired about the old and present inhabitants and found old Mrs. Shimmon who recognized Mercy quickly. She got the visitors some tea and the best she had with great pleasure. Her husband was in the Bedford Infirmary nearly blind. It began to rain, and they got rather wet before they got back to Honidon; so Mercy did not go upstairs at the old house. She got Mrs. Eat to give her a root of houseleek "off the old oven tiles." On their return,

Mary Fielding Smith pioneer home with added protective roof and rock-columned portico.

Graves of Mary Fielding Smith and Mercy Fielding Thompson, City Cemetery, Salt Lake City, Utah.

Courtesy of N. Ross Beatie

they stopped again at Mrs. Smith's—got bread and cheese and some wine. She sent her son to take them home in her gig.[17]

Mercy Thompson was a spiritual minded person and breathed into each letter to her loved ones a prayer for their well-being. In one letter to her niece, Martha Ann Harris, she said she wondered so many times how people dared to ask for blessings at the hands of the Lord when they daily disobeyed his commandments ". . . and it really seems to me that those who are apparently the most blessed with good things of the world are the most careless and ungrateful. But we may well say, let him that is without sin cast the first stone. Do try to speak an encouraging word to the young; they have many temptations. Tell your loved ones that Aunt Thompson prays for them every day. I do hope that they will never forget their prayers. I say God bless them with all my heart. Amen."[18]

She was a firm believer in the mission of the Prophet Joseph Smith. In her twilight years, she lived with the memories of her association with him and other great ones. She remembered one occasion in particular—the day in Nauvoo when Joseph and his wife Emma graciously called to take her and little daughter for a ride in their carriage. The Prophet drove out on the prairie. Suddenly, he stopped, got out, and picked a bouquet of wild flowers. He returned to the carriage and presented the bouquet to the little girl, Mary Jane Thompson. It was one of those simple acts, yet, it was done with all the courtliness of a nobleman.

---

[17]Mercy Rachel Thompson, Journal, May 1873.—Courtesy of Josephine Burton Bagley.

Note:The old Fielding home, on Manor Farm Honidon, was of the type known as "stud and plaster" built around a huge central chimney which supported the great rough-trimmed oak beams that crossed the house. Downstairs were two rooms, kitchen, and dairy. Upstairs were four bedrooms, crossed by big beams which left many painful recollections to one who did not stoop low enough when passing from one room to another. The house, which is no longer standing, was built about 200 years ago—the roof thought to be of straw thatch because of its high pitch, then later covered with tile. There was also an outbuilding with a big open hearth and a brick oven in which the weekly batch of bread was baked.—Courtesy of P. W. Bailey, Huntington, England, whose family lived on the place for sixty years.

[18]Mercy R. Thompson's letter, April, 1886, to her niece, Martha Ann Harris.

For many years, Mercy was an active member of the Relief Society of the Sixteenth Ward. She passed to her final rest at her home at 103 North, Second West Street, September 15, 1893. She was at the time of her demise one of the oldest members of the Church, eighty-six years old.[19]

* * *

The curtain, now about to close on the story of Mary Fielding Smith, remains apart a moment longer to record some observations of her by men of affairs. In an L.D.S. conference, held out of doors on April 5, 1908, Ben E. Rich said of her, in part: "This woman planted the faith of the gospel so deep in the hearts of her children that all hell has not been able to root it out of a single one of them." Also, Osborne J. P. Widtsoe said of her: "Mary Fielding was one of these women whom men not only love but honor."[20] In a recent Oakland-Berkeley Stake Conference, Thorpe B. Isaacson said of her that a great and powerful faith—a faith stronger than understanding—a faith pure and supreme in concept—guided Mary Fielding Smith over a rocky road and exalted her above the hills.

It is quite certain that men will continue to extoll her because she was a woman who had fortitude and would not give up. Certainly, each reader will appraise her in his own way.

We now salute her and leave her to the ages. Her virtues live on even as do the sego lilies that continue to wave in the spring air on the foothills of the Wasatch mountains.

---

[19]Jenson, *op. cit.*, 726.
[20]Widtsoe *op. cit.*, p. 50.

Bronze plaque in memory of Mary Fielding Smith on fountain at site of pioneer home in Salt Lake City, Utah—sculptured by Gilbert Riswold.

Inscribed stone commemorating pioneer mothers of inter-mountain country—on fountain at site of Mary Fielding Smith pioneer home, Salt Lake City, Utah. Courtesy of N. Ross Beatie

In a Western Setting.
Courtesy of Utah State Historical Society

Bibliography

Corbett, Pearson H., *Hyrum Smith—Patriarch,* Deseret News Press, Salt Lake City, 1963.

Cowley, Matthias F., *Wilford Woodruff—History of His Life and Labors,* Deseret News Press, Salt Lake City, 1909.

Evans, Richard L., *A Century of Mormonism in Great Britain,* Deseret News Press, Salt Lake City, 1937.

Gregg, Thomas, *The Prophet of Palmyra—Mormonism,* John B. Alden, Publisher, New York, 1890.

Jakeman, James T., *Daughters of Utah Pioneers and Their Mothers, Biographical Sketches,* Salt Lake City, 1915.

Jenson, Andrew, *Latter-day Saint Biographical Encyclopedia,* Salt Lake City, 1914.

Nibley, Preston, *Joseph Smith the Prophet,* Deseret News Press, Salt Lake City, 1946.

Roberts, Brigham H., *Comprehensive History of the Church of Jesus Christ of Latter-Day Saints,* Salt Lake City, 1921.

Smith, Joseph, *History of the Church,* (Documentary), 7 vols., Salt Lake City.

S[mith], J[oseph] F., "A Noble Woman's Experience," *The Heroines of Mormondom, Noble Women's Lives Series,* Bk. 2, 1884.

Smith, Joseph Fielding, *Essentials in Church History,* Deseret News Press, Salt Lake City, 1928.

Smith, Joseph Fielding, *Life of Joseph F. Smith,* Deseret News Press, Salt Lake City, 1938.

Smith, Lucy Mack, *History of Joseph Smith,* ed. Preston Nibley, Salt Lake City.

Smith, Ruby K., *Mary Bailey,* Deseret Book Company, Salt Lake City, 1954.

The Doctrine and Covenants.

Tullidge, Edward W., *The Women of Mormondom,* Tullidge & Crandall, New York, 1877.

Whitney, Orson F., *Life of Heber C. Kimball,* Printed at the Juvenile Instructor Office, Salt Lake City, 1888.

Bennett, Archibald F., "Solomon Mack and His Family," *The Improvement Era,* LIX.

Brigham Young University, Dedication and Naming of 22 Buildings, Provo, 1954.

"Dedication of Monument to Pioneer Woman," 1927, *Deseret News,* June 5, 1927.

Harris, Richard P., "Martha Ann Smith," *The Relief Society Magazine,* XI, 1924.

Holmes, Bernice Burton, Sketch, MS, "Great-Grandfather Joseph Fielding."

Irvine, Arnold J., "Mary Fielding Smith Mothers Future President of Church," *Deseret News, Church News Section,* Nov. 9, 1963.

Fielding, Joseph, Journal, 5 Books, L.D.S. Church Historian's Office, Salt Lake City, 1839-1859. Reproduced in mimeographed form, June 1963.

Linford, Henry, Autobiography, MS, pp.10-12.

Lund, A. William, "Our Cover Picture," *The Instructor,* Sept. 1948.

"Mary Fielding Smith, Mother of President Joseph Smith," *The Instructor,* May, 1955.

Matthews, Ann Fielding, "Memoir of Mrs. Rachel Fielding of Honidon, Bedfordshire," *Wesleyan—The Methodist Magazine,* Aug. 1830.

"Mercy R. Thompson Describes the Parting Prior to the Martyrdom," *Juvenile Instructor,* XXVII, 1892.

Norman, Mary B., Autobiography, MS.

Roberts, Brigham H., "Truth Told Regarding Prophet's Burial Place," *Deseret News,* Sec. 2, Jan. 1928.

Russell, Samuel, "Laying the Foundation of the Church in Canada," *Deseret News, Church News Section,* July 1937.

Smith, John, "Patriarch Smith Summoned Home," *Deseret News,* Nov. 1911.

"Temple Workers," *Young Woman's Journal,* IV, Apr. 1893.

Thompson, Mercy Fielding, "Recollection of the Prophet Joseph Smith," *Juvenile Instructor,* XXVII, Salt Lake City, 1902.

Tibbutt, H. G., "Westward Across the Atlantic," *Bedfordshire Biographies XXII, Bedfordshire Magazine,* Spring—1956.

Webb, Kay, "Not Alone," *The Instructor,* July 1960.

Widtsoe, J. P. Osborne, "Hyrum Smith Patriarch," *The Utah Genealogical and Historical Magazine,* II, 1911.

Fielding, Rev. James, letter, Aug. 27, 1838, to Joseph Fielding in England.

Fielding, Rev. James, letter, Nov. 23, 1839, to Joseph Fielding in England.

Fielding, John, letter, Dec. 19, 1837, to Joseph Fielding in England.

Fielding, Joseph, letter, Aug. 12, 1839, to Rev. Timothy R. Matthews in England.

Fielding, Mary, letter (undated) to Mercy Rachel Thompson in Canada.

Harris, Martha Ann, Centennial-Jubilee letter, Mar. 22, 1881, to her posterity.
Matthews, Ann, letter, Mar. 22, 1833, to Joseph Fielding in Canada.
Matthews, Ann, letter, Aug. 20, 1837, to Joseph Fielding in England.
Matthews, Ann, letter, Mar. 24, 1841, to Joseph Fielding in England.
Matthews, Rev. Timothy R., letter (undated) to Joseph Fielding in England.
Smith, Mary Fielding, letter, June 1839, to Joseph Fielding in England.
Thompson, Mercy Rachel, letter, Apr. 20, 1841, to Joseph Fielding in England.
Thompson, Mercy Rachel, Centennial-Jubilee letter, Dec. 20, 1880 to her posterity.
Thompson, Mercy Fielding, letter, Sept. 5, 1883, to Joseph Smith, son of the Prophet Joseph Smith.
Wright, Sarah M. (Lillie), letter, Feb. 8, 1915, to Pearl Vilate Burton.
Wright, Millicent F., letter, Oct. 22, 1964, to author.

Index